Writing Short Stories

Writing Short Stories

A Writers' and Artists' Companion

**Courttia Newland and
Tania Hershman**

Series Editors: **Carole Angier and Sally Cline**

Bloomsbury Academic
An imprint of Bloomsbury Publishing Plc

B L O O M S B U R Y
LONDON • NEW DELHI • NEW YORK • SYDNEY

Bloomsbury Academic

An imprint of Bloomsbury Publishing Plc

50 Bedford Square	1385 Broadway
London	New York
WC1B 3DP	NY 10018
UK	USA

www.bloomsbury.com

BLOOMSBURY and the Diana logo are trademarks of Bloomsbury Publishing Plc

First published 2015
Reprinted by Bloomsbury Academic 2015

British Library Cataloguing-in-Publication Data
A catalogue record for this book is available from the British Library.

ISBN: PB: 978-1-4081-3080-3

Library of Congress Cataloging-in-Publication Data
A catalog record for this book is available from the Library of Congress.

Series: Writers' and Artists' Companions

Typeset by Fakenham Prepress Solutions, Fakenham, Norfolk NR21 8NN
Printed and bound in Great Britain

Contents

Contents

Part 3

Foreword

by Kate Clanchy

When writers start writing, it is very often with the short story. It can seem the least daunting of forms: more modest than the novel; less formally demanding than the poem. It is a lovable shape, too: almost everyone has a short story they treasure, that seems to speak to them with special intimacy and directness. Then, too, stories are wonderfully flexible: they can equally well be detective mysteries, science fiction, modernist or entirely surreal; they can be told by anybody from a mute child to a garrulous ancient prophet; and they can be as highbrow as Lydia Davis and or as entertaining as Dashiell Hammett. And above all, for writers who have just discovered what amazingly hard work it is to keep a sentence, let alone a paragraph, in perfect order, short stories are short.

Short stories, though, are no sort of foothill. In fact – and I am writing this just as I finish my first collection – I think they are what the Scottish Munros are to the Swiss Alps – considerably smaller, but every bit as hard to climb. A poem, after all, can hold the new writer, as it held me when I set out to write, in its firm grip, giving ancient shapes to raw thoughts and impressions; novels, meanwhile, are baggier, more forgiving of the odd duff sentence or flag in the plot. The short story, in contrast, shines a harsh light on every word you write and neither gives you a shape nor forgives you for getting the shape wrong. It makes you, to paraphrase Hamlet, king of infinite space yet bounded in a nutshell, and sometimes, that can give you bad dreams. Or rather it can leave you floundering in the pit of anxiety which stopped you writing in the first place.

How to get out of that pit is something all writers have to learn, and constantly relearn. Probably the best cure is a writing course, with a tutor, fellow writers, and this book as a companion, resource and guide. But if no course is instantly available, *Writing Short Stories* can be all three.

Some of Britain's most passionate writing teachers and practitioners of the short story have come together here to create a lively, personal and very practical guide to get you started and to keep you writing to that all-important ending. It will take you all the way to the top of your particular Munro, and show you how fabulous the view can be from here – on a fine day, every bit as good as Mont Blanc. And then set you off on the next climb. You might even find you write a book-full.

Preface

by Carole Angier and Sally Cline

Writing Short Stories is the sixth in our series of Writers' & Artists' Companions, and one of the most exciting.

It's by two young voices, both of whom share with us their adventures as short story writers. Courttia Newland read Sam Selvon's *Lonely Londoners* as a teenager, and knew he wanted to capture the lives of inner-city West London kids, as Selvon had captured their grandfathers'. He started to hammer out his first book on a friend's word processor, he tells us – until one day she needed it back. He knew he'd write the rest some day, but not when or how. He trusted to luck; and eventually it came. Tania Hershman also beat a lone path as a short story writer, reading all the best books on writing, and struggling for a long time with secret shame that she couldn't follow their rules. Finally she realized she didn't have to: she had her own vision to follow, and that of a few kindred spirits.

Give yourself permission, take risks, endure – that is the heart of Courttia's and Tania's message. No method works for everyone. Or rather, only one method does. American writer Ron Carlson, one of Tania's kindred spirits, sums it up: *'The writer is the person who stays in the room.'*

Like all the Writers' & Artists' Companions, *Writing Short Stories* is original in its content, but shares its form with the others. Part 1 is by the two authors: essays on their personal reflections and experiences, such the ones above; a history of the short story; and two fascinating chapters in which each analyses the development of one of their own stories. Part 2 is, as always, the guest section, this time with guests from around the world: the US, Canada, South Africa and New Zealand as well as the UK. And Part 3 (once again by the two authors) is a hands-on practical guide, complete with exercises, for writers working alone or in groups, with or without a tutor.

The short story is the up-and-coming form, with the Nobel Prize in Literature going to (Canadian) Alice Munro in 2013, and the first new Folio Prize to (American) George Saunders in 2014. Courttia, Tania and their guests are in the forefront. We hope you'll join them.

Part 1

The history of the short story

Tania

This can be only a potted history, with many omissions. But the short story understands, if anyone does, that things must be left out. So, let's carry on.

The history of the short story is by necessity tied to the question, What is a short story? If you don't have a definition how can you pinpoint the first instance of one? Tricky, even today. Let's not attempt to answer that yet, and start instead with storytelling. As William Boyd writes in his excellent 'A short history of the short story' (*Prospect Magazine*, 2006), 'You could argue that storytelling in one form or another is hard-wired into our human discourse'. He imagines early humans telling fanciful tales around cave fires, and this leads him to speculate that 'the short form is, conceivably, more natural to us than longer forms: the anecdote that lasts several hours is going to find its listeners drifting away pretty soon'.

In order to retain the listener's attention, our ancestors learned editing skills, an understanding of what to omit, and, of course, that all-important ending – all vital aspects of a great and successful short story.

In 'The Short Story: An Overview of the History and Evolution of the Genre' (included in *Short Story Theories: A Twenty-First Century Perspective*, Viorica Patea [ed.]), Viorica Patea peers almost as far into our past: 'The origins of the short form go back to myth and biblical verse narratives, medieval sermons and romance, fables, folk tales, ballads and the rise of the German Gothic in the eighteenth century.' She quotes Mary Rohrberger, one of the first 'theorizers of the genre', as saying that while 'short narrative fiction is as old as the history of literature', the short story 'as we know it today, is the newest of literary genres'. William Boyd: 'The cultural history of the published short story is only a few decades longer than that of film.'

The *Encyclopaedia Britannica* mentions both the tale and the sketch as forerunners of the short story. The tale, says the EB, is the older form and 'provides a culture's narrative framework for such things as its vision of itself ... tales are frequently understood only by members of the particular culture to which they belong'. The sketch is the opposite, 'depicting some phenomenon of one culture for the benefit or pleasure of a second culture'. The tale is generally spoken and the sketch written, but also, says the EB, by nature the sketch is 'suggestive, incomplete' and it came to the fore around the sixteenth century.

Aesop's fables in the sixth century BC are considered by many to be ancestors of the modern short story. The Greeks were also the originators of romantic fiction, often told in brief tales, such as *The Love Romances of Parthenius of Nicaea*, a collection of '36 prose stories of unhappy lovers', says the EB. The Romans were more wedded to longer forms, perhaps, suggests the EB, because of their love of rhetoric!

The Middle Ages were a fertile time for short narratives, which provided much-needed diversion and entertainment with, according to the EB, 'even the aggressive, grim spirit of the invading Germanic Barbarians ... amenable to expression in short prose'. Whereas these and the Scandinavian and Icelandic invaders' tales were rather violent, the short prose of the Celts had a more romantic and magical aspect. One popular medieval short story collection, *The Seven Sages of Rome*, was published in almost all European languages. And then around the same time, of course, is *The Arabian Nights*.

Chaucer and Boccaccio refined the short narrative. Chaucer experimented with many forms, from animal fables to sermons. Where Chaucer 'reveals a character through actions and assertions, Boccaccio seems more interested in stories as pieces of action', says the EB. Boccaccio's *Decameron* is what we'd now call a linked short story collection: ten people meet and tell each other ten stories each. This spawned imitators, with 50 writers of what were called at the time 'novelle' in Italy alone. The Italians seized upon short narratives with gusto for three centuries. Says the EB: 'Almost every Italian in the 16th century, it has been suggested, tried his hand at "novelle" ... In the early 17th century, Giambattista Basile attempted to infuse stock situations (often of the fairy-tale type, such as "Puss and Boots") with realistic details.

The result was often remarkable – a tale of hags or princes with very real motives and feelings.'

France joined in with a rather steamy collection, *Les Cent Nouvelles Nouvelles* (*The Hundred New Short Stories*, 1460). Spain, one of the most influential nations in Europe in the fifteenth and sixteenth centuries, played its part with, among others, Miguel de Cervantes' experimental *Novelas ejemplares* (*Exemplary Novels*, 1613). Says the EB: 'Cervantes' short fictions vary in style and seriousness, but their single concern is clear: to explore the nature of man's secular existence. This focus was somewhat new for short fiction.'

Short fiction's popularity begins temporarily to wane in the seventeenth and eighteenth centuries for many reasons, from the emergence of the novel to a renewed interest in drama and poetry; also, because, 300 years after Boccaccio, nothing new was apparently being written. 'Travel books, criminal biographies, social description, sermons, and essays occupied the market. Only occasionally did a serious story find its way into print, and then it was usually a production of an established writer like Voltaire or Addison', says the EB.

The short story seems to have been hardest hit in England, where it hadn't become as popular as elsewhere, maybe because people were more interested in their social conditions, and short stories didn't address these issues.

It was in the nineteenth century that short fiction re-emerged as the 'modern short story'. When was the first modern short story published? William Boyd claims it was Sir Walter Scott's 'The Two Drovers', published in 1827 in *Chronicles of the Canongate*. Scott was an inspiration internationally, he says, not only to George Eliot and Thomas Hardy in Britain but to 'Balzac in France, Pushkin and Turgenev in Russia and Fenimore Cooper and Hawthorne in America', who in turn influenced Flaubert, Maupassant, Chekhov, Poe and Melville.

Scott doesn't get a mention in the *Encyclopaedia Britannica*, which does agree that the modern short story emerged at around this time, simultaneously in the US, France, Germany and Russia, and that this new type of short story took on some of the realist aspects of journalism. 'What is a short story', Goethe asked, 'but an event which, though unheard of, has occurred?'

Others in Germany also seemed to require the short story to be realist, which, of course, did not mean that everyone concurred. German writers such as Heinrich von Kleist and E. T. A. Hoffman called their fabulist stories 'tales'. Ludwig Tieck in the preface to his 1829 collection, says the EB, 'envisioned the short story as primarily a matter of intensity and ironic inversion. A story did not have to be realistic in any outward sense, he claimed, so long as the chain of consequences was "entirely in keeping with character and circumstances". By allowing the writer to pursue an inner, and perhaps bizarre, reality and order, Tieck and the others kept the modern story open to non-journalistic techniques.'

A similar two-stranded evolution – realist and non-realist – was happening in the US. Regional stories of the second half of the nineteenth century such as those by G. W. Cable, Bret Harte and Sarah Orne Jewett, dealt with real places, people and events. But Edgar Allen Poe's stories, such as 'The Tell-Tale Heart' (1843), are less realist. Another American, Washington Irving, didn't confine himself to one school or the other, writing both realistic sketches and not-so-realist stories such as 'Rip Van Winkle' (1819).

It wasn't until the short story was included in discussions of literary theory, argues Viorica Patea, that it became a genre in its own right – and the first people to do that were not literary critics but writers themselves, soon after Scott published 'The Two Drovers'. The most notable was Poe, who started off the discussion about the short story's 'form, style, length, design, authorial goals, and reader effect, developing the framework within which the short story is discussed even today', says Patea. In his 'The Philosophy of Composition' (Edgar Allen Poe, 1846), Patea says he 'was the first to consider endings as crucial elements in compositional strategies and defined the short story in terms of reading experience'.

Now we get into definitions: it is the novel that the short story is compared to and differentiated from. A short story according to Poe was simply 'a narrative that "can be read at one sitting"'. This sounds rather piece-of-string-like, but Boyd thinks it's spot on: 'What Poe was trying to put his finger on was the short story's curious singularity of effect, something he felt very strongly came from its all-in-one-go consumption', which, when the story is well written, for Poe led to 'a sense of the fullest satisfaction'.

Boyd takes this further himself: 'The great modern short stories possess a quality of mystery and beguiling resonance about them – a complexity of afterthought – that cannot be pinned down or analysed', he says. 'Bizarrely, the whole is undeniably greater than the sum of its parts ... We cannot summarise or paraphrase the totality of effect of these stories.' Rather than Poe, it is Herman Melville who, for Boyd, caused the short story to come of age with *The Piazza Tales* (1856).

In *The American Short Story Since 1950*, Kasia Boddy pinpoints the first instance of the term 'Short-story' in print as 1885, in an article by American critic Brander Matthews, who deliberately used a capital letter and a hyphen 'to distinguish short stories from stories which merely happened to be short'. Boddy argues that the Americans seized upon the short story as a 'national art form' because the country was so young and the short story best reflected newness, lack of a lengthy 'narrative arc'.

Also the pioneering spirit: 'At the end of the [nineteenth] century Frank Norris advertised "great opportunities for fiction-writers in San Francisco"', writes Boddy. 'Unlike Eastern cities such as Boston or New York, San Francisco was "not settled enough yet for the novelist". Why? Because the novelist, he argued, "demands large, co-ordinated, broad and simple lines upon which to work, something far more unified than we can yet give him".'

Short story writers, the implication seems to be, thrive in chaos, in uncertainty, within limits. 'For Norris, the form best suited to retain, or promote, unsettled manliness was short fiction. Only the short story, he claims, would allow the writer to express "growing and living ... in spots, here a little, there a little, scattered bits of life and movement, quite independent of each other".' (This begs the question – what of unsettled womanliness?)

A similar claim is made by Argentine short story writer, novelist and essayist Julio Cortázar, in an essay entitled 'Some Aspects of the Short Story' (first published in 1971 and included in *The New Short Story Theories* edited by Charles May): that the short story is given great importance in 'almost all the Spanish-speaking countries of America ... As is natural among younger literatures, in our countries spontaneous creation almost always precedes critical examination.'

Paul March-Russell puts forward a theory in *The Short Story: An Introduction* about 'postcolonial short fiction', which he says is rarely referred to in discussions of the 'cultural products of either the colonial past or the liberated present'. He talked about dissidence and the short story: 'merely electing to write in a less dominant form, such as the short story, sets writers against the norm', and the postcolonial short story is 'potentially a more dissident form than the major genres, especially with regards to rethinking the post-colonial'.

Examples March-Russell adduces include Franz Kafka, born in Prague, then part of the Austro-Hungarian empire, and writing in German: 'Kafka's strange and alienating fictions mediate the criss-crossing fractures of geography, history and language', he says. Others include Kenyan writer Ngugi wa Thiong'o, the Canadian writers Alice Munro and Margaret Atwood, Nadine Gordimer in South Africa, exiled South African writer Bessie Head, and the Caribbean-born writer V. S. Naipaul. Here is where women writers surface in the short story's history, towards the mid-twentieth century.

There's one name that always comes up in any short story discussion: What is it about Anton Chekhov (1860–1904)? William Boyd says: 'Chekhov saw and understood the life is godless, random, and absurd, that all history is the history of unintended consequences ... By abandoning the manipulated beginning-middle-and-end plot, by refusing to judge his characters, by not striving for a climax or seeking neat narrative resolution, Chekhov made his stories appear agonisingly, almost unbearably lifelike.'

Chekhov, says Boyd, represents 'the end of the first phase of the modern short story', arguing that all the greats who came after him (James Joyce, Katherine Mansfield, Raymond Carver) 'are in one way or another in his debt'.

Says Viorica Patea: 'Chekhov's dictum – "In the short story it is better to say not enough than to say too much" – anticipates by several decades the modernist aesthetic agenda and Hemingway's famous iceberg theory.' Hemingway explained his theory – also known as the theory of omission – in his book on bullfighting, *Death in the Afternoon* (1932): 'If a writer of prose knows enough of what he is writing about he may omit things that he knows and the reader, if the writer is writing truly enough, will have a feeling of those things as strongly as though the writer had stated them.

The dignity of movement of an iceberg is due to only one-eighth of it being above water. A writer who omits things because he does not know them only makes hollow places in his writing.'

Well, we've now reached the twentieth century, and quite a lot is happening. Instead of quoting people talking about the early twentieth century short story, I bring you a voice directly from that time: William Patterson Atkinson, vice-principal of Lincoln High School, Jersey City, US, in the introduction to his textbook, *The Short-story* (1916):

> The latest stage in the development of the short-story is due to
> Rudyard Kipling, who has made it generally more terse, has filled
> it with interest in the highest degree, has found new local colour,
> chiefly in India, and has given it virility and power. His subject matter
> is, in the main, interesting to all kinds of readers. His stories likewise
> fulfil all the requirements of the definition. Being a living genius
> he is constantly showing new sides of his ability, his later stories
> being psychologic. His writings fall into numerous groups − soldier
> tales; tales of machinery; of animals; of the supernatural; of native
> Indian life; of history; of adventure; − the list could be prolonged.
> Sometimes they are frankly tracts, sometimes acute analyses of the
> working of the human mind ... So in the course of a little less than
> a century there has grown to maturity a new kind of short narrative
> identified with American Literature and the American people,
> exhibiting the foremost traits of the American character, and written
> by a large number of authors of different rank whose work, of a
> surprisingly high average of technical excellence, appears chiefly in
> the magazines.

While Atkinson's textbook was aimed at readers, around this time another kind of textbook emerged: creative writing handbooks. These were based on Poe's theory about the short story, which 'gave editors both a model and a standard by which to judge the work of writers', says Paul March-Russell. However, there was a problem: Poe's ideas were taken to be the 'formula' for writing short stories, leading to the concept of the 'well-made story', which sounds like a compliment, but was a term first used in the nineteenth century, says March-Russell, 'to describe French drawing-room dramas that used the classical unities of time, character and plot, but which were mechanical in construction and devoid of feeling'. So while short story theories led to books encouraging writers to write short stories, they were being encouraged to write one type of short story – the type which British writer A. S. Byatt recently said 'can be mildly admired and taken or left'.

While there was criticism in the US and Britain of 'formulaic' short stories – criticism that continues today with regard to the ever-growing number of creative writing courses – is there something so wrong with the well-made story? Its British practitioners include Somerset Maugham, H. E. Bates, V. S. Pritchett and Elizabeth Taylor, beloved both by readers and critics.

Perhaps it's a question of fashion or personal preference. As March-Russell points out, 'While these writers were aware of the effect that modernism had upon literature, for example Maugham's debt to [Joseph] Conrad, they preferred to stay within the more familiar realms of plot and character. [They] were undeniably modern but they chose against the more disquieting possibilities in narrative form that the effects of modernity had opened up.'

Modernist literature refers to the late nineteenth century and early to mid-twentieth century, to short story authors including Gustave Flaubert, Joseph Conrad, Virginia Woolf, James Joyce and Katherine Mansfield. Some of the features that define them as 'modernist' are: unreliable narrators, stream of consciousness narration, futility, anarchy, ambiguity and absurdism, influenced by Sigmund Freud's and Carl Jung's theories of the mind and consciousness, and developments in physics.

One example Paul March-Russell focuses on is the short story 'Bliss' by Katherine Mansfield, which he describes as 'anti-transcendent: it returns both [the main character] Bertha and her readers to the ambiguity of human relations ... Running through Mansfield's oeuvre ... is the belief that self may also be an illusion that deludes and incarcerates the individual.'

Irish writer Elizabeth Bowen's introduction to the 1936 *Faber Book of Modern Short Stories* illuminates what was happening at that time (reprinted in full in Charles May's *The New Short Story Theories*).

The short story is a young art. As we now know it, it is the child of this century ... The cinema ... is of the same generation: in the last thirty years the two arts have been accelerating together. They have affinities – neither is sponsored by a tradition; both are, accordingly, free; both, still, are self-conscious, show a self-imposed discipline and regard for form; both have, to work on, immense matter – the disoriented romanticism of the age.

Bowen talks about how 'the short story as an art has come into being through a disposition to see life in a certain way', but claims that short story writers almost always need to look for some guidance from those who came before. While admiring stories by James Joyce and Thomas Hardy, she believed that the modern English short story took inspiration from abroad, specifically from Chekhov and Maupassant, who had very different approaches to the form.

Chekhov, says Bowen, 'opened up for the writer tracts of emotional landscape ... His hero was the sub-man, he crystallized frustration, inertia, malaise, vacancy, futile aspiration or sly pretentiousness.' Whereas Maupassant's writing, according to Bowen, is 'energetic, ruthless, nervous and plain ... his hardness and capability made him that rare thing – the first-rate unliterary writer'.

Even in 1936, Bowen was cautioning writers against using Chekhov as a model, because he's been done to death. 'We have suffered outpourings of minor dismay, or mediocre sentiment. From the dregs of his influence our most vital short story writers now seem to revolt.' She suggests that English writers could learn from the Americans, whose claim that the American short story is superior might not be untrue. 'The American level of workmanship is higher; also, to-day, from the American pen our used language starts with new vitality.'

Bowen distinguishes between the 'commercial short story' and the 'non-commercial short story', where the latter is 'not meant to be suitable for the popular, well-paying magazines, and free, therefore, not to conform with so-called popular taste'. Clearly, the commercial short story writer could make a decent living in 1936 – and Bowen is definitely not denigrating the hard-working writers of these stories. The non-commercial story was on the rise, and Bowen was happy that writers were being freed from tradition and commercial conventions. But non-commercial doesn't make it art, she argues, and worries about the new set of conventions that are springing up around the 'free' short story which might 'prove as dangerous to living work'.

Now, just before World War II, the postmodernist period begins, and things take another turn in the short story world – or, rather, it expands.

Postmodernist literature is associated with notions such as fragmentation, collage, pastiche, experimentation and metafiction. By the end of the 1960s, writes Kasia Boddy in *The American Short Story Since 1950*, 'the short story's reputation had shifted from that of most conventional of contemporary literary genres to a position at the "forefront of the avant garde"'.

Why had the short story become so conventional? One reason was the influence of *The New Yorker* magazine, which, by the 1960s, was one of only a handful of magazines still regularly publishing short stories. *The New Yorker* was accused by its critics of trying to 'iron out all the writing', says Boddy: 'Strict adherents to the rules of "modern English usage", the magazine's editors added commas and informative sub-clauses to avoid the very ambiguities and uncertainties that their fiction contributors had worked so hard to cultivate.' But contributors couldn't complain, since there were so few paying venues for their work.

Teachers and students on the growing number of creative writing programmes in the US decided to create a revolution from within. Says Boddy: 'Some writers revived pre-modern forms such as the fable or fairy tale or drew upon short fiction's links to the discursive essay and Kafkaesque philosophical parable. Others looked further afield. Why not write a story in the form of a questionnaire or footnotes or a TV game show? Why not make collages combining words and images? Why not write fiction for "tape" and "live voice" as well as for print? In other words, just about anything went – except, that is, the mood-driven, slice of life realist short story.'

Experimental fiction seemed to be the mood of the age, taking a stand 'against' anything and everything. Experimental postmodern American short story writers included Richard Brautigan, who often employed metafiction to comment on his own stories, such as the beginning of 'A Short Story About

Contemporary life in California': 'There are thousands of stories with original beginnings. This is not one of them.'

Many postmodern short stories seem to be about the difficulty of writing short stories. John Barth's 'Lost in the Funhouse', says Boddy, 'seems to be narrated by a writing-school student trying to remind himself how to go about the task. He often interrupts his narrative with passages that might have come from his lecture notes.' Postmodern short stories might be in the form of a list, such as William Gass's 'In the Heart of the Heart of the Country', which Boddy describes as consisting of '36 discrete blocks of prose, each clearly labelled and each describing, or rather inventing, some aspects of the town' that Gass is writing about in Indiana. Boddy quotes Gass talking about his attraction to lists because lists 'are for those who love language, the vowel-swollen cheek, the lilting, dancing tongue, because lists are fields of words'.

Donald Barthelme wrote stories which were often, says Boddy, 'about a thwarted quest for structure and meaning'. Barthelme became one of *The New Yorker*'s regular fiction contributors, which Paul March-Russell explains thus: 'Due to a personal connection, Barthelme's mix of collage, allusion and pastiche found an amenable venue at *The New Yorker* ... Initially, though, Barthelme's fiction was greeted with incredulity and derision by several of *The New Yorker*'s readers, but the magazine offered Barthelme a regular contract because the controversy had helped recast *The New Yorker* as an innovative journal, thereby re-emphasizing its leading status.'

Experimentation and postmodernism were also thriving outside the US, with Angela Carter reinventing the fairy tale in England, and Gabriel García Márquez in Colombia pioneering magical realism, combining realism with fantasy.

We are pretty much up to the present day. Are we still in postmodernist times? That might not be for us to say. There are more creative writing programmes worldwide than ever, and thousands of markets for the short story writer; although in the UK and the US the novel is the dominant form for mainstream publishers.

It is an interesting time for the short story: the awarding of the 2013 Man Booker International Prize for her achievements in fiction to American writer Lydia Davis, who often writes extremely short stories with metafictional elements, was swiftly followed by the 2013 Nobel Prize for Literature for Canadian short story writer Alice Munro, writing at the longer end of the short story spectrum.

What might happen next? That's for this generation of short story writers to explore. Yes, that means you. Shall we carry on?

Further reading

Boddy, Kasia, *The American Short Story Since 1950* (Edinburgh University Press, 2010).

Bowen, Elizabeth, 'Introduction', *Faber Book of Modern Short Stories* (reprinted in *The New Short Story Theories*). Charles May [ed.], (Ohio University Press, 1994).

Boyd, William, 'A Short History of the Short Story' (*Prospect Magazine*, July 2006).

Cortázar, Julio, 'Some Aspects of the Short Story' (first published in 1971, included in *The New Short Story Theories*, Charles May [ed.], Ohio University Press, 1994).

Hansen, Arlen J., 'The short-story (Literature)', *Encyclopaedia Britannica*.

March-Russell, Paul, *The Short Story: An Introduction* (Edinburgh University Press, 2009).

May, Charles (ed.), *The New Short Story Theories* (Ohio University Press, 1994).

Patea, Viorica (ed.), *Short Story Theories: A Twenty-First Century Perspective* (Rodopi, 2007).

Patterson Atkinson, William, *The short-story* (1916).

Crime, tricks and tales: genre and the short story

Courttia

It might seem strange, but it's not easy to find much information on the history of science fiction and crime writing in the short story. There are pages of speculation as to the origins of the story itself, and its links to the awakening of human consciousness. As Tania has noted, William Boyd imagines a band of Neanderthals or similar humanoids hunkered around a fire, recreating their day to an enraptured primordial audience, complete with gnawed bones and the darkened maws of their respective caves. Charles May speaks of the wellsprings of the form being as old as 'the primitive realm of myth' (May 1). Arthur Asa Berger, writing in *Media, Myth and Society*, explains how ancient myths continue to permeate modern storytelling efforts. From this point onwards, with regard to the literary short story at least, there is often a great leap forwards, usually depositing us in nineteenth-century Europe and America, deep in the realm of ghost, horror and revenge stories such as Edgar Allen Poe's 'The Cask of Amontillado', published in 1846. Poe is credited with the creation of the first fictional detective, an unknown word at the time. He even invented the Watson-style sidekick. Fascinatingly, gentle digging unearths the appearance of short form crime fiction during the Middle Ages, placed curiously alongside tales of speculative fiction and abstract, fantasy worlds not too unlike our own.

The short fiction tale, that ancient precursor to our modern genre story, is steeped in fantastical elements described as 'a manifestation of a culture's unaging desire to name and conceptualize its place in the cosmos' (*Encyclopaedia Britannica*). Tales enabled the nations of the world to form narrative frameworks that either helped to encapsulate their visions of themselves, or expressed their conception of their narratives and gods.

Led by characters like Elegba and Shango, Krishna and Kali, Prometheus and Hercules, ancient heroes were the Supermen and Superwomen of their times. Their imagined exploits gave rise to our use of the word myth, derived from the Greek mythos, 'meaning "word", "speech", "tale of the gods"' (Berger, 2). Tales were epic in scope, highly speculative, and their stories enrapture readers to this very day.

While it's true that most early speculative tales were spoken in verse to aid memorization, it's not true that they were exclusively oral. Of course, the common man or woman of the times could not imagine what it might be like to walk around with a paperback in their pocket. That came centuries later with the invention of the printing press. But some of the oldest narratives in the world — the famous Babylonian tales *The Epic of Gilgamesh* and *The War of the Gods, The Heavenly Bow* and *The King Who Forgot*, both Canaanite, were written, or better yet inscribed in cuneiform on clay, sometime during the second millennium BC. Egyptian tales recorded on papyrus during the Twelfth Dynasty were more prosaic, such as 'King Cheops [Khufu] and the Magicians'. Early Indian tales came later, circa 700 BC, and were mostly theological appendixes to the Four Vedas. One of the world's most popular books, *The Pañca-tantra* (c. 500 AD), was a collection of moral animal tales akin to Aesop's Fables, and has been translated into Persian, Arabic, Greek, Hebrew and Latin. The Hindu epic, the *Mahabharatha* (eighth and ninth centuries BCE), details the story of King Revaita, who travels to heaven to meet Brahma and is shocked to learn that many ages have passed when he returns to earth, predicting the concept of time travel.

Hebrews wrote sophisticated, fantastical narratives that became fused into the Old Testament, including the Books of Tobit and Judith and the story of Jonah, one of the most famous stories of all time. The early Japanese tale *Urashima Tarō* is equally fascinating. A young fisherman named Urashima Taro visits an undersea palace and stays there for three days; after returning to his village home, he finds himself three hundred years in the future, where he is long forgotten, his house is in ruins, and his family are long dead. The tenth-century *The Tale of the Bamboo Cutter* features a princess from the moon who is sent to earth for her own safety during a celestial war. She is found and raised by a Japanese bamboo cutter, and later taken back to the moon by her real, extra-terrestrial family. A manuscript illustration depicts a round flying machine that looks remarkably like a flying saucer. Because of their themes, motifs and speculative technology, both stories are considered proto-science fiction.

It goes without saying that the contribution of the Greeks changed the short story forever, yet they also refined the concept of the genre story. There were Aesop's animal fables, collected in the sixth century, and Homer, Euripides and Hesiod's tales of love and war. As well as these infamous stories, the Greeks are also credited with the invention of the romance genre, which often took place as a series of short tales. *The Love Romances of Parthenius* and *The Milesian Tales*, an erotic collection by Aristides of Miletus, now extant, were two popular texts of the times. The Romans contributed less in comparison. Ovid's *Metamorphoses* reshaped over 100 short tales which were popular at the time to fit a thematic pattern of transformation. In both Roman and Greek writings, the didactic themes of early narratives were replaced with what we might recognize as a distinctly modern moral position.

In the Middle Ages there was the violent short prose of Germanic barbarians, whose myths and sagas held sway throughout Iceland and Scandinavia, perhaps as an early precursor to dark crime fiction. Meanwhile the Celts' romantic nature also influenced their tales, producing magical stories from Ireland, Wales and Brittany. On the opposite side of the world, sometime in the late Middle Ages, came *The Arabian Nights*, most famous for its use of the structural framing device of Scheherazade.

The basis for this device – one central storyteller who recites a range of diverse stories – is reputed to be the lost Persian collection *Hezar Efsan* (Thousand Romances), although some stories are reputed to have their origins in India. Other stories in this collection are the earliest known examples of crime fiction; these include 'The Three Apples', known in Arabic as 'Hikayat al-sabiyya 'l-muqtula' ('The Tale of the Murdered Woman'), and 'The Hunchback's Tale', a comedic courtroom drama laced with suspense. 'The Tale of Attaf' also concludes by introducing elements of crime writing. Some tales possess elements of horror, fantasy and science fiction. There is the first-ever mention of ghouls (in 'The History of Gherib and His Brother

Agib'). 'Ali the Cairene and the Haunted House in Baghdad' is a story of paranormal activity. 'The Adventures of Bulukiya' follows the protagonist on an epic journey in search of the herb of immortality, braving the seas, Paradise and Hell, before taking to the cosmos and exploring worlds larger than his own. There he encounters djinns, talking trees, talking serpents, and mermaids. Not content with being confined to one gender, another protagonist, Abdullah (in 'Abdullah the Fisherman and Abdullah the Merman'), also gains the ability to breathe underwater and discovers an undersea society that's an inversion of that on land, following a primitive form of communism where money and clothing do not exist. There are Amazonian societies dominated by women, lost technology, advanced ancient civilizations, and stories of epic catastrophe. No wonder these tales influenced the likes of Stephen King (Scheherazade's frantic storytelling to save her life is echoed in the chilling *Misery*), and H. P. Lovecraft, who read them as a boy and attributed some of his work to his fascination with these fantastic stories.

It's widely perceived that the short story went through a lull after the high of the Middle Ages. The common man and woman used them as a form of ribald entertainment rather than instructions for life, or even serious art. During the Ming Dynasty in China, around the eighteenth century, Gong'an fiction, a genre of crime fiction, was very popular. 'Di Gong An' was translated into English as 'Celebrated Cases of Judge Dee' by the Dutch sinologist Robert Van Gulick, who later wrote his own original Judge Dee series. Van Gulick outlined several major differences between Chinese crime fiction and its Western counterpart. The detective was usually a local magistrate; the criminal was introduced at the beginning of the story; the story had a supernatural element, where ghosts gave their own version of events; there were digressions into philosophy, which created very long books; there was a huge cast of characters; and not many pages are spent on the details of the crime, with more focus given to the execution and torture of the criminal, including their time spent in various hells for the damned.

While there must have been genre stories produced during this time in Europe, a quick scan records nothing of note. There was Chaucer and the Italians Boccaccio and Franco Sacchetti, but these were realists for the most part, framing their stories around the inescapable presence of the Black

Death. Following this was the decline of the subsequent three centuries, owing as much to the inability to escape Boccaccio's powerful influence as it did to the rise of the novel. Finally, in the mid-nineteen hundreds, there came an almost simultaneous acknowledgement of two types of stories on two sides of the world: the realistic story, largely a modern form, and the surrealist, with origins in the tale. Goethe, after publishing 'entertainments' for 32 years, concluded that the short story had to be realistic. Ludwig Tieck, on the other hand, wholly rejected realism, thus making available non-journalistic techniques to writers and their stories.

Early crime stories began to appear in 1829, when the Danish novella *The Rector of Veilbye* was published. Other crime writing included the English novel *Confessions of a Thug*, published by Phillip Meadows Taylor in 1839 (incidentally, 'thug' is a Hindi word adopted into English after the success of that bestselling book), and *Mordet på Maskinbygger Rolfsen* (*The Murder of Engine Maker Rolfsen*) by Maurits Christopher Hansen, a Norwegian writer who is said to have introduced the novel to Norway. That novel, written in 1839, is reputed to be the world's first crime novel, beating Poe by two years; interesting in light of the Scandinavian dominance of the modern crime novel in recent times.

In the United States came impressionist stories by Washington Irving and Edgar Allen Poe, where the hallucinations of their central characters shaped the reader's understanding. Irving and Poe's surreal ghost stories went on to influence generations of writers. There's little doubt these writers were the precursors to the science fiction, fantasy and horror writers who emerged in the twentieth century. Poe loved to genre-hop, writing science fiction short stories, a novel, *The Narrative of Arthur Gordon Pym of Nantucket*, as well as the world's first locked room mystery, published in 1841 (*The Murders in the Rue Morgue*). The 'locked room' technique was adopted later by Agatha Christie and Arthur Conan Doyle alike. Well-known authors such as Joseph Conrad, Sheridan Le Fanu and Dick Donovan all wrote crime novels during this time, although later critics found their efforts formulaic.

Then, in 1887, came Sherlock Holmes. Though Conan Doyle wrote novels in the main, his influence is immeasurable; from him came the concept of the client, who hired the detective to solve the crime, and also logical deduction – a staple tool of the modern detective. There could not be a history of the genre without mentioning him.

The Golden Age of crime fiction arrived in the 1920s and 1930s, and was led by the British: Agatha Christie, Dorothy L. Sayers, and many more. Again, these were largely novelists, but most also wrote stories for magazines, periodicals, journals and their own collections. Christie penned 14 collections under her own name, featuring Poirot and Miss Marple, and Sayers wrote several featuring her own key protagonist, Lord Peter Wimsey. Their use of conventions, such as the English country house setting, and stock characters such as the handsome young gentleman and his rich fiancée, gave rise to the US response: the hard-boiled school, or noir fiction. Dashiell Hammett, Raymond Chandler and Mickey Spillane are its most well-known exponents, but writers like Jonathan Latimer also contributed to the form. Hammett had actually worked as a private eye, and a majority of the writers lived and worked in the areas they wrote about. It was this sense of authenticity that gave rise to a new, alternative set of conventions. The PI worked alone. He was aged 35 to 45. He was a loner and a tough guy. He was a heavy drinker who fought back when required and always carried a gun. He knew the urban landscape like his own front room. He was dirt-poor. He didn't trust the police. His mission was to rescue America from itself. The writers of this new breed of crime story had a plethora of pulp magazines that had been publishing war and cowboy adventure stories ready and waiting to publish their tales of seedy LA, New York, Chicago or San Francisco. Some of this intensely American work, such as Jonathan Latimer's *Solomon's Vineyard* (1941), wasn't published in Britain until during the Second World War.

Science fiction's Golden Age occurred a few decades later. Until then such stories and novels were being published, but the genre was not yet called science fiction. Whether its slower ascendance was the result of a cross-genre work ethic most writers adopted at the time or simply of the circumstances of the era is difficult to tell. Science fiction jostled next to adventure, murder mystery, horror and fantasy. It is noteworthy that Edgar Allen Poe is mentioned as a founding member of modern science fiction, alongside Jules Verne and H. G. Wells. Yet there were also Mary Shelley's *Frankenstein* (1818), Felix Bouden's *Le Roman de l'Avenir* (1834), Edward

Bulwer-Lytton's *The Coming Race* (1871), and countless other novels published during this time, including George Tucker's 1827 satirical novel *A Voyage to the Moon*, often cited as the first American science fiction novel. But due at least in part to the proliferation of magazines, science fiction short stories were also being published at an astonishing rate.

Thus Edward Page Mitchell wrote science-based stories for *The Sun* for more than a decade. Jack London wrote a number of stories that involved extra-terrestrials, invisibility and an irresistible energy weapon; his contribution is said to have changed the landscape of science fiction. Edgar Rice Burroughs started writing science fiction stories before World War I, publishing his first, 'Under the Moons of Mars', in 1912. Sir Arthur Conan Doyle also made forays into early science fiction, with the character Professor Challenger. There was even Bengali science fiction. Rokeya Sakhawat Hussein's 'Sultana's Dream' is one of the first examples of feminist works in the genre. The story was written in 1905, and published in *The Indian Ladies Magazine* of Madras, in English. It depicts a feminist utopia run by women, where men are secluded, and therefore crime is eliminated (as men are responsible for all of it). Female scientists have discovered solar power and how to trap the weather, and there is 'electrical' technology that allows labourless farming and flying cars. 'Sultana's Dream' has since been published as a Penguin Modern Classic, together with the related work 'Padmarag' (1924).

The development of the American science fiction magazine finally ensured the rise of the genre proper, when Hugo Gernsback founded *Amazing Stories* in 1926. Although similar magazines had been published in Sweden and Germany previously, *Amazing Stories* was the first in English to devote itself entirely to science fiction, which Gernsback called scientifiction. He encouraged stories that were scientifically realistic, although these were often published besides others written with no basis in reality.

Although scientifiction stories were viewed as sensationalism, and not real literature, *Amazing Stories* found itself competing with several more magazines by the 1930s; these included *Weird Tales, Astounding Stories* and *Wonder Stories*. The tales in these pages inspired a whole generation of science fiction writers (Stephen King, for example), no doubt due, at least in part, to the 'Letters to the Editor' columns, a medium eventually taken on by comic book publishers like Marvel and DC.

By now, many writers were attempting to respond to the changes that had taken place globally after World War I. Some who had been unconnected with science fiction and wanted to explore new storytelling forms found an original voice through the genre. Kafka, Joyce, T. S. Eliot, Woolf, Forster and many other authors all wrote stories playing with time and individual identity. Though these works were largely classified as literary fiction, they dealt with the impact of technology and science on the people of the time. The effects went both ways, with some of the genre writers adopting modernist literary techniques in turn.

The late 1930s saw the rise of the Futurians, a group of science fiction fans who assembled under the editorial guidance of John W. Campbell, who ran the magazine *Astounding Science Fiction*. These fans soon became professional writers, and included Isaac Asimov, Damon Knight, Frederik Pohl, Judith Merril and many more. The period also saw the emergence of Arthur C. Clarke, Robert A. Heinlein and A. E. van Vogt, and led to what is considered by most to be the Golden Age of science fiction. This was a time of hard science writing, characterized by a celebration of scientific achievement and success. It was said to have lasted until post-war technological advances, when a new generation began to turn against this mode.

These younger writers, who sought freedom of expression and new ideas, moved towards other magazines that had sprung up in the 1940s and 1950s: *The Magazine of Fantasy and Science Fiction*, *If* magazine, the resurrected *Amazing Stories*, and *Galaxy*, under the editorial stewardship of H. L. Gold and Frederik Pohl. Their focus was on a more literary form of science fiction, less concerned with plausibility than Campbell's *Astounding*, and taking its cues from mainstream fiction. Many believed that *Galaxy's* rise signalled the end of the Golden Age. Writers like Asimov and several others left the genre entirely and turned to writing almost exclusively science fact.

As the decades moved on, the detective story underwent a slow metamorphosis to eventually become the crime novel. Stories did not disappear altogether, but as more magazines became defunct, apart from a few scant publications in the UK, the novel began to hold sway. Character analysis took the place of plot-driven works. New themes, such as the spy thriller and historical mysteries began to emerge, and there have even been futuristic cross-genre mysteries in the work of Phillip K. Dick. Writers like Val McDermid, Nancy Sanra and Sarah Peretsky write stories featuring lesbian sleuths. The police investigation novel – or the procedural, as it has become known – is today by far the most popular form of crime writing. While short stories are still published online by writers like Ray Banks, and there were the early print collections of Ian Rankin, there is nowhere near as much call for stories as there was in the genre's heyday. Still, close attention is still being paid to the magazines, online and print, by agents and editors on the hunt for new talent, and so it's always worth sending stories to magazine editors. Crime writing has never been more popular, whether in film, TV or books.

For the science fiction story, which has arguably waned in popularity in comparison to crime writing, it would seem that the advent of science fiction in TV and film has forced the printed story into decline, even while on-screen representation has enjoyed major success. Curiously, this has forced writers into fierce experimentation for a number of decades, and science fiction's themes and tropes are still inspiring literary novelists to this day. Auspicious beginnings can be found in Kingsley Amis's *New Maps of Hell*, published in 1960, a literary history and examination of the form that introduced short story writers like Robert Sheckley to a wider reading public. At the same time, a British 'New Wave' was experimenting in the magazine *New Worlds*, under the editorial control of Michael Moorcock. The magazine had been a fanzine called *Novae Terrae*, first published in 1936, changing its name in 1939. During his tenure, Moorcock published stories by Brian Aldiss, J. G. Ballard and Thomas M. Disch, who all went on to become major names. By 1970 the magazine was heavily in debt, and it ceased publication by issue 200.

In the US, Harlan Ellison's *Dangerous Visions* anthology set stories by Americans beside those of British authors. Asimov wrote an introduction that called this the second revolution, the first being the movement that produced the Golden Age. The anthology went some way to producing a transatlantic New Wave of writers whose concerns were highbrow and more stylistic than the previous generations. Sexuality was brought to the fore, in the writings of Samuel R. Delany, Ursula K. Le Guin and Theodore Sturgeon. Political issues were also voiced. Phillip K. Dick explored the metaphysical mind and the social landscape of the modern world. This work was soon called soft science fiction, less interested with the hard scientific fact than with socio-political context and how that affected individual human beings, trapped in mostly dystopian worlds.

By the tail end of the 1980s, New Wave had faded from view to be replaced by cyberpunk. William Gibson, Bruce Sterling and John Shirley were in the vanguard of a movement that became a major influence on Japanese Anime (*Ghosts in the Shell, Akira*). Since then, the cyberpunk movement, once likened to a 'tribe' by John Shirley, has been commonplace in mainstream science fiction: think Matrix, Johnny Mnemonic, and video games like Metal Gear, and its influence is easily spotted.

Yet for the science fiction writer, much as for the crime writer, even as mainstream dividends for the long form have grown, the pickings in the short story have become increasingly slim. Notable collections, anthologies and standalone stories include Octavia Butler's *Bloodchild* (1995), winner of the Nebula Award for the title story and the Hugo award for best novelette; *The Dark Matter* series (2000–4), which published prominent African American writers of the time and twice won the World Fantasy Award for best anthology; the luminary ascendance of China Mieville, his loosely formed New Weird movement and his collection *Looking for Jake* (2005); Neil Gaiman's seminal collections, *Angels and Demons* and *Smoke and Mirrors* (1993, 1998); Jonathan Lethem's *The Wall of the Sky, the Wall of the Eye*, winner of the World Fantasy Award in 1997 (though by now Lethem is largely considered a 'literary' author); Vardana Singh's *The Woman Who Thought She Was a Planet* (2008), a collection inheriting the themes first outlined by Rokeya Sakhawat Hussein over a century ago; and the anthology *Afro SF* (2012), the first-ever compilation of science fiction from the African continent, heaving with established names alongside burgeoning talent.

While by no means exhaustive, this list is an example of genre fiction's popularity, and the fine work being done in short crime and science fiction writing. While arguments still rage over the merits of 'entertainment' and 'literary' works, there are a number of writers who are committed to crossing those unhelpful barriers in order to prove how defunct they actually are. Their tenacity is reflected in the work of the generation that is coming to the fore, emboldened by the great leaps and widened possibilities of their predecessors. The future of genre fiction, in the short story especially, is as promising as the imaginations of the writers themselves.

The shorter end of short stories – boundaries with poetry

Tania

What is a short story? Well, here's what it isn't. It isn't a whole novel squashed into five, 15 or 25 pages. It isn't a poem without line breaks. (I'm not even dealing with the question of how to define 'novel' or 'poem'.) It may be novel-like in scope, poetic in tone or rhythm, or filmic in style, dramatic in pacing. But a short story is a creature unlike any other. Not only that: each great short story writer takes it and makes it her own, does something new and different with it that no one has done before, that only he can do.

A poem may be book-length, a film may fill ten hours, a play can stretch over several days, a novel can strain the wrist to lift it. The one thing a story must be – and in this it is different from almost every form (except the novella, bounded at both ends) – is short. How short? Some would say down to six words and up to around 20,000, and anything in between.

This leads to my first point when discussing short stories and poetry, which is a political one: in bookshops (remember those?), short story collections are generally shelved under Fiction, alongside much heftier-looking novels. Apart from the issue I've already dealt with – that these are two completely separate forms – how can the word 'short' in this placing fail to imply 'less than' slimness leading to feelings of insubstantiality? However, were the short story collections shelved nearer to the Poetry section, wouldn't most ideas of quantity being related to quality dissolve? It's all about context.

If we are obliged to label, to pigeonhole, to create a family tree here, the short story has always, for me, been on a branch nearer to poetry than the novel. In her introduction to the 1936 *Faber Book of Modern Short Stories,*

Irish writer Elizabeth Bowen says of the short story: 'Poetic tautness and clarity are so essential to it that it may be said to stand on the edge of prose; in its use of action it is nearer to drama than to the novel.'

American short story writer Mary Gordon, in her introduction to the 2001 O. Henry award-winning short story 'The Deep', by Mary Swan, says:

> Prose fiction is the bastard child of poetry and journalism. If we, arbitrarily perhaps, but perhaps not, name poetry as the mother, and journalism as the father, it seems to me that current prose fiction suffers as a child who takes too much nourishment from its father's hand, an insignificant amount from its mother's. But 'The Deep' triumphantly insists on fiction's kinship with poetry.

On a more personal note, for several years now people have been suggesting that my very short stories, flash fictions, may actually be poems. At first I was resistant; I wanted rigid boundaries – a short story is a short story and a poem ... well, I didn't really know what a poem was, and so who was I to say whether I might be writing poems?

But over the years, as I have begun opening myself up to reading poetry, learning to write it, I have been letting down my guard and accepting that the borders are porous. At a major poetry event in London a few years ago, I heard award-winning British poet Simon Armitage read from his collection, *Seeing Stars*. His poems did not sound at all like my idea of 'poetry', an opinion which was formed from little more than studying the war poets at school when I was 14. His poems sounded like the kind of stories that I love. So I bought the book, and was astonished to see that on the page, these poems looked like prose, too.

When I later took a course (in radio drama) with Simon, he directed me towards one of his favourite poets, the Pulitzer-prize winning American, James Tate – and, lo and behold, all of Tate's poems look like this, too, and read like surreal short stories! I began to think, Well, if these can be poems ... then there is really only the thinnest of veils separating our two worlds. But, in England anyway, the formal worlds of poetry and the short story are mostly kept separate, which seems like a shame.

If not always brevity, then what we often share, short story writers and poets, is manifold: economy of words, implication rather than overt statement, the idea of creating an atmosphere and evoking feeling in the reader or listener, an embrace of the fragmentary nature of life, of focus on the miniature in order to illuminate the world.

Now that I am writing short stories as well as entities that I think of from the start as possible-poems, I can see where the similarities may be in the writing, too. I can hold the whole of a short story or a poem in my head at once, I can see its shape. I can get down a draft of either in one day, or even less. Then, for me, the process differs. A poem is something I seem to need to work on far more consciously, almost like a crossword puzzle, finding each right word. My 'poetry-writing head' is different from my 'short story-writing head'.

Have I turned a flash story into a poem and vice versa? Yes, I have, but for me this has required a complete re-thinking, not a simple removal or insertion of a line break. I use repetition and rhythm to create a certain effect in a short story, but I've found that a poem is far less forgiving when it comes to repeating words – it almost won't stand for it, demands to know if it is absolutely necessary. A poem that used to be a short story is a cousin of the original, but turns out to have a different atmosphere, to convey another thought about the world.

Here are two quotes from writers:

If the end of ... [X] arrives at a place that did not exist, was not conceivable before this particular [X] began then I think ... [X] is exciting, creates an impossible destination.

I don't think in terms of ideas. I have some sort of starting point. And I never know where ... [Y] is heading. The first thing I have to do is press my gas pedal and take my hands off the wheel. If I crash, maybe I'll get to somewhere interesting. It can't be premeditated.

Who is talking about what? I won't keep you in suspense. The first quote is from former American poet laureate Billy Collins, talking about poems; and the second is Israeli short story writer, Etgar Keret, talking about stories.

I'm not saying we can't label anything at all, that we should dissolve all definitions. But let's loosen our grip. We are all word-builders, and I don't really mind what you call my structure once I have put it out into the world. Take it; it's yours.

Further reading

Armitage, Simon, *Seeing Stars* (Faber & Faber, 2010).

Bowen, Elizabeth, 'Introduction', *Faber Book of Modern Short Stories* (reprinted in Charles May [ed.], *The New Short Story Theories* (Ohio University Press, 1994).

Collins, Billy, 2007 Writers on Writing podcast (2007) http://writersonwriting.blogspot.co.uk/2012/11/poet-billy-collins-on-writers-on.html

Dark, Larry (ed.), *Prize Stories: The O. Henry Awards 2001* (Anchor Books, 2001).

Keret, Etgar, *The Observer* http://www.theguardian.com/books/2012/mar/04/etgar-keret-interview-short-stories (4 March 2012).

Tate, James, *Return To The City Of White Donkeys* (Ecco Press, 2005).

Stories: those little slices of life

Courttia

Just last night, when my son was getting into bed, I was pondering what we would read. We'd exhausted Winnie the Pooh (although he still loves him deeply), and Beatrix Potter, and Harvey Moon, and the Mr Men. In fact we'd pretty much read everything on his shelf, apart from a large, fat, old-style book with a woven cover and periodic illustrations. I wasn't sure whether he was ready for it, at four and a half years old, but I decided to give it a try. The volume was *Aesop's Fables*. As we settled down in the bed and I opened the pages, I could picture myself, albeit a little older, lying on my mother's bed leafing through my own Ladybird edition of Aesop's cautionary tales. I'd read it so many times the spine was broken and exposed. The stories and accompanying illustrations were dark and wonderful moral tales – perfectly suited for my burgeoning imagination. As I read the fables to my son, I became aware that these were probably the first short stories I had ever encountered. Or, to use a modern term, the first 'flash fiction'. Most are no more than a page long, some less than a paragraph. They excited and delighted me as a child, doing what the very best art does, becoming deeply embedded in my psyche. When I got a little older, just before primary school, my uncle Trevor gave me a heavy edition of *Lord of the Rings*. I forgot about Aesop and his fables for many years.

Discovering short stories

Of course, my son loved Aesop's tales, responding with an enthusiasm that surprised me. When I said I'd read one last story, he said 'One more'. When I read another four at his prompting, he said I had to, because 'They're very short.' He said this with a smile, but his nose was also wrinkled in puzzlement; he'd never imagined stories could be told in such a small space on the page.

My own journey through literature must have been somewhat similar – it's difficult to remember back that far! I do know that after reading *Lord of the Rings* and *The Hobbit*, and many other long-form stories, I was blinded by the bright light that was the novel. The tales I wanted to tell were long. I thought that's what you had to do. That was as far as my reasoning went – stories had to be long. I didn't even particularly want to be a writer back then. When I was told by my English teacher that's exactly what I would be, aged 11, I responded with anger (I wanted to be a musician). But secretly, in my bedroom, I read all the novels I could and started on what was really a long short story of my own, in as much as I didn't have a plot, just six pages that I expanded. And expanded. And expanded. Character development? What for? Narrative voice and point of view? Variable. Authenticity? Who needs it? I wrote until I could write no more, 111 now long-lost pages about a kid who wins a competition to go and live with Michael Jackson (don't laugh), saves his life, and finds the King of Pop forever indebted to him. When I finished that, I put it away somewhere and looked at it just once more, when I gave it to my English teacher. Those words, 'You're going to be a novelist when you're older', still make me shake my head in wonder. Was it that obvious? Was I that bookish? There I was, trying to do everything I could not to be one, and the truth was written in those pages. None of that wanting to be a writer all my life for me. I wanted to be anything but.

I began to write my own short stories when I'd finished my first novel. In writing those stories – 15 in quick succession, before I began to read them as a 'collection' and make a close analysis of what I had done – I began to see that there were certain 'rules' to take note of when considering writing your short story, things that make it a short story and not anything else. These 'rules' are by no means prescriptive – indeed most of the fun and originality we seek can come from sometimes breaking them. But when you're starting out it's good to test whether you can adhere to the form by playing along with what's expected, before branching out and beginning to bend the form to shape your own needs.

What makes a short story?

Character — It's often said that the short story writer should use minimal characters and stick to one point of view, whether first person, second, or third. Some advice warns that you will not have room for more than one or two of what E. M. Forster terms 'round characters' (see his essay 'People' in *Aspects of the Novel* for a more detailed description of what this means). Economy is vital in the short form, so your protagonist should not be characterized too heavily, and the mention of minor characters must be brief. This means that you will not have much chance to switch perspectives and realize, in a balanced way, more than one point of view. Although this is a limitation in terms of perspective, it can also be an asset; you have a justifiable reason to withhold important information, thus channelling the reader's thoughts and feelings in the direction you choose.

Time — The economy of character also applies to time. There are some stories that manage to cover years of the protagonist's life (Daphne Du Maurier's 'Monte Verita', for example) but these often tend to be longer in word count as a result. It's often wise to decide that your story will cover a Moment in Time, a window into a direct portion of the character's life, with some allusion to what might have gone before, and very little of what may come after. In such a confined space, it is often important to focus on the specific events that make up your narrative.

Location — I tend to know that the story in my head will become a novel or a short story quite early on. One of the telltale signs is location. If I have a central setting the protagonist visits, or call their own, and they don't move from that place during my chosen Moment in Time, then I either have a short story, or a play. If I have multiple locations, over a longer period of time, then I probably have a novel or a screenplay. The idea of having one environment to work from that is tethered to the central character as a way to examine their psyche, or move the plot forwards (or in the best case, to do both), is one I find deeply stimulating as a means of generating material. What is the location? What does it mean to the character? Does it cause conflict or peace? How is the character's emotional state reflected in the place they find themselves in? Answering these questions is integral to building a compelling story.

Economy – so, if you haven't guessed it yet, the overall aim of the story is to minimize at all costs. To do this, it's often helpful to think of the short story as a push-and-pull mechanism between two modes of writing: character and action. To put it another way, every word you write should advance either our knowledge of the character, or our knowledge of the story. If it doesn't do those things it should go. Fancy descriptive passages that last half a page have to be cut down, or out. Long monologues from minor characters are superfluous; they can be problematic even when spoken by your protagonist. These are not things you have to worry about particularly at first draft stage, but when you get to the redraft and edit, you must be as merciless as Ming. Poets are famed for their ability to make every word count. A short story writer must be equally vigilant.

Why write short stories?

An easy question. After all, I started to write my own short stories because I didn't want to get stuck into another novel. I was drained, but I still wanted to write. I was limbering up for the day when I would be struck by a long-form idea and until that happened, I would keep my hand in by writing stories. My primary focus was the novel; after all, nobody reads shorts, right?

Wrong.

Well, to be fair, not totally wrong. I did begin writing stories because I believed all of the above (I hope that doesn't get me kicked out of the short story union). But by the time I'd written 15 practice runs, and delighted in stories and collections that quite frankly blew my mind, while reminding me how far I had to go to learn the craft (Jess Mowry's collection *Rats in the Trees*, and James Baldwin's story 'The Rockpile', for example), I realized the form had become less of a means to an end, and rather the end itself. I wanted to tell stories. And I wanted to tell them well. Part of that meant I had to scrap the original 15 stories I'd written and start again, using the things I had learned and discarding what hadn't worked. I had to think about why I wanted to tell these stories, what they meant to me and therefore, possibly, others. I had to define the urge.

So what are some of the reasons we might write stories? These are very particular to me and by no means exhaustive, but they might serve as impetus for you to think about some of your own reasons for wanting to write the short form.

- To Articulate the World – to be a writer, I believe you need to be an observer. Twenty-four hours a day, seven days a week, you must be prepared to receive information that could help the formulation of your story. Even when you're resting, you must be on standby; pen in pocket, notebook in a bag or on a table if you're at home, just in case your senses pick up something that can help you write. Yes, it is exhausting. Now it's become a habit, it's difficult to switch off and not notice every little detail around me. But equally, it's exhilarating. Every day since I have started to write seriously I feel more alive than I did before. As if I'm really living, instead of ambling along putting one day behind another. Life is way stranger than fiction, and it's those little daily coincidences and oddities that feed into the writing and help to create the urge.

- To See the Good in People – one of the reasons I like to write is because I can get into someone's head. When I write stories this is multiplied, usually by 12 if I'm writing a book. I don't know why I always tend to have a dozen stories in my collections; I suppose I'm odd that way (or even). So I often have 12 different characters, each with their own point of view based on age, race, gender, sexuality, religion, class and all the other permutations that make up the people of this world. In telling their stories I believe I'm trying to find their unique point of view, and defend it. No other person has exactly that point of view, because no other person has precisely that mix of perspective and experience. Invariably, most people believe they are right; or failing that, that they are a good person even when they are wrong. I like to try and pull back the curtains, and reveal the soul of the character, the person who emerges when no one else is around, so that we may understand them better. It's not up to me to judge them, at least not overtly. It's up to me to show as much of their character and experience as possible, so the reader can understand why they hold their unique perspective. And in doing so I tend to understand them a little more myself. The biggest leap I took in order to do this came from a short story in my first collection *Music for the Off-Key*, entitled 'Suicide Note', written from the point of view of a paedophile. From my own perspective, especially as the father of a child, paedophilia is a particularly heinous crime. But if I could create empathy for such a character while leaving my own distaste at the door and present him as a fully rounded human being, then I would have achieved a major win as a writer. And so I tried, and was pleased with the result.

- To Learn About the World – way before my writing helped me fill my passport, I travelled the world via books. As a child, I was always baffling adults and children alike with my knowledge of subject matters that surprised them, or more often confused them. It didn't help that I was allowed to read adult books, and so I was presented with concepts and emotions that were sometimes way over my head, and contributed, I believe, to my growing up a little too fast! But I've learned so much from the reading and writing of books, and not just from far afield. Sometimes I've discovered very interesting things about my locality by being given a free rein to write. One of the most memorable occasions was a tour by the Friends of Kensal Green Cemetery for my short story 'Underground', which included a visit to the church crypt filled with ancient coffins wall to wall. I've come to relish research, to love it and welcome it as part of my process, which means I'm one of those writers who never turns off wi-fi (as long as I don't read email or fall below my word quota, Google is a wonderful thing). Writing has become a great excuse for reading books about subjects that fascinate me, or having deep conversations with people who would usually never tell me their secrets, or travelling across the world, or watching documentaries and films – and most of the above is non-taxable if you're self-employed!

- To Enhance Your Craft – though I do despise the idea that stories are just gateways to writing the most important of prose forms, the novel, I do believe that they can stimulate your craft. The practice of not only writing prose, but reading, thinking and researching are all necessary tools of the trade that need to be sharpened regularly lest they become blunt. This is why I believe it's important to write in various forms. Who knows what story will come to you tomorrow? What character will demand, in a loud voice, that their story must be told? A desire to wrestle with form, style and genre will become a desire to speak in tongues other than your own, and will enhance your ability to pen the story no matter who tells it. Age, race, sexuality, religion, and time, will all become irrelevant as a result of such immersion.

- For the Thrill of It – there's no doubt about it, you should be enjoying yourself. The thrill is what makes it fun. That's not to say that you should not be a) anxious; b) doubtful; c) fearful of making mistakes; but this is part of what makes the whole process thrilling. The anxiety, doubt and fear will not go away.

In fact, as I've become more experienced, I've come to welcome them. In the times when I've sensed an absence of those emotions, when I've felt no thrill so to speak, I've never performed particularly well. The writing, or reading, or whatever it is I'm doing, tends to emerge flattened like one of Forster's lacklustre characters, devoid of life. Emotions tend to flavour the words so the reader feels them too. It sounds like basic common sense, but if you're managing to have fun on the page the reader probably will too.

● Because You Can't Stop Yourself – and that's the crux of it really. For most of us, we write because there's a niggling feeling, day after day, saying 'What if…?'. And the worst of it is that the feeling doesn't stop if you ignore it. I've tried. The niggling feeling goes on and on, saying that line, or picturing that place, or showing that window of action over and over again like a glitch in a DVD; or else you can smell something, or taste something, or otherwise hear a song that dredges up some memory that won't get out of your head. Someone commented not so long ago that they'd noticed my Twitter page was subtitled, under my name, 'literary procrastinator'. And they wondered why I'd written that when I didn't seem to be suffering from that affliction. I replied that actually, I did; the tongue-in-cheek subtitle was my acknowledgement that most of the time, the last thing I want to do is sit in front of the computer and type. I'd rather do anything else. Really. I can think of a lot of things that are a great deal less arduous and time-consuming. Like rock climbing. But being serious for one moment, I really do hate sitting in front of the flashing cursor for roughly the first 15 minutes or so. But then the urge that has brought me to the computer is the same one that gets me typing, and by the time approximately 15 minutes has gone by, what I want to say and how to say it in the best possible way is more important than anything else I might have done. And way more exhilarating. So I do it again, and again, because I can't stop myself. And hopefully you feel the same way, which is why you're reading this.

Where do stories come from?

Of course, that's a vast and complex question, coloured very much by those side-by-side components of life: experience and perspective. The following is my answer, although you'll probably have your own, and in some places we might even converge. It's the kind of question most writers don't like to be asked, and most, including me, have developed some pat answer that closes the questioner down and attempts to avoid the complexity of what's being asked. Mine is, 'The world around me'. And although it sounds frivolous, it's really not meant to be. I mean it. To reiterate my thoughts about articulating the world, I believe all stories, but most importantly, short stories, come from everywhere. All the time. Which is why I find them exhausting. Even today, when I woke up, an idea that had been niggling me ever since I read another short story and thought, 'But what if I did that?' forced me to roll over in bed, and write down a series of notes, which became four bullet-point descriptions about the central object in the character's orbit, which then became the first paragraph of my story – where I discovered my protagonist's name is Clay Wiltshire, and he's an avid gardener.

The most obvious answer to our question is that stories come from us. Of course. That goes without saying. But let's look a little closer at what that means, bearing in mind the pointers I have outlined above. One of the most influential writers of the modernist avant-garde was James Joyce. His collection of stories, *Dubliners*, has been widely heralded as a modern masterpiece since its publication in 1914. In this collection Joyce draws heavily from a location, Dublin, that is not only known well to him, but is as much as part of himself as his own voice. He charts many differing aspects of humanity; from death, to young love, to a failed literary dream, the stories are sure-footed and insightful in their depiction. But it is his invention of a literary device that has brought Joyce as much fame as the stories themselves, and this invention has not only served as a tool for his own fiction, but has become a prose staple – and some might even argue one of poetry and drama too: the literary epiphany.

Up until the age of 16, Joyce was a devout Catholic. As a writer, he began to fashion a modernist writing style centred on inward revelation. To do this in a manner which suited not only his own life experiences, but those of his characters, he turned towards the religious epiphany. In a traditional Catholic context, an epiphany is the witnessing of the divinity of the Christ child, governed by a sense of heightened awe. For Joyce the word meant a sudden consciousness of the 'soul' of an object, or person. *Dubliners* is composed of stories told from the point of view of child protagonists, and his characters eventually grow older with each progressive story until they reach maturity. Thus, the collection is divided into three informal sections – childhood, adolescence, and adulthood – mirroring his growth in the city. The epiphany as a literary device is used by Joyce as the moment when a character reaches self-understanding or illumination. Sometimes this is achieved by using the character's immediate environment to illustrate their moment of revelation, as in the final passages of 'Araby' when the boy, who has gone to the fair to buy a gift for the girl who lives on his street, stands before a vendor:

> I lingered before her stall, although I knew my stay was useless,
> in order to make my interest in her wares seem more real. Then I
> turned slowly and walked down the middle of the bazaar. I allowed
> the two pennies to fall against the sixpence in my pocket. I heard
> a voice call from one end of the gallery that the light was out. The
> upper part of the hall was now completely dark.
>
> Gazing up into the darkness I saw myself as a creature driven
> and derived by vanity; and my eyes burned with anguish and anger.

In these few, deft lines, Joyce conveys the loneliness of adolescence and the boy's growing awareness by a slow descent into darkness, leaving him to believe he is illuminated, exposed in isolation. This belief is not borne out by the facts. The remaining light is focused on the lower section of the hall, but the boy's feeling of being singled out belongs to him alone, driven by inner revelation. He has seen the world this way because of his feelings at that precise Moment in Time. It is a powerful use of outer and inner experience converging to subtly enlighten the reader.

In his posthumous novel *Stephen Hero*, completely rewritten and published during his lifetime as *Portrait of the Artist as a Young Man*, Joyce explicitly describes this device:

> By an epiphany he meant a sudden spiritual manifestation, whether
> in the vulgarity of speech or of gesture or in a memorable phase of
> the mind itself.

So it would seem that for Joyce the literary epiphany is an acknowledgement of the inner self. In the years following the publication of his seminal collection, this device has been lauded, emulated, and in more recent times questioned and re-evaluated by authors, critics and readers. In one of my fiction classes I proposed the idea that maybe the literary epiphany in its traditional form has had its day, becoming less of an illumination than a cliché. That more experienced writers, once they had learned the ropes by using this valued technique, had to find other ways to articulate this inner illumination, or even – wait for it now – cease using it at all, as least for some of their stories. What surprised me most was the almost uniform opposition from my students, even if it meant putting the epiphany aside for just one piece. To put it dramatically, they were horrified. They believed the modern story could not work without it. But, as *Dubliners* was published in the early twentieth century, story in general has done without it for most of its existence, and the short story, reputed to have come into critical being in 1837 with the publication of Nathaniel Hawthorne's *Twice Told Tales*, has also got along pretty fine.

To write what you know isn't just about writing the things you see around you, although it is that too. It's a self-conscious act of uncovering yourself, making every day epiphanies in order to discover what makes you believe, what you feel, how it makes others feel about you, what stands out for you in the world, how you once lived, how you live now, what surprises you, what you accept, have no truck with ... the list goes on – but in other words, what makes you, you. I have no doubt Joyce engaged in such rigorous examination. A lot of great artists do. When asked why he was preoccupied with writing about Dublin even though he hadn't lived there for many years, Joyce said, 'For myself, I always write about Dublin, because if I can get to the heart of Dublin I can get to the heart of all the cities of the world. In the particular is contained the universal.'

In my own experience as a short story writer, my first attempts were the selection of 15 short stories that made up my first collection, *West Side Stories*. As I said before, the majority of those stories were scrapped, never to be published. I think that two were published in a journal, and another two were published in my book of interlinked shorts *Society Within*. The scrapped ones have been lost for years, which I'm glad about, as I try to remember what they were like and almost recoil with horror. The published ones, 'Small Island Mindedness' and 'The Yout' Man and the Ki', I'm actually pretty proud of in a 'Look at how silly I was as a child' kind of way. Stumbling, trying to gain forward momentum. But those stories (and I went on to write another 15, plus the 12 that made up *Society Within*) were almost exclusively about West London working-class teenage life.

In his essay 'Fan Fictions: On Sherlock Holmes', the novelist and non-fiction author Michael Chabon claims 'Influence is bliss'. This idea revises Harold Bloom's longstanding opinion on the subject in his 1973 book *The Anxiety of Influence: A Theory of Poetry*. Bloom's central thesis is that poets are hindered by the necessary but problematic literary relationship with the poets who preceded them, which renders their work derivative and unoriginal. Chabon argues that this influence can instead become a vital part of a writer's arsenal, citing Arthur Conan Doyle as a positive influence on his novel *The Yiddish Policeman's Union*. I would tend to agree. Raymond Carver famously regarded Chekhov as a major influence. Angela Carter wrote *A Company of Wolves* after being influenced by Isak Dinesen's *Seven Gothic Tales*, and Borges was a fan of the stories of Kipling and Poe, so much so that he had them read aloud to him in his old age, after he had become blind.

When I noticed I had been unconsciously returning to Greenside stories in my own shorts I immediately realized what form a book of these stories might take. The reason for my confidence was that I had three 'blueprints' or 'templates' from which to draw: Jess Mowry's *Rats in the Trees*, Eden Robinson's *Traplines*, and Richard Price's *The Wanderers*.

All three collections are composed of interlinked stories that make up the whole. All three focus on disaffected teenagers living inner city lives: respectively Oakland, British Columbia and New York City. They are dark, sometimes shockingly so, told in a simple, pared-down style. The authors' refusal to censor their characters' actions sometimes made me hate the people I was reading about. But they were real. I could empathize with them even when I didn't like them, and even better, I could feel their pain, their joys and their loves. There was a freedom and a certain majesty in the authors' ability to wring beauty out of stark places. Reading their works made me giddy with possibility. Other writers helped too. Randall Keenan's *Let the Dead Bury their Dead* gave massive insights into how I might harness an interlinking narrative structure, and Roald Dahl was still beguiling me with the art of the twist. But those three books were absolutely pivotal in terms of guiding my way, and reassuring me that the path I was about to set out on was not crazy, or impossible, or doomed to failure. I could hold the success of another in my hand, and know it could be done.

What is a short story?

Critics seem to have got themselves into a real muddle with regard to what constitutes or does not constitute a short story. On the one hand you have Charles May, a US professor of English and short story aficionado, who says: 'A genre only truly comes into being when the conventions that constitute it are articulated within the larger conceptual context of literature as a whole.' I take this to mean that the genre truly becomes a genre when the important components that make up a short story – Character, Time, Location and Economy by my own reckoning – can already be found in other 'established' literary forms such as the novel and the poem. One tick for the story. On the other hand, some critics argue that the story is not distinct enough from the novel to be a literary form in its own right. An anonymous reviewer of Brander Matthews's *Philosophy of the Short-Story*, published in the 1901 *London Academy*, claims: 'The short story is a smaller, simpler, easier, and less important form of the novel.' A sure-fire x against, if I've ever heard one.

The crux of both arguments seems to be that the form should have a number of original characteristics that cannot be found in any other genre, plus the opposite idea that it should display a clear literary lineage. Fortunately I believe we are living in a time in which the short form in the UK is finally being regarded as an important genre in its own right, precisely because of its perceived ability to fulfil those two requirements concurrently. Europe and the US, I think it's fair to say, came to this conclusion far sooner. The story, while using all of the tools that a novel brings to bear in order to compel the reader to read on, also has the uncanny ability to do what the novel cannot – primarily, to harness consistent intensity, tension, brevity, and ambiguity to heightened effect.

All four can be found in the novel – that is true. But it is the first – intensity – that makes the other three so magical in the short form. The novel is like a long piece of music, and because of that, there must be changes in pace, rhythm and force, or volume. It must rise and fall like the tide, or risk becoming monotonous. The confined space of the short story means that its intensity produces a heightened concentration of an experiential occurrence – a Moment in Time.

In his essay 'Against Epiphanies', Charles Baxter writes that he doesn't believe a character's experiences have to be validated by conclusive insight, or a brilliant visionary stop-time moment. He says that stories can arrive somewhere interesting without claiming any wisdom or clarification beyond their wish to follow an interesting chain of thoughts to a conclusion. And I agree. A contradiction? I think not. Every short story follows the precise Moment in Time of a different character, and so it follows that every character's journey will be different from the last. Some might contain epiphanic insights, others may not. It depends on who's 'speaking', or who's telling the story. Sometimes there's even an opportunity for a character to reach a point of what they believe is momentary insight, and act on that, only to have events conspire against them, landing them even deeper in the mire than when the story began. Personally, I love this type of conclusion, to read and to write, and it definitely doesn't make the story less of a story.

My first real and true short story collection wasn't published until seven years after I'd written the first. I'd been stuck between trying to move on a little from the work that had made me known and feeling that I owed it both gratitude and respect. I didn't want to kill the goose. *Music for the Off-Key* took just under nine years to write. In hindsight, that was the flaw. The earlier stories tended to stray from the project remit, and seemed a bit out of place, at least to my eyes. And there was fact that in those nine years my skills as a storyteller had grown along with my experience. I see now that I was too eager to publish, especially as there had been a long gap since my last book. I should either have cut those early stories out, or waited longer and written others to replace them. Learning from your mistakes is another part of being a writer. You always make them. In some ways I believe it's the mistakes that spur you on.

Music for the Off-Key entered the world with very little fanfare or fuss. Such is the nature of short stories. We are the jazz soloists of the literary world – well-trained, respected, yet not much noticed in a world obsessed with Miley Cyrus. I had a few great reviews, but I was happy with all of them. When one mentioned a flaw, I thanked the reviewer, because I would be sure not to make that mistake again.

I'd become comfortable with this notion that some projects would either be reworked and made good, or left to slumber indefinitely, possibly forever. So I began to write as ideas came to me. And these short stories began to grow into something that had cohesion. I hadn't chosen a theme, but I think getting married and having a child impacted greatly on me, not as much in the focus of the stories, but underlying them. Once I had noticed a central theme – love in times of conflict, or trauma – I began to write more. In that time I wrote a sci-fi novella and two short stories themed around my concerns of the time: class and how it plays out in my community. Then I got very lucky and was given a commission to write three stories, all set in the same area of West London; and went on holiday to Kenya, which inspired another story.

And that's how it happened. Travelling, thinking and writing, not much concerned about what the outcome might be. But when I read the stories back, they all worked satisfactorily; and even better, the connection was more organic than my last attempt. A collection had snuck up on me like a friendly spirit. I named it *The Book of Blues*, and later revised that to *A Book of Blues*. It just felt better. I don't know why.

That last collection is probably my favourite, mainly because it crept up on me so quietly, but also because it's stories, a form I never imagined I'd write when I started out. And I love stories. They have rescued me in so many ways, as a reader, a writer and a human being. As sources of inspiration and strength; as entertainment, a blueprint, a way of understanding the world. They're not neat and tidy. They're the exact opposite and that what's thrilling and exciting. They demand to be understood for what they are. They refuse to give easy answers. I love the magnitude contained in such a small form. I hope to capture that magnitude in my own work.

Reflections on writing and on books on writing

Tania

I've always had the feeling that while everyone else was doing it 'properly', this writing thing, I was 'doing it wrong'. I was muddling through, getting lucky when stories actually got written. (This is about writing, not publishing, the 'business' part.)

What is this Right Way that had lodged in my subconscious? Well, it has several elements:

1 Write every day.
2 Blurt out a first draft, get it down without worrying about it.
3 If you're stuck, write about yourself, your childhood, what's around you.
4 Focus only on your writing, eliminating distractions.
5 When you've got your messy first draft, then, with your analytical 'editor' head, revise it into shape.

Even writing that list makes me feel funny, like an imposter. I don't do any of those things. None. We'll come on to what I do do later. But where had I got this from? From books on writing I'd been recommended at writing workshops (mainly in America): *Bird by Bird* by Anne Lamott, *Wild Mind* by Natalie Goldberg, and others. They purport to be about fiction writing, about unleashing your creativity. But they also mostly focus on novels, and peddle some variant of my five-point plan above.

What if that doesn't work for you?

It doesn't work for me. It's never worked for me. Hence, for years, despite having some success, I felt I wasn't a Proper Writer because I wasn't following The Method. I'd get embarrassed when asked how I revise. Or if I write every day. Or whether I turn the internet off. I can't even go near writing about childhood – that makes my skin crawl. I just want to Make Things Up. Isn't that what fiction means, goddammit?

At first, when I realized the source of the 'wrongness' that had dogged me all these years, I was angry. Why had I been given these books? Why were they so fixated on one way of doing things? Why didn't they talk about the unique needs of short story writers, drawn to this form because we perhaps don't want immersion in just one world? Or, in fact, the unique needs of EVERY writer?

Then I realized something. Maybe these books were a gift. The fact that they hadn't given me a 'method' that worked for me, that there's no paint-by-numbers formula (there isn't. I thought I should let you know that. It's a good thing), meant I had to invent my own.

If I wanted to be a writer, I would have to find my own tools. We all want help when we start. We have no clue what we're doing, which is why the internet is awash with 10 Tips to Be A Better Writer, etc. ... (As a fledgling poet I understand this feeling very well.) But I had to make up my own way. Which goes something like this:

- write fast
- write slowly
- don't focus directly on or think too much about what I'm writing
- do something else while I'm writing (play online Scrabble, tweet, write emails)
- write on the computer
- write by hand
- write at home
- write in cafés and on trains
- don't necessarily write every day
- let my desire to write build up
- let stories swim around my head before getting them down
- use prompts to get stories started
- create characters out of my imagination and put them in situations I've never experienced

Do some of these contradict one another? Yup. Even within this one writer there are different ways that work – so how can there be just one way across all writers? There's a reason my list says 'my' rather than 'your'. It's my list.

When I finally decided to ask other writers how they do it on my blog, several writer friends said: 'Thank goodness, I thought it was just me, that I was doing it wrong.' I discovered that almost no one I know does it the way those books describe, and many of them found that trying to do it that way destroyed their stories.

Trawling through all the *Paris Review* author interviews, I found more evidence for Doing It Your Way. Dorothy Parker: 'It takes me six months to do a story. I think it out and then write it sentence by sentence – no first draft. I can't write five words but that I change seven.' Eudora Welty: 'Often I shift things from the very beginning to the very end ... Small things – one fact, one word – but things important to me. It's possible I have a reverse mind and do things backwards.' Jorge Luis Borges: 'At first I did [revise a great deal]. Then I found out that when a man reaches a certain age, he has found his real tone. Nowadays I try to go over what I've written after a fortnight or so, and of course there are many slips and repetitions to be avoided, certain favourite tricks that should not be overworked. But I think that what I write nowadays is always on a certain level, and that I can't better it very much, nor can I spoil it very much, either.'

Okay, I'll give these writing books a break. Really, they are just sharing *their* way in case it helps. But is it any wonder that I – and most beginners – cling on as if these are commandments? This is the danger. Despite the fact that I was writing and doing quite well, I couldn't say proudly, 'This too is a Right Way to Write'.

After I started writing this chapter, I found the book I wished I'd read back then: *Ron Carlson Writes a Story*, by American short story writer and novelist Ron Carlson (Greywolf Press, 2007). Ron, where were you when I needed you? Ron was writing, and figuring out his own writing process.

This book is specifically about short stories. And, more specifically, one particular Ron Carlson short story. He says that all he's doing is taking us through the writing of one story, not laying down rules. But this slim, 100-page book does more than that. So much chimed with me, told me that the way I do things is okay; I can only imagine the permission it might have given me had I read it ten years ago.

There was one major revelation for me. Carlson says his writing process has nothing to do with a possible reader of the story but is aimed at preventing one thing: him getting up from the computer. (Just before I wrote that, I got up and wandered off.) He knows his main battle is against that urge: to leave, to stop writing. This happens to me constantly. All I want to do is not write. Even though writing is all I want to do, is when I am happiest, inside words, everything flowing. But when I start – instant twitchiness. How much better do I feel to hear Ron Carlson has this!

Carlson says: 'The most important thing a writer can do after completing a sentence is stay in the room. The great temptation is to leave the room to celebrate the completion of the sentence or to go out into the den where the television lies like a dormant monster and rest up for a few days for the next sentence ... But. It's this simple. **_The writer is the person who stays in the room_**' (my italics, bold and underline.)

This is worth saying again: _The writer is the person who stays in the room._

If I put a symbol throughout a story-in-progress whenever I got twitchy and did something else, it would be unreadable. One reason may be because many of us don't know what we're writing. Says Carlson: 'Beginning a story without knowing all the terrain is not a comfortable feeling. It's uncomfortable enough in fact to keep most people away from the keyboard.' American short story writer Donald Barthelme said in _Not Knowing: The Essays and Interviews of Donald Barthelme:_ (Vintage, 1999). 'Writing is a process of dealing with not-knowing, a forcing of what and how ... At best there's a slender intuition, no greater than an itch. The anxiety attached to this situation is not inconsiderable.'

Discomfort. Anxiety. It's enough to put you off. Anne Lamott, in _Bird by Bird_, points out that her writer friends 'do not go around beaming with quiet feelings of contentment. Most of them go around with haunted, abused, surprised looks on their faces, like lab dogs on whom very personal deodorant sprays have been tested.' Those of us who write must have some kind of compulsion. And a knowing, deep down, that it'll be worth it.

It does get better. Carlson: 'The single largest advantage a veteran writer has ... is this tolerance for not knowing. It's not style, skill, or any other dexterity.

An experienced writer has been in those woods before and is willing to be lost; she knows that being lost is necessary for the discoveries to come.'

After doing this for years, I do stay in the room, and Ron Carlson's book helped me see how I do it. I thought the other things I often do while writing – playing online Scrabble, emailing – were to distract my Inner Editor, the voice that immediately starts telling you you're rubbish. But they also keep me in the room. (These are clearly connected – it's my Inner Editor trying to get me to leave.) If I play one Scrabble turn, I'm still here – it subdues my twitchiness enough to write another sentence. It works for me.

I realized something else – working like this gets me into the dream-like state I need to write the kind of fiction I want to write. I have a science background; my natural tendency is for everything to make sense, problems solved. I'm introverted so I think a lot. But I've found that thinking in this logical, scientific way doesn't let me express what I want to express through my stories: the messiness of life, lack of solutions, uncertainty. What helps is this frequent jumping from one thing to another, not looking directly at what I am writing, not thinking. This befuddles me just enough to allow me to write without inhibitions.

Once again, this has taken years. Letting go of inhibitions, quieting the Inner Critic, is a lengthy process, one that for this short story writer at least is helped by the validation of getting published. Someone appreciating what you write enough to publish it is enormously helpful, and one of the joys of being a short story writer: you get frequent little shots in the arm to spur you on, give you permission to do what you're doing, and to take risks, try something new. (See my section on Permission and Risk.)

So, no book can tell you how to write. But books might 'allow' you to try new things. Find your own way to stay in the room. An artist friend recently told me he listens to novel-length audiobooks while he draws: they have to be long enough to keep him sitting there. What keeps you there?

One of the delights of thinking about writing is that I get to come up with my own analogy! Writers are word-builders. Is there one way to build a house? There's the traditional way, bricks and mortar. But even within this there are options – brick size and arrangement of bricks, mortar-spreading techniques, which wall first. Do you work on the blueprint then lay bricks, or do you put one brick down and see where the next fits? And then, oh my, there are tents, huts, skyscrapers, bungalows ... And the amazing bubble houses I heard about on a *99% Invisible* podcast! You inflate a half-grape-fruit-shaped balloon, coat it in cement, then remove the balloon. (I suspect I'm a bubble house word-builder; I want to be.)

I believe whatever you do in life, you need to learn how to do it. I spent six years in writing classes learning bricklaying basics. But then you have to decide what you're going to build and find your way. Otherwise your house will look like the one next door, and when someone's wandering around the neighbourhood only the gnome in your front garden distinguishes it from the others; do you really want to be known only for your gnome?

Okay, I think the analogy has been fully exploited. But Courttia and I are firm in our conviction that this is a No-Rule Book. No 'shoulds', no 'musts'. This ain't a science.

In the rest of my sections, I quote writers whose short stories I love, because why take advice from someone whose writing I don't love? I focus mostly on contemporary writers, the authors of most of the thousand or so stories I read every year. If you want Chekhov, Carver and O'Connor, there are plenty of books doing that. The short story is thriving and it's important for me to bring current voices into the discussion.

Feel free to read this book and disagree. At least you'll know what you *don't* want to do, and that helps in your experimentation, the seeking of your own processes (plural for a reason). Something that worked today might leave you cold tomorrow. So cast your eye over a new brick. Move that wall. Or build yourself a bubble house.

Further reading

Barthelme, Donald, *Not Knowing: The Essays and Interviews of Donald Barthelme* (Vintage, 1999).

Carlson, Ron, *Ron Carlson Writes a Story* (Greywolf Press, 2007).

Goldberg, Natalie, *Wild Mind* (Bantam, 1990).

Lamott, Anne, *Bird by Bird: Some Instructions on Writing and Life* (Anchor Books edition, 1995).

The Paris Review Interviews, Vols 1–4 (Picador, 2009).

Reflections on the what, when, how, why and where of it for me

Tania

As a journalist, I was trained in the importance of What, When, How, Where and Why, so what better way to reflect on my short story journey. It's not quite that easy, but let's begin … at the beginning.

When

I first started becoming a writer by becoming a reader. My mother told my brother and me stories about Rosemary and Marjory, and although I can't remember them now, this was where the seeds were planted – of narrative, of investment in someone else's life, of being desperate to Find Out What Happens Next.

I read everything. On Saturday trips to the library I would wander down, then up, amassing as many books as I was allowed to take home and devour. When I ran out of books for my age group – as happened to voracious child readers in the 1970s – I started on grown-up books. I couldn't *not* read.

And fiction seemed to come naturally to me. I invented a character, Caroline (my middle name) and would ask my mother to let me walk ahead, then act surprised to see me and ask me about myself. (My mother certainly didn't wish a career as a fantasist for me, she was hoping for medicine, or law. Ah well.) I also attempted to write a novel about triplets, which, fortunately, has been lost.

This might be how many writers begin, but here's where I perhaps diverge: I didn't like English at school. I didn't 'get' English literature: I loved books, but couldn't accept my teachers' assumption they knew why Dickens chose the name Estella, say, in *Great Expectations*. Or that he made a conscious choice at all. Maybe he just liked the name?

I loved maths. The rightness-or-wrongness, no grey, no room for interpretation. Quadratic equations, oh my! I was pushed towards the sciences, took maths, physics and chemistry at A Level and studied maths and physics at university, where I quickly discovered that university-level science is not the same. The maths was a mystery, I didn't have the head for it. Physics, while fascinating, was also a struggle. I just didn't speak those languages. Words were my tools.

So, after getting an MSc in philosophy of science — fascinating, but another language I struggled with — and a diploma in journalism, I became a science and technology journalist. And emigrated to Israel.

Why

Why did I love short stories? After reading all the usual children's novels, the first short story collection I came across as a teenager was *Kiss Kiss* by Roald Dahl. How many short story writers is he responsible for birthing! How can he do this in only a few pages? I thought. This was the beginning of a fascination with brevity, economy, what can — and must — be left out.

The second seminal short story reading experience for me, in my mid-20s, was Ali Smith's *Other Stories and Other Stories*. Here were no murders, no twists, but intimacy, as if I was intruding on a conversation between two characters (rarely named, just called 'I' and 'You'). And there was a quiet power, shocking as electricity. Where Dahl's stories entertained, Smith's stories made me feel. I hadn't experienced the events she described, but something was familiar: confusion, loneliness, yearning for connection, joy when it works, despair when it doesn't.

As I read more short stories, I began to see everything a short story might be. But the basic answer to why I love the short story is this: Because it's short. Because you know when you start, with absolute certainty, that in 15 minutes or less it will end. And, if it's a great story, the end will leave you satisfied without being hermetically sealed – and will linger in your mind for much longer than it took to read it.

Our world is ever more attracted to infinity, endlessness. You slay one email and another pops up. Twitter and Facebook feeds replenish every millisecond. Television series rarely end, only when a show is cancelled; films are often sequels, remakes or prequels. And it turns out our universe is even expanding and the idea of parallel universes may not be so fantastical after all!

In all this endlessness, the short story is an oasis of the finite, a refuge of completeness. A great short story is great due to, not despite, its limits. This is not understood by many book reviewers. How amazing that this writer can do 'all that' in such a small space! A short story is excellent precisely *because* of the small space, the boundaries which the writer has chosen.

Doesn't knowing that something is scarce, imminently ending, make it more precious? 'While stocks last' and 'limited availability' send us rushing to get hold of whatever it is. Perhaps the short story is the 'while stocks last' of fiction – make the most of these characters, this world, because it's going to end. Great short stories remind us what is precious, what must be savoured. They remind us of the weight of each single word.

How

So, I was reading short stories but despite being a journalist, I didn't think of myself as the kind of writer I'd wanted to be as a child, dreaming of having a book filled with made-up stories, with my name on the spine. In my late twenties the little voice in my head got louder. What about your creativity? You're writing about other people's creations, where are yours?

Then I met my first Real Writer, Nathan Englander, also living in Jerusalem and a friend of a friend. Now the author of two award-winning story collections and a novel, he had already had many individual stories published, in the excellent (and now, sadly, defunct) *Story* magazine, no less. Proper publication. Proper short stories. Proper writer.

He kindly took me for coffee and gave me a reading list (the only name I remember is John Cheever ... I should have kept that list!). Nathan had an MFA (Masters in Fine Arts, the American equivalent of an MA) from the renowned University of Iowa's Creative Writing program. I decided to go to their Summer Writing Festival, so in 1998, I headed from Israel to Iowa.

As befits a short story writer, I'll skip my first experience of the Midwest and go straight to the workshops. First, 'Reading as a writer' – a revelation. Far from frustrating school English class, we learned close reading, looking at structure on the page as well as content, pacing, tense, characters, every element that makes up prose. I met 'white space': a blank line indicating passage of time or change in location, stronger than a paragraph break. I had my first taste of American short stories such as Tobias Woolf's astonishing 'Bullet in the Brain'. Most of all, I started to understand how much a would-be writer (all writers) can learn from reading.

The second workshop was 'Writing Short Stories for Beginners'. The tutor guided us gently through the writing of what was my first short story. One day we wrote a scene, the next some dialogue with backstory woven in, then a flashback. It may sound simplistic, but for me, aged 28 with no fiction writing training, it was invaluable. It was as if I wanted to build a house but had never held a hammer or explored the difference between screwdrivers. If you don't have the tools, you can stare at houses, you can wander from room to room, but can you build one?

I went back to the Summer Writing Festival the following year, enjoying not just workshops but evening talks by Big Names such as Joyce Carol Oates, Annie Proulx and Richard Ford ... and for the next five years went to more, mostly in America, where they have writing festivals that weren't available at that time in the UK.

Through these workshops I was introduced to anthologies that became very important to me: *Sudden Fiction* (W. W. Norton, 1983) edited by Robert Shapard and James Thomas, and the follow-ups, including *Sudden Fiction International* and *Flash Fiction Forward*. A love for extreme brevity began to take hold.

I want to stress this: I spent seven years learning to write short stories and not submitting anything anywhere. I wasn't ready for the rejections that are always part of this process. It was easier then, the internet was in its infancy, I didn't know many writers, I lived in a country with no English-language literary magazines. I had time and space that I fear nowadays new writers don't give themselves, to learn the nuts and bolts and then to start to do it my way.

In 2002, I heard about Arvon, the wonderful organization running residential writing courses around the UK. To my amazement, I saw a course on how to slip science into fiction and poetry. I thought I was the only person who wanted to do this. I booked a place. That, once again, changed everything. Until someone shows you a way to do something, it can seem unfathomable. I had no idea how to transform scientific fact so it became inspiration for – or part of – fiction. During these five days in Yorkshire, I began to understand how.

In 2003, I studied for an MA in Creative Writing in the UK, another step in the transition between 'I'm trying to write' and 'I am a writer'. The MA gave me deadlines, a peer group of writers to share work with, and something vital: critiquing skills. I learned how to read someone else's work and, even though it wasn't how I might write that story, learned to see it from within what they wanted to do, and offer neither praise or criticism but ask questions, drawing attention to elements of their piece in a useful way.

My MA thesis was a short story collection. My tutors suggested I find a theme to make them commercially viable. (I didn't believe I might publish a book. A far-off dream.) I had always thought that *New Scientist* magazine's articles would be great inspiration for fiction, and this was the point at which I started letting my imagination off the leash. I would let an article roam around my brain until something sparked. And it sparked, in very odd ways! I ended up with 12 short stories all inspired by *New Scientist* articles, from 1,000 to 7,000 words.

Then, expecting nothing, I submitted my short story 'The White Road' to radio production company, Sweet Talk, looking for new voices for BBC Radio 4's *Afternoon Reading*. I really expected nothing, because my MA colleagues all told me the story didn't work (I made up something medical that may or may not be 'true'). Looking back, I'm astonished I didn't let that throw me. Despite being inexperienced – or perhaps because of that! – I decided everyone was wrong because the story worked for me. That was a useful lesson: writing is not democratic.

Sometimes everyone *is* wrong. Sweet Talk chose my story, which was broadcast on Radio 4 in January 2005, a highlight of my life. An actor takes your character, whose voice only you have heard, and makes her real, so that you hear and everyone listening hears her. I cried. 'The White Road' also became my first story in print, chosen by Route for their anthology, *Wonderwall*. Without the confidence boost of the Radio 4 broadcast, I'm not sure I would ever have submitted it.

After my collection came out, I wrote the piece below summing up what happened next. Here it is, slightly abridged:

How Tania Hershman achieved her dream and got a book

- The young woman develops a wonderful relationship with the radio production company who produced her story, they produce a second story, and commission her to write a third. Her confidence is rising. Someone likes what she writes.

- The young woman goes on another Arvon course with Ali Smith, one of her favourite writers, who tells her: 'Give up your day job. You can do this.' The young woman, astonished, does.

- In 2007, she submits three short stories to Salt, a small press known for poetry and beginning to publish story collections. She waits. She befriends Salt's editor on MySpace.

- A message through MySpace! The editor loves the stories, wants 'everything else'. The young woman lays out all the stories on the kitchen table, arranges them, then sends them off. She waits.

- The young woman, and her friend are on a writing retreat. The young woman pulls the internet cable out of the only computer. A succession of technical support guys cannot fix it. Finally, it's fixed. And there it is: THE email. Salt: 'May we publish your book?'

- The young woman is in shock. She can't stop grinning. She can't write. She doesn't believe it is really true, won't until she holds her book.

- 31 August 2008: the woman is agitated. Her book has not reached her in Israel and tomorrow is publication day! It's as though her child is being held in another country. How can she celebrate?

- 1 September 2008: Publication Day. The woman is calm, elated, ecstatic. She may not have the book but she feels what this day means. She is floating. When the books arrive a few days later, she feels it all over again.

- She gets in touch with *New Scientist*, worried they might not like how she used their articles. They do. They publish the title story on their website, where it receives many and varied comments. To the woman's delight, they include the book in their Best Books of 2008.

- Through a Google alert, the woman discovers she's been commended by the 2009 Orange Award for New Writers. She cannot speak. She had no idea her book had been entered. This unexpected vote of confidence from those who had no obligation to read her book fills her with the feeling that she can do anything.

- In August 2009 she moves back to England, to talk about short stories to her heart's content. She meets writers, is asked to do readings, to judge competitions, to write about short stories. This, she thinks, is it.

How (2), what, when (2) and where

The second *How* is *How Do I Write*, not a simple question to answer. It involves a *What*, another *When* and a *Where*.

I first discovered really short stories or flash fiction in the *Sudden Fiction* anthologies. What is sudden fiction? Well, say editors Shapard and Thomas in their *New Sudden Fiction* (2007), '[W]hen we first began to see short-short fictions cropping up in literary magazines, we didn't know what they were ... [They] didn't end with a twist or a bang, but were suddenly just there, surprising, unpredictable, hilarious, serious, moving, in only a few pages.' I fell in love with this suddenness, this economy, which tied in with my journalism training: Why use ten words when you can use two? Surely this applies to any form which involves words? It worked for me as a reader so I began to try it as a writer.

My first collection included a number of very short stories, but during the time I waited for the book to come out – and after it was published – flash fiction was almost all I wrote. The shock of the book deal, of publication, of the attention (wonderful, unexpected, but also stressful) left me without the focus to write longer stories.

What stimulated me were the weekly challenges run by the online flash fiction writing groups I belonged to, such as: Write a story in under 250 words in which each sentence begins with the letter 'M'. Or: Write a story of less than 500 words where someone dies in the first sentence. I thrive on deadlines, and this was also my first taste of the benefits of constraint. Instead of acres of blank page and no idea what to write about, I was given parameters, a frame, and this helped me write 150 flash stories over four years, 56 of which are collected in my second book, *My Mother Was An Upright Piano: Fictions* (Tangent books, 2012).

So, how do I actually write? As mentioned, I write on computer, but also by hand. I sometimes write fast but occasionally slowly. I write at home, in cafés, on trains. I often get a first line in my head and everything comes from that. Last thing at night is a very fertile time. Or I write from prompts set by writer friends when we write together – in the same physical or virtual space – or for themed competitions or literary magazine submissions.

After years of practice, of building up my writing muscles, I can get a first draft of a flash story down in 20 minutes. Sometimes it's a story I've had in my head for a while – I let it develop in there until it feels right to write it out. Much of the process often happens in my head.

When writing a longer story, I tend to write more slowly. Writing by hand helps. I can only write a certain amount in one go, only as much of the story as I know then – if I carry on beyond that point, I feel it's me telling the story, not the story telling itself. It gets clunky. I've learned to trust 'story sense', something I believe we all possess, fed and driven as we are by stories. I let myself go into uncertainty, knowing I've emerged from it before, that the story will come.

American short story writer George Saunders talked about this in *The Paris Review*:

[S]o much of that process is intuitive. Just deciding minute-by-minute, over and over again, over the period during which you're writing the story … the difference between a good writing day and a bad one is the quality of the split-second decisions you made ... [W]henever I feel myself formulating or invoking something that is conceptual/ theoretical I veer away from that so fast. I just know from experience that my instincts are better than my cerebration.

I've learned to wait, sometimes for weeks or months, until my character tells me what happens next. This is not procrastination. Says Natalie Goldberg in *Wild Mind*:

> You've worked on something for a while. You are excited about it, even happy, but you are wise and step back. You take a walk but this walk isn't to avoid the writing on your desk. It is a walk full of your writing ... You are letting writing work on you ... Procrastination is a cutting off. It diminishes you. Waiting is when you are already in the work and you are feeding it and being fed by it.

Something else that helps, as I mentioned earlier, is not focusing too closely on what I am writing. I play online Scrabble, switching between that and writing – while my logical brain is figuring out the best Scrabble word, the story-creator is whirring away behind the scenes. Scholarly articles have described the benefits of distracting yourself from what you are trying to do, especially if it's something 'creative'. Jonah Lehrer, in an article in *The New Yorker* entitled 'The Annals of Science: The Eureka Hunt', writes:

> While it is commonly assumed that the best way to solve a problem is to focus, minimize distractions, and pay attention only to the relevant details, this clenched state of mind may inhibit the sort of creative connections that lead to sudden breakthroughs. We suppress the very type of brain activity we should be encouraging ... letting the mind wander is essential ... Concentration, it seems, comes with the hidden cost of diminished creativity.

Canadian short story writer and Nobel Prize-winner Alice Munro referred to this in a *Paris Review* interview about writing a story:

The whole process might take up to a week, the time of trying to think it through, trying to retrieve it, then giving it up and thinking about something else, and then getting it back, usually quite unexpectedly, when I am in the grocery store or out for a drive. I'll think, Oh well, I have to do it from the point of view of so-and-so and I have to cut this character out, and of course these people are not married, or whatever ...

Why (2): why do I write at all?

If I knew what was going to happen in the story before I wrote it down, I wouldn't bother writing it. I write to surprise myself, to find out what I think, to make myself laugh and cry (often at the same time). I write to slip inside someone else's head and be The Other, whether woman, man, older, younger, from another planet, an animal or piece of furniture. I write to go places and experience situations I will never experience.

As a short story writer – and especially as a short-short-story writer – I can get inside many Others' skins and go to many places because I write lots of stories, using up many of the ideas I have. I work on a number of stories simultaneously, hopping between worlds. This suits me; I've never had the urge to immerse myself.

Writing is how I deal with life, and although I never write about myself (that makes me highly uncomfortable), it is how I process what has happened to me and investigate what-ifs and what-might-have-beens.

My stories seem to pre-empt my need of them; I wrote a story two years ago about grief before I'd experienced it, and it helped me when I did. Ron Carlson says:

> Let's agree that we know more than we can fully express, and writing is a way of touching, tapping into the heart and finally locating that knowledge, ending up with more resources than we started with ... We write to present questions, sometimes complicated questions, not to offer easy or not-so-easy answers. If we're really writing we are exploring the unnamed emotional facets of the human heart.

In *Bird by Bird*, Anne Lamott says:

> We write to expose the unexposed. If there is one door in the castle you have been told not to go through, you must. Otherwise you'll just be rearranging furniture in rooms you've already been in. Most human beings are dedicated to keeping that one door shut. But the writer's job is to see what's behind it, to see the bleak, unspeakable stuff and to turn the unspeakable into words – not just into any words but if we can into rhythm and blues.

And I write to be read. This is not a given. There are writers who simply want to write. But I write stories to connect with strangers. As I said, I'm introverted, not good at small talk. I can't hold forth at a dinner party (except about short stories, on which subject I am an interminable bore). I reach out through my fictions. Nothing means more to me than a message from someone telling me how something I'd written spoke to them.

I've also learned to let the story go; I have no say over how it's read or what gets read into it. I think this is particularly true of short stories – a form that, because of its succinctness, invites the reader to be actively involved, fill in the gaps. A story almost becomes a different story to each reader. I would never say what I think my stories are about. I love hearing readers' takes on them.

Working in this 'non-dominant form', which doesn't get huge media attention, unlike novels, say, or Hollywood screenplays, I don't worry much about the marketplace. Literary agents aren't interested in short story writers, so – although it took a few years to accept this – there is freedom in being a short story writer. I can write whatever I want. Yes, I need to promote myself and my work, which isn't the easiest thing for most writers, but it's what I chose when I worked as a freelance journalist, so I think that it suits me!

What do I write?

At first I was adamant: I wrote short stories. I wanted to clearly define the boundaries, to state my passion for the form. Then I expanded this to short stories and flash fiction, although is flash fiction separate? Are they just short short stories?

Over the years, people have commented on the fact that some of my very short stories seem like poems. I have no background in poetry, so I couldn't be writing poems, could I? I started sneaking towards poems, taking some classes, trying to understand.

Now I don't think it's up to me what I call my writing. My second collection is of 'Fictions': all I can say is that they are fictional. Some of them were published as prose poems. I am letting go here, too. Are my fictions experimental? Sure, if you think so. Are they prose poems? If you'd like to call them that. I don't mind. As long as I'm writing.

Further reading

Dahl, Roald, *Kiss Kiss* (Penguin, 1962).

Daley, Ian (ed.), *Wonderwall* (Route, 2006).

Englander, Nathan, *For The Relief Of Unbearable Urges* (Faber & Faber, 1999).

Goldberg, Natalie, *Wild Mind* (Bantam, 1990).

Lamott, Anne, *Bird by Bird: Some Instructions on Writing and Life* (Anchor Books edition, 1995).

Lehrer, Jonah, 'The Annals of Science: The Eureka Hunt', *The New Yorker* (28 July 2008).

New Scientist magazine.

Shapard, Robert and Thomas, James (eds), *Sudden Fiction* (W. W. Norton & Company, 1983).
  - *Sudden Fiction International* (W. W. Norton & Company, 1989).
  - *Flash Fiction Forward* (W. W. Norton & Company, 2006).
  - *New Sudden Fiction* (W. W. Norton & Company, 2007).

Smith, Ali, *Other Stories and Other Stories* (Penguin, 1999).

Reflections on the evolution of a short story

Courttia

I had a novel I wanted to write that had been bugging me for a long time – many years actually. I'd been inching towards the concept, my Big Idea, putting it off, getting quick flashes of inspiration but not writing anything, just turning it over in my mind. I'd written one completed short story ('Underground', published in *A Book of Blues*) and one failed one ('The Return' – half-written, still on my hard drive). Neither was quite the Big Idea itself, but over a two-year period I had begun to realize that I'd been unconsciously circling the concept of reincarnation. I'd always loved the zombie films of George Romero as a child – the original *Night of the Living Dead* is still a classic for me, combining sharp storytelling, sci-fi horror, and biting yet understated political commentary in a manner I've always wanted to emulate. Dystopian fantasies were an endless wasteland of imaginative joy. My adult tastes range from *Mad Max* 1 and 2 and *The Stand* to the wildly successful *Fallout* computer game series. Maybe it's my morbid nature. I'm known in the main for inner city novels – so what could possibly be better than a dystopian 'zombie' speculative horror, set in present-day Shepherd's Bush?!

So, the novel was awarded the title of my half-finished short story, 'The Return', and my sights became set on a short story to test out the world, its themes and its framework. I began with a series of ideas, or rules, if you like:

- Like the novel, the story would be set in a world where the dead have come back to life as living, sentient beings – more like vampires than zombies, although there would be no sucking of blood. They seem as though they live, although they're not alive. They speak and have all their memories intact. They're just dead. Some have 'returned' as they were, gentle, loving and compassionate, flawed but essentially stable of mind. I called these Symps, short for sympathetic. Others are scarred mentally, psychotic; these would be nicknamed Sykes. This second group likes to murder for fun. A small percentage were violent without limit, but most would prefer elaborate tactics: setting traps, either mechanical or home-rigged, with ropes and the like; shooting at people from hidden places, or poisoning their victims. Most lie and charm their way towards murder. They are loved ones, friends and family. Worst of all, no one can tell the difference between the Symps and the Sykes.

- While my novel would chart the fall of humankind and how this situation came into being, the short story would take place many months afterwards, focusing on a couple who are trying to survive in this insane new world. It would be a first-person story, told from the point of view of an adult female protagonist, as my novel's protagonist would be a teenage girl. Unlike my novel, which would be set in Lewes (moving as far from my inner city haunts as possible), the location of my story would be Shepherd's Bush.

- The characters would all be of Caribbean heritage, although there would be scant mention of this. This was intended as part of an ongoing literary experiment. And although I hadn't actually made this next decision until I wrote the first line, my protagonist would tell the story in present tense, in as much real time as possible, set over the course of a single climactic day – which meant no scene breaks, and that I could only use flashbacks sparingly: in memories or dreams.

I'm looking back through my collection of used notebooks and although I can find notes for most of the speculative fiction stories in my growing collection, I struggled to find any for this story. Sod's law, I suppose. Since I've been using the iPhone I've got used to writing ideas on the notes facility; the novelist Teju Cole also does this, although he told me he tends to write ideas for metaphors rather than outright stories. The beauty of this method is that some of the notes get saved to your email address (it's in the notes section of Gmail – I'm not sure where you'd find it for other email accounts). Please be careful with this. I've noticed it can be quite arbitrary, and so if I really care about the importance of a certain note, I tend to write it in my notebook anyway, or save it as a Word file just in case.

Today I seem to have got lucky, because I've found something. It's a note dated 28 March 2012. I suspect that's not when I started the story, for two reasons: 1) when you write a new note, or edit what you've written already, the iPhone automatically changes the time and date; 2) I only started to take notes halfway through my story – the rest of the 'working-out', unfortunately for the purposes of this exercise, was done in my head.

I do recall a few things. I remember the central image, my opening, playing in my mind before I began, nagging almost. I saw a woman holding a blue plastic bag, walking along the central white lines of Ladbroke Grove – the main road in the west London area of Ladbroke Grove/Notting Hill. The streets are bare of people and vehicles. The tarmac is glistening and wet – it has not long finished raining, and that sharp smell is rich in the air. A pub on the corner of Westbourne Park Road and Ladbroke Grove – The Elgin – has boarded windows. The traffic lights before her are dark eyes. The sky is pasted with grey clouds and yet lit by a harsh sunlight. Where there are no clouds, the sky is blue. The woman wears a grey hoodie and jogging bottoms and although her back is turned to me, I can see that her head is moving left to right in jerking fits. She's scared.

I now realize that the image I saw in my head was an intertextual nod to the *28 Days Later* movie poster. I also know my story is set in Shepherd's Bush, not Ladbroke Grove. I saw the woman in the wrong location, because she was walking yards from where I once lived. For both of those reasons the image was useless to me. But it did so much in other ways. In the main, it got me started. I mentally deleted her from that lonely road, and deposited her back where she belonged, in a two-bedroomed flat someplace between Shepherd's Bush and Hammersmith. I thought about what she does before the story begins. It is early morning. She would be getting up, slipping from her bed without her boyfriend's knowledge. She'd be dressing, peeking through the wooden slats they've used to board up the windows, unlocking the flat door and creeping along the worn carpet of the communal passage, opening the front door, tentative as an escapee. She'd be sitting on the front steps with her hood up, lighting a cigarette with a nervous hand. She'd be smoking with quick, halting sips. That's when we'd see her, and the story would begin.

In that precise Moment in Time, my as-yet nameless protagonist would be thinking:

Some days are full-on nightmares, others are troubling dreams. I
never know which one I'll get, so this morning I wake up early, put
on simple clothes and go out on the front steps. The air is cloying
and smells of far-away bonfires. The flats around me are empty
now, most of them anyway, and I don't worry about my neighbours.
I light a cigarette and keep an eye out for strangers. There aren't
many of those, but I watch anyway.

The date I saved this finished story to a Word file was 29 March 2012. I
suspect not having scene breaks helped me power though this story but
even so, I'm surprised. I honestly had no plan, just a vague outline I hadn't
even written down. It doesn't always work so well. When I tried that with my
story 'The Return', also told from the point of view of a first-person female
protagonist, I petered out and never got started again.

This is the thing with stories. Some work. Others end up as half-finished
ideas that never leave the drawing board. Lorrie Moore, author of numerous
stories and editor of The Best American Stories (2004), describes the short
story as a love affair, and the novel as a marriage. I agree. The point is not to
become attached. Create your stories, love your stories, move on. I try not to
be beholden to any, the good or the bad. I use them for my own purposes,
which are dual: to be a better writer, and to create the perfect story. I know
I'll never achieve the second, yet there's fun to be had in the trying.

Somewhere during this time I also read Jose Saramago's Death with
Intervals, a novel in which, from the stroke of midnight on 1 January, no one
in an unnamed country (I'm guessing Portugal) dies any more. It shares very
little with my own story, except being about some form of reincarnation,
and that's the main reason I read it. Unlike many authors, I always read
around my subject before, during and sometimes even after my own writing.
This goes back to Chabon's theory of 'influence is bliss'. You cannot erase
influence. It's like trying to drown out the voices of other people and the
myriad sounds of the outer world. It's impossible. And why would you?

So I read science fiction/horror, fiction and non-fiction concerning death
and reincarnation, mythical and religious texts such as the Tibetan and
Egyptian Book of the Dead, and all the articles and scientific papers on the

subject I could get my hands on. I always try to make this reading and absorbing information a daily habit, which results in the happy accident that when I'm not reading for work, or writing, I'm collating a library of sources that can be draw on when the time comes.

I'm not sure whether anything I read got 'used', in the material manner most people think of research being used, but that saturation gave me confidence. That's vital for a writer: to feel as though they know everything they need to about their story. It gives them the confidence to leave things out by choice, not ignorance.

Back to my story. My unnamed protagonist is sitting on the front steps of her house smoking a cigarette – a crazy, death-defiant act in a world gone rabid. But the reader doesn't know that yet. Everything is allusion. I call it the carrot-on-the-stick method. I have to get her up and doing something in order to get the plot moving. I already know what that is, from the image I saw in my head. She was holding a blue carrier bag. Why?

The answer was simple; she's going to the shops.

So I get her up and walking down the road. I write that short ten-minute journey quickly, in the space of a sentence. I want her to get there soon. A look to the left and she sees the Goldhawk pub, which helps me retain some of my initial imagery: the boarded-up doors and windows of a former public house. Once she's standing outside a similarly boarded-up corner store, she knocks on what's left of the shop door. No answer. She continues to knock until a slat of wood is removed and an eye appears.

I write my first line of dialogue: the woman introduces herself as Dana and asks for 12 eggs. The eye disappears and leaves Dana waiting, pacing on the spot, desperate to leave. The transaction happens with little or no further conversation. She swaps a brown paper bag filled with the eggs for household batteries (I see six AAs, but don't give that detail), and she leaves to tread the empty high road back to her house.

That's when I decide to give her a 'Chandler Moment'.

The 'Chandler Moment' comes from the seminal crime writer Raymond Chandler's introduction to his short story collection, *The Simple Art of Murder*: 'When in doubt, have a man come through a door with a gun in his hand.' Although this gets a laugh in my classes, I don't think Chandler meant it literally. I've always understood it to mean that the writer should do something that surprises them. Take a wild leap of faith and introduce a character or idea that you hadn't thought of until that point. Make someone act in a manner contrary to what you had planned. Interesting things happen when you write spontaneously, and it keeps the prose fresh, and the writer on their toes. What's more, if you're managing to surprise yourself, there's a strong chance you're wrong-footing the reader too.

My 'Chandler Moment' was to introduce a mysterious stranger. He's staring at Dana as she walks home, standing on a corner dressed in a duffel coat, hood raised. He scares her. She speed-walks along the main road, then as soon as she turns down a side street she's running, holding her bag of eggs away from her – a ridiculous attempt to maintain some illusion of normality – all the way to her flat. Danny, her boyfriend, is waiting for her on the front steps. He's holding a gun.

At this stage of the story, a number of things were starting to happen. I've called writing a battle between instinct and the intellect, but to be honest it's less of a battle and more of a see-saw. I had created an 'in' that I liked. I had managed to create a tension that made me feel tense, raised questions that made me want to know the answers, had worked on nothing more than vague instinct and a random collection of images. Now I had to consolidate what I had in the world so far, what I'd like to do next and how the two ideals might come together to reinforce certain themes I had in mind. I had to think intellectually. This is how I tend to 'shape' stories, balancing one mind state against the other, trying not to let either one dominate. One of those objects I introduced into the world was eggs. Another was a man with a gun. I had a female protagonist, something once novel in horror and fantasy, but since the days of Ridley Scott's *Alien* pretty commonplace. How could I do something new with that?

Well, I could go against type. Instead of making her a swashbuckling, kick-ass heroine, which has fast become the norm, I could show her attempts to become a reformed domestic goddess. After all, it was a tragic fantasy horror story, wasn't it? What could be more horrific, subliminally, for female readers in particular, than a couple trying to deal with a post-apocalyptic world by reverting to tired gender roles? And so Dana became the domestic goddess, and Danny the warrior hunter-gatherer.

So she goes inside the flat with Danny and makes eggs Florentine as best she can with only the barest of ingredients. While she cooks, Danny needs something to do. Keeping in mind the role I wanted him to play, I thought it might be good to have him say, 'I'll go and check the scarecrow'. I remember looking at that sentence for a long time. It reminded me of *Dark Night of the Scarecrow*, one of those 1980s video nasties that flooded the VHS market when I was a teenager; one I'd loved. Scarecrows were a great horror trope, I told myself, and provided an even better title. My characters' scarecrow was the dead body of someone who'd occupied another flat in the building and turned feral. Danny had shot him in the head, hauled him up onto the roof and left him to stand guard to scare the undead.

And then that other thing happened that most writers will know so well. As I progressed with the story, reintroducing the mysterious stranger whom Danny spies from the roof when he checks on their decomposing scarecrow, introducing Dana's brother Sherwin (who turns out to be the Syke in the story), I began to change my mind. The dream-like plot I'd anticipated began to drift away and another, more solid form took its place, complete with the tragic, dark ending I'd imagined, but much less obvious. And it all came from the scarecrow, something I hadn't even considered when I began writing, but quickly became all-important. It made me ask questions, of my characters, of my story, and of myself. In deciphering the answers, I could move ahead with a plot that felt more true and more natural than the idea I'd first imagined. But I couldn't have got there without that first loose framework. And that's why I believe that always, the most important thing a writer can do is write – work it out on the page. There's no better way to get it right.

Of course, I can't tell you what I discovered. That would ruin the story. But the result was that I rewrote the first half to reflect what was going to happen with my new ending. That makes it sound a big job, but it was more like a sculptor chipping away at precise places, laying the foundations of the eventual structure. Along the way I tidied minor issues, like Dana and Danny being my main characters' names. That was never going to work, yet in the throes of writing I hadn't noticed; I changed the woman's name to Nicole. Once I'd tidied up the first half the second came very easily. Within two days, the story was done.

When Tania and I discussed the idea of writing about the evolution of our stories, we decided it might be best to use one I hadn't published. *Scarecrow* hasn't been; I'll be honest and tell you that it's been rejected once or twice. But this story pleases me whenever I look at it, because I imagined something that became a physical presence on the page. So don't worry if your story's not published. If you write it well enough, and it pleases you, it will be.

You can read the full story here:

www.bloomsbury.com/writing-short-stories-courttia/

The evolution of a short story: 'Under the Tree'

Tania

I'd never looked at one short story's evolution from conception to publication. But when Courttia and I decided to do this, I knew which story to pick, one that took me years to 'get right'. I began it in 2006 and it was published in 2012. It changed substantially over that time – and represented a major turning point in my writing.

First, I thought I'd give you a stark example – to me, at least – of how my writing shifted. While searching through back-up disks, I unearthed the first short story I ever wrote, 'A Dog's Life', during my first workshop at the Iowa Summer Writer's Festival in 1997. Here's the first paragraph:

> 'I simply don't know what to do with him,' Mrs Morrison said to her friend Vera. They were sitting facing each other in their usual booth in Lyons for the Wednesday tea appointment. 'I don't like dogs.' She set her teacup back heavily into its saucer, which wobbled.

And here's the opening to 'All Activity is Silent', a story I wrote in 2011, published in *Kill-Author* journal:

> She forgets. He forgets. She screams like a baby. He screams like a fish. They forget the screams. They forget the baby.
> 'Fish,' she says.
> 'I've been,' he says, and inside him a billion microbes are at work.

Fourteen years separate these two – would anyone reading them blind know they were written by the same person? The first story is 'traditional': in language, setting, character names, even in its title. There's little doubt what's going on, who and where they are, what they're doing. (I even used an adverb, 'heavily'!) The second story also has two characters but is bizarre and confusing – the title gives nothing away and the opening has two unnamed people (perhaps?), but not much setting or explanation of what's going on.

Whether readers prefer one over the other is not my concern. What's important is that I feel the second story is far closer to expressing on the page, in structure, language and content, the writer I want to be. That took years to get to. And the story I am going to dissect was vital in helping me get there.

This story began as 'Garden Baby' in 2006 and was published as 'Under the Tree' in 2012. I happen to have kept seven drafts of the story otherwise I wouldn't remember how I started writing it.

First draft

The story came to me as an image and an idea: a boy sits under a tree in his garden and doesn't want to get up; his mother has no idea why. The first version, December 2006, is 1,499 words long and starts like this:

> He spends all his time out there, sitting under the tree, our big old oak, his back against its trunk, looking out towards the house, but not seeing it, seeing through it, over it, beyond. If I come out and bring him tea, he seems normal, he takes the cup, we talk, he asks what I am doing but I don't ask him what he's doing. I don't want to hear the answer.

I wrote this trying to figure out myself what was going on. The title is intriguing but vague, and potentially misleading – the opening would be weird if you think that 'he' is a baby. Also, starting with 'he' and only bringing 'I' in in the second sentence might wrong-foot the reader. There is no hint here in language or content about the strangeness of what he's doing. Or the relationship between 'he' and 'I'. There's more detail about the tree!

The second paragraph is a flashback to when 'he' was a baby, so we learn what the title refers to, and that 'I' is his parent. I remember this line being important to me:

'My Garden Baby,' I said to Alice, who had a little girl who screamed when she saw a butterfly. 'It's like he came out of the earth instead of out of me.'

Once again, I'm trying to explain to myself what he's doing under the tree, but before I've even established the story. Where's the tension? Who wants what? The main characters have no names, but Alice does. Why?

The third paragraph mentions 'John': 'Before John died, we had a barbecue every week, even when it was raining.' John's death – might be important.

It's only on page 3, almost the end of this first draft, that the central issue surfaces: 'he' refuses to come into the house and 'I', his mother, has no idea why or what to do. There's a hint of what is to come:

I thought back to when it began, a summer day, a morning like many other mornings where I came downstairs, put the kettle on to make us tea, and saw through the window someone sitting under the tree. I stood for a moment, wondering if they had climbed over the fence, should I call the police, but then I realised that it was him. He was sitting very still. I didn't have my glasses but I felt, even from that distance and in the bright light, that he was smiling.

Then his mother talks to a psychiatrist about whether this was to do with John's death and there's a section on the boy applying to study botany – this is me still grasping for an explanation (grief, love of plants) for why he's under the tree. A rushed final scene with mother and son happily under the tree together – and the story ends.

One major problem is that the boy is not a fully fleshed character. He's talked about and he speaks but doesn't seem three-dimensional. So, even though I sent the story out, that was mighty premature because I wasn't happy with it at all.

Second draft

A month later the story has the same title but a different opening:

> *When he was a baby, he loved grass.* If he was having a crying fit,
> I would take him outside and lie him on the ground among the
> ants and the daisies, and he would grab at it all with his fat hands
> and giggle. I watched his eyes move from one thing to the next,
> a flower, a bee, a clump of weeds, delighting in it all. 'My garden
> baby,' I said to Alice, who had a little girl who screamed when she
> saw a butterfly. 'It's like he came out of the earth instead of out of
> me,' I said, but I don't think Alice heard; her girl was crying in the
> sandpit, sand stuck to her cheeks as she rubbed her eyes with her
> caked hands.

I moved paragraph 2 to the top to explain the title, but what does it actually do? Looking ahead to the new second paragraph, which is in the present tense, the story now starts with a flashback. We're not even in the present and already we're in the past. Why did I italicize the first line? It could indicate someone is speaking but it doesn't seem to make sense with the story. (The italics will be something I need, but I don't know that yet.)

There's still the problem of 'he' introduced before 'I', although we know their relationship straight away; neither of them have names, but Alice does, which gives her prominence although she never reappears.

The second paragraph is:

> Now he sits there under the old oak and that's all he does. He
> sits with his back against the trunk, looking out towards the house
> but not looking at it: it's as if he looks through it and beyond. Or
> perhaps he's seeing something else, something I can't. I come out
> and bring him tea, lunch, dinner, and he takes the mugs, the plates,
> and we chat. He asks what I am doing, but I don't ask him. I don't
> want to hear the answer.

Better. I've introduced the central issue and the mother's anxiety. The story's now 1,700 words long but the remaining parts are the same as Version 1, padded a bit. The ending's the same.

Third draft

A month later, and now we have the name of Alice's daughter in the opening, but still no main character names! The story has grown to 2,000 words, and we have a twist, on page 5 of the six-page story:

> Then this morning, I woke up and he was gone. I stood at the
> bedroom window for I don't know how long, just staring at the
> tree, wondering if it was my eyes. Then I ran downstairs, calling
> his name. My voice echoed back to me. There was nothing on the
> kitchen table, no note saying 'Gone for a walk', or 'At the shops,
> back later'. I felt disaster in my bones and I rushed out into the
> garden.
>
> The tree looked the same, the grass was thick, there wasn't even
> a patch where you could see he had been sitting. More than a
> week he sat here and then the grass just springs back as if he was
> never there?

The story ends with him gone and the mother sitting down under the tree.

Hmm. Interesting. Mysterious. But still the same problems. Still not feeling I've hit it, I'm not telling the story I want to tell. Which is why, in July 2007, I take it to the Tin House Summer Writers Workshop in Portland, Oregon, with one of my favourite writers, Aimee Bender, and things start to shift.

I wrote this blog post when I came home:

> [Aimee] gave us permission not to tie up our stories neatly and
> end with everything fixed; she talked about the media's obsession
> with finding the causes of someone's behaviour, showing the
> psychological 'reason' why they are doing what they are doing,
> and told us that we don't need to explain why our characters do

what they do. Life is more complicated than that ... This last point, although I thought I knew it, when clarified so simply, led me to a major revelation about a story I have been banging my head against for several years ... I'd always felt something was 'clunky' and suddenly I realized it was because I was trying to explain the reason for my main character's weird behaviour, trying to draw a straight line between incidents in his childhood and what he was now doing. But I don't need to explain anything. I can just cut all that out. Ohmigod. What a relief.

This has informed my writing ever since. How often do we know what motivates our *own* actions? There's rarely one cause for anything, so why try to ascribe something so simplistic to our characters? If we want them to be complex, real, we have to allow them to do what they do without explanation. Leave that to the reader to fill in.

I'll say that again: leave that to the reader. Readers are clever, let them do some of the work. As legendary screenwriter Billy Wilder wrote in his *Ten Tips for Writing a Great Screenplay*: 'Let the audience add up two plus two. They'll love you forever.' It's easier for me, the writer, too – I can let go of needing to know, and it makes the reader feel involved in the story. Win-win.

Fourth draft

November 2007. My story is now called 'Underneath the Tree', and here's how it starts:

I wake up early, although it isn't early really, it's my normal time, but there's nothing to do now in the morning now that Duncan's not a child and John isn't here. But still I wake up at that same time, can't fight it so I put on my dressing gown and head off to the kitchen. I walk past Duncan's room and the door's open, and the bed's neatly made and he's not there, so I call out, Duncan, love, put the kettle on! No answer. Boys. But he's not in the kitchen, and as the water's boiling I wander around the house, and he isn't anywhere. Not in the loo, or watching breakfast TV. And no note, no Mum, popped out to the shops, or something. And I can't help it, I start sweating and my heart is banging away and I hear the switch on the kettle pop and I go back into the kitchen, my head full of thoughts of kidnappings, even though who ever heard of a grown eighteen-year-old who might not have a lot of muscle but can certainly look out for himself, who ever heard of an eighteen-year-old being grabbed from his bed? And what kidnapper would make the bed, no, no, stop with that nonsense, calm down, drink your tea.

We're immediately inside our main character's head, and we're in the present tense, no more flashbacks to him as a baby, no Alice. No italics either. Also, her voice is stronger: finally, I could hear her, and hoped the reader would too. We're instantly told she is his mother and made aware there's some sort of mystery, some reason why this day isn't like all the others: Duncan (he has a name and age) isn't where she expected. We sense her anxiety.

It's a really long first paragraph, over 200 words, and it's stuffed full! The story itself is now over 2,200 words.

Here is the second paragraph:

As I rummage for a clean spoon in the sink, I look up and out into the back garden, and there's someone there, someone under the tree, is it, what's he doing ...? Duncan? Morning, mum, he says as if I wake up every day at 7am and find him sitting fully dressed under the oak tree. What are you doing? I say, trying to keep my voice from getting higher, keep him from hearing my stupid anxiety, all my stupid thoughts about night-time abductions, all the mother-stuff. Nothing, he says, and he grins at me and I wonder why I don't understand him even though he came out of my body. Want to join me? he says, looking up at me from where he's sitting and I say, Aren't you cold? Isn't it damp? And he just grins, and leans back against the trunk, and says, Will you make me a cup of tea? And I nod, of course I will, and I go and put the kettle back on.

Here we nearly have the story's central issue. The major change is that I can hear Duncan too. He's real. He wants tea and he's grinning. Then, at the beginning of the third paragraph, on page 1 instead of near the end, we get the tension of this story, in one simple line: 'The thing is, he doesn't come in.'

Later on, a new character, Muriel, the mother's friend, is mentioned but doesn't actually appear, but mostly what is striking in this draft is what's gone: All attempts at explaining why Duncan is there – the father's death, a love for plants. What's here is what the mother does: she takes him his meals as if being under the tree is normal, while she slowly falls apart. This is definitely now *her* story. What's still here, though, is the realist tone, despite the oddness of the premise.

There's a new part, halfway through:

When it starts getting dark, I go back out. I can't not go, can I, with
my son under a tree and no explanation? I stand there, he sits,
and I know that I am standing in mother-is-anxious position, arms
folded over my chest, legs a foot apart as if I'm bracing myself, as if
someone's about to hit me in the chest.

That compound word, 'mother-is-anxious', is the first hint of a language shift that will be important. And there's a new ending: Duncan becomes part of the tree.

I move to touch him but I pull my fingers back. Duncan ... I say.
Duncan, don't ... and his eyes look into mine and I reach in as if
I can pull him back, but as I look I see him fade and then he is
gone.

I remember liking this magical realism, but the problem is there's no hint at the beginning that this is going to be *that* kind of story, in *that* genre.

Robert McKee, in his excellent screenwriting book, *Story*, says that 'the audience is already a genre expert. The genre sophistication of film-goers presents the writer with this critical challenge: He must not only fulfil audience anticipations, or risk their confusion and disappointment, but he must lead their expectations to fresh, unexpected moments, or risk boring them. This two-handed trick is impossible without knowledge of genre that surpasses the audience's.'

Substituting 'reader' for 'audience' and 'film-goer', how does this apply? What I've done is establish it as a realist at the beginning, then at the end it turns into a different genre, with no hint this might happen. This is unfair to the reader – if you've managed to keep them reading your story, they may feel cheated. The rules of this world were clear, how could he just turn into the tree! Exactly.

Permission and structure

To recap: the first revelation in the writing of this story was Aimee Bender's 'permission' not to know why my character does what he does. This is about *content*. The second revelation, between November 2007 and April 2008, is to do with *structure* (I touch on this in the section on permission and risk). Structure and language.

Looking back, I see now that a lot was happening in my writing life at this point. Salt Publishing had offered to publish my first collection, and I went into shock, couldn't really write at all. I left this story. I didn't know how to 'solve' the problems so I put it away.

Then I read and reviewed two short story collections which helped me see what to do next. The minimalist, funny and odd stories in *All Over*, by Roy Kesey, gave me permission to leave things out and play with language; a story divided into headed sections in *The End of the World*, by Paddy O'Reilly, opened my eyes to structure.

Fifth draft

Next came some drastic changes, possible, I think, because I let it lie for five months – setting a story aside makes it easier to feel less attached, see why it isn't working. Draft 5 (April 2008) now called 'Under the Tree', is a skinny 800 words, less than half the previous version, and begins thus:

Under the tree
He sits and I come and I feed him, breakfastlunchdinner, and he
says, I'm fine Mum, don't worry Mum, but he doesn't get up, doesn't
come in. Just sits. Under the tree. And I sit, in the kitchen, opposite
the window, and watch him. Then, when it's too dark to see
anymore, I stumble upstairs, fall onto the bed. The next morning I
get up and we do it all again.

First day
I was curious, wondering, asked him in a jokey way, was he trying
out for the local drama club, was that it? Make a great plant, you
would, I say, trying for a laugh, for a fightback, for a getting-up-
standing-up-stopping-all-this-nonsense. But what I got was a grin, a
nod, nothing at all, no answers, all open, everything hanging, falling
apart.

We immediately have a subheading, a repeat of the title, in italics, indicating
that something 'non-traditional' is going on. The reader can see from the
three headed sections on page 1 that the whole story will be structured
like this. Second, the tone's changed: the pace of the opening is almost
breathless, you have the compound word, 'breakfastlunchdinner' conveying
time passing in a blur, taking us inside her head. Her state of mind is there
on the page. It also hints that we're departing from strict adherence to
grammar, to 'rules'. We immediately know who they are, their relationship,
and the central issue is – he's under the tree and his mother doesn't know
what to do.

The second section is a flashback, the subheading 'First day' tells the
reader exactly where we are in time. The structure really does some work
here, the sections are not a gimmick, they help progress the story. And – as
Ron Carlson discusses in his book, *Ron Carlson Writes a Story* – most importantly, they helped me write my story the way I wanted to write it. I don't
believe I could have done it without them. (Once I'd written the story, I might
have chosen to remove the sections; but in this case I didn't want to.)

Here's the next section:

Ghost

Help me, I say at night, lying in the lonely bed, the marriage bed of not-John and me. Where are you? And there's a whispering in my ear, a shuffling of John-ness, and I know I'm ungripped but I stay with it. It's Duncan, I say, but the John-ness, the -ness of him, it knows already, it knows about our boy, fixed onto the earth outside. And then there may be words, maybe, justforme words, some sort of sense saying Sit with him, Be with him, Be him, See him, ABC him, and I'm sleeping and the John-ness is holding on, holding on, until I drift.

More non-traditional language: she's falling apart. We have John, but he's there for her, not for the boy. I've ditched all attempts at explaining any of it. I'm telling the story but not commenting on it. (We could mention 'show versus tell' here but I don't find it useful; some writers are fantastic at 'telling not showing'.) This, perhaps, is a good definition of minimalism. It's not up to me to tell you what the story is about.

The ending is different. He doesn't turn into a tree. There is no neat tying up, and in fact the ending seems to embody two contradictory states at once (I won't spoil it by explaining why, you can read it for yourself). As I read more and more short stories, I came to understand that the kind of story I love and want to write doesn't have an ending where everything's solved. What's most important to me is to make myself – and a possible reader – feel something. I upset myself writing this story. I remember that when I hit it, with this, almost the final version, I was moved. Not just because I felt I'd finally got the damn thing. But because it was so sad. I hoped – and this is all we can ever hope – that if it moved me, it might move one person who isn't me.

Sixth and seventh drafts and submission

In the next two drafts over four months, I made only minor tweaks. For a reason lost to me now, I made 'breakfastlunchdinner' into three separate words in the first line, and saved the compound word for the third section. That's pretty much it.

Because it was clear to me now – and, I hoped, clear to a reader from the start – that this is not a realist story, after several rejections from traditional venues, I submitted to *Electric Velocipede* (sadly now closed), whose submission guidelines said:

> We want to see stories that are a little weird ... Science fiction is fine; we just don't care for hardcore nuts and bolts. Fantasy is fine; we're just not all that comfortable with elves, dwarves, unicorns, etc. Cross-genre is more than fine, and weird is just about perfect.

(An aside: do read submissions guidelines; often a publication will tell you exactly what it wants, and if you send something it doesn't want you are wasting your own time and energy, and they'll probably bin it.)

I knew my story was weird so I sent it. In December 2009 I got the thrilling news – it was accepted! It was eventually published in 2012; it took a while. But without getting this acceptance, I'm not sure I would have had the confidence to include the story in my second collection.

Summing up

The writing of this story took two and a half years. It went from 1,400 words up to 2,200 words and ended up at 804 words. It changed radically. I was putting in things I needed to know to write it, to make these characters real, but the reader didn't need, they didn't have to be on the page. I was not removing these elements consciously though. I didn't announce 'Oh, Alice has to go'. I felt my way through it, more instinctual than logical. As Ron Carlson says, I had to not think but 'watch instead. Occupy. Many times a story will get twisted when a writer knows where she wants to go, what irony or point she wants the story to achieve, and she's got her eye on that goal and can't see or hear the opportunities arising in the current scene ...'

Through grappling with this story I learned so much. I learned to play. To break rules like 'Don't squish several words into one new word not found in the dictionary'. To trust that in the kind of short story I love, less is much more; to leave out enough both to let me write it and allow my clever reader to fill in gaps. That how the story is set out on the page helps me write it, as well as contributing to the story. I learned that I like writing weird stories. That I don't like neat endings.

I kept working on this story until it was the way I wanted it, and then, miraculously, found another person, *Electric Velocipede*'s editor, who liked it enough to publish it.

It's been fascinating looking at my own writing in this way. I hope it's interesting for you, too. You can read the final version of the story on: www.bloomsbury.com/writing-short-stories-tania/

Further reading

Carlson, Ron, *Ron Carlson Writes A Story* (Greywolf Press, 2007).

Electric Velocipede http://www.electricvelocipede.com/

Kesey, Roy, *All Over* (Dzanc Books, 2007).

kill-author http://killauthor.com/

McKee, Robert, *Story: Substance, Structure, Style and The Principles of Screenwriting* (Regan Books, 2007).

O'Reilly, Paddy, *The End Of The World* (University of Queensland Press, 2007).

Wilder, Billy, 'Ten Tips for Writing a Great Screenplay', from *Conversations with Wilder* (Crowe, Cameron, Knopf, 2001).

Reflections: permission and risk

Tania

As I mentioned earlier, the gift Roy Kesey and Paddy O'Reilly gave me was permission – to take risks, do something I might not otherwise have done. Once I became aware of how I can get permission from others' work, it happens again and again. Each time I find a new short story I love, it cracks opens a window and lets fresh air into my own writing.

I read Roy Kesey's short story collection, *All Over* (Dzanc Books, 2007) and I loved what it made me do as a reader. What was it that was so eye-opening? *Kesey made me work. Hard.* His stories were fabulously minimalist and often surreal. They confused me, deliciously, making me simultaneously read and figure out what was going on. It was as if I wasn't watching the story unfold but was part of it, complicit in the act of creation. Less-is-more at its very best. I thought: Could I take the risk of doing to a reader what Roy Kesey did to me?

The first story I wrote immediately after reading *All Over* was 'Vegetable, Mineral'. For the first time, my characters had no names, just 'you' and 'I'. (I'd seen Ali Smith do this ten years earlier, but thought I was 'not allowed' to try it myself.) For the first time, my story wasn't set anywhere. For the first time, it was mostly dialogue and you didn't always know who was speaking. It was odd, and I loved writing it. Then it won a flash fiction contest and was a finalist in another. So, *was* I allowed to try this? Not only allowed, but being actively encouraged. Roy Kesey's stories gave me permission. I took that risk, and I've never looked back.

The second permission-giving experience came from Australian writer Paddy O'Reilly's wonderful collection *The End of the World* (2007). As I mentioned in the section on the evolution of 'Under the Tree', I was struggling with this story. Then I read one of Paddy's stories which was divided into sections with subheadings. Hers has a completely different plot, but something clicked. *Structure*. A writing teacher once said that when you are having problems, structure can ride in like a knight on a white horse. When I rewrote my story in sections, with subheadings, everything fell into place.

Is it worth taking risks? When I judge a short story competition or guest-edit a literary journal, taking risks is a quality I prize – even if they don't quite pay off. I prefer to be confused by a brave writer than bored by a perfectly crafted story. Nicholas Royle, editor of the *Best British Short Stories* series (Salt Publishing), agrees. In his introduction to *BBSS 2011*, he says: 'I'd rather be left with questions than answers. With a vague feeling of uncertainty rather than one of satisfaction at how neatly everything has been tied up.'

Taking a risk doesn't necessarily mean embracing minimalism or experimental structures. There are stories I've loved that took risks in looking anew at an overused plot, or using humour, which, if not done deftly, can derail a story. Others take risks by not making the main character entirely sympathetic, for example. Risk means something different to everyone. As does taboo – what *don't* you want to write about? You might be comfortable writing about sex or politics, for example, but not about family life. What are your taboos?

You might think: Why should I take a risk instead of keeping life easy and doing what I've done before? There's no simple answer – but since you're reading this book, I suspect you are the kind of writer that pushes him or herself, doesn't want to get too comfortable. I would argue that it's not just for the benefit of readers or judges, it is about the essential question: Why are you writing? I write to try to make sense of the world, and, for me, uncertainty is part of life. If quantum physics taught me anything, it was the limits of knowledge: we can't see everything, measure everything, pinpoint cause-and-effect. Subatomic particles pop in and out of existence; people behave in strange ways that have no apparent reasons. It's complicated.

The nice, neat stories where everything is explained and ties up at the end – the 'well-made stories' I mentioned in the History of the Short Story, many of which have become classics – are popular, but how do they resonate with someone who lives in this world, this uncertain, complicated world? I would argue that if you really want to touch a reader, to reach into their guts, it's a messy business. Get your hands dirty.

The first person I want to affect is myself. Grappling with chaos, ambiguity, letting go of a need for resolution – this is what affects me, widens my perspective, helps me understand life isn't about fixing things but about catching what's flung at you while struggling to stay standing. That, for me, is what makes a story truly great. So, take that risk. Jump.

Further reading

Hershman, Tania, 'Vegetable, Mineral' (*PANK magazine*, 2010 http://pankmag-azine.com/piece/tania-hershman-2/).

Kesey, Roy, *All Over* (Dzanc Books, 2007).

O'Reilly, Paddy, *The End Of The World* (University of Queensland Press, 2007).

Part 2

On being brief

Jenn Ashworth

Jenn Ashworth is the author of three novels, *A Kind of Intimacy* (winner of the 2010 Betty Trask Award), *Cold Light* and *The Friday Gospels*, as well as numerous short stories. She also reviews fiction for the *Guardian*. She lives in Lancashire.

A short story is a sliver of light between a pair of half-drawn curtains. It is a laser heading for an eyeball. Or it is a torch flashing wildly around a darkened auditorium. It is a fight seen out of a car window; a drive-by sort of thing. Or half of a telephone conversation, overheard on the train. It is something and nothing: presence and absence, detail and space. It may be brief but it is ultimately the most generous and respectful of literary forms. It won't describe an intergenerational saga, nor examine its theme from a thousand angles. It might provide an epiphany, but is just as likely to trip the reader up by dramatizing a moment of realization that is not quite right; cracked, somehow, to let the light in, to let the unwritten parts of the tale shine through the silence.

Because it is such a generous form, a really great short story doesn't lead us by the nose; it provides us with the essentials and sends us on a journey. *Off you go*, it says, *make of this what you will*, and while we are looking to be moved we are left alone to move ourselves. We travel light, with only a handful of possessions to take with us. Everything we need to know about Katherine Mansfield's Miss Brill comes to us in the narrow gap in time and space between her worse-for-wear fur and her unbought slice of honey-cake. Shirley Jackson's 'The Lottery' terrifies us with Bobby Martin's pocket full of stones, Donald Barthelme surprises and discomfits us with a single 'new gerbil' in 'The School'. Readers of short stories can be trusted: they don't need much.

Short stories are uncanny: they contain ghosts. They haunt us because of what they require from us, but they ask us to haunt them too, making ourselves uncomfortably at home in a strange place by filling in their spaces and scribbling round the margins with our own anxieties and wonderings. There's nothing as frightening as the monster you're seduced into inventing for yourself, after all. With no room for exposition or repetition, the horror of possession, of sexual betrayal or perhaps something else, is communicated to us perfectly in Emma Unsworth's story 'In' merely by the sound of a clanging gate. We are maddened by it. Alison Moore's short story 'When the Door Closed, It Was Dark' is puzzling: the violent and erotic undertones only hinted at, or perhaps provided by us. In Nabokov's 'Symbols and Signs' the horror and sadness take place in another room, in a hospital on the other side of town. All we are presented with are two elderly parents eating fish, looking at photograph albums, regarding an undelivered birthday present and waiting for the phone to ring.

A few pieces of advice for short fiction writers. Don't tell everything. Construct a story that gifts the reader with the apparatus they need to do the work themselves. Particularize like mad and let your reader generalize, if she wants to. Use objects carefully. There's no formula for fiction. But here's one anyway: a short story = language + silence + a reader.

Whose epiphany?
Julia Bell

Julia Bell is a writer and Senior Lecturer at Birkbeck College, London, where she teaches Creative Writing and is Project Director of the Writers' Hub. She is the author of three novels, and the co-editor of the Creative Writing Coursebook and several volumes of short stories. She also writes poetry, occasional essays and journalism.

For me the word epiphany is always associated with the Bible story of the three wise men who saw a star in the sky that led them to the infant Jesus. As a child I always imaged three wise men, dressed in swags of Arabian clothes, leading their camel train full of treasure across the desert until they looked at the sky and had a – ping! – light bulb moment. Never mind that light bulbs and ancient Middle Eastern mystics were a historically inaccurate combination. As I grew older, T. S. Eliot's narrative poem 'Journey of the Magi' – 'A cold coming we had of it ...' – started to take its place. Then in the writing workshop – an epiphany was something that happened in a short story, although it wasn't always clear what on first reading. A shift in the character, a tone, a phrase where the story opened up rather than closed down, a realization that dawned – but for whom?

To me it seems that there are two distinct types of epiphany. Two kinds of stories, one in which the epiphany happens within the story to the characters, who are either left in the light of that realization about to change something, or, if it's a tragic story, to acknowledge too late the reality of their situation. Then there is another kind of story, in which the character continues blithely on in error off the edge of the page without realizing anything at all, but instead it's us, the readers, who have the light bulb moment about the character. We are led by the story to a moment of truth about the life of the character, but the epiphany lies entirely with us, rather than in the action on the page.

Take the Lorrie Moore story 'You're Ugly Too', in which a Midwestern college professor who uses humour as a defence, who is lonely and possibly sick, is left at the end of the story pretty much as we found her, almost more tragic than at the start. The story ends with a question, which throws the character at the reader and asks us to think about who she is, but at no point do we get a sense that she has had moment of understanding about herself. It happens entirely to the reader, who is placed in the psychiatrist's chair.

In Raymond Carver's story 'They're Not Your Husband', by contrast, we witness the humiliation of Earl Ober, unemployed and frustrated and taking out his disempowerment on his wife. After overhearing some obscene comments about her physique at the diner where she works, he puts her on a diet, obsessing about her body instead of about getting a job. Once she has lost some weight he revisits the diner and says lewd things about her to the customers. The other customers turn away from him for being a jerk, and he is humiliated. Here, the epiphany belongs to the character. And we realize something by watching him – about the control of women; about Earl's desperate attempt to control his life.

A good short story should always deliver an experience for the reader, and in this way an epiphany could also be seen to be the physiological effect of reading a good piece of writing: the heart rate quickens, the synapses crackle as the mind expands. We are left in a different place from where we were when we began reading, and that's the best we can ask of all great art.

On generosity
Anthony Doerr

Anthony Doerr is the author of two short story collections, *The Shell Collector* and *Memory Wall*, and the novels *About Grace*, *Four Seasons in Rome* and *All the Light We Cannot See*. He has won four O'Henry awards for short stories and been anthologized in *Best American Short Stories*. He lives in Boise, Idaho.

'A Worn Path', Eudora Welty's famous story about a grandmother's walk to retrieve medicine for her ailing grandson, begins like this:

> It was December – a bright frozen day in the early morning. Far out in the country there was an old Negro woman with her head tied in a red rag, coming along a path through the pinewoods. Her name was Phoenix Jackson. She was very old and small and she walked slowly in the dark pine shadows, moving a little from side to side in her steps, with the balanced heaviness and lightness of a pendulum in a grandfather clock.

Eighty words, none of them fancy, and yet look at what Welty does with them. We learn that it's December; that we're 'far out in the country', a place where people can have names like Phoenix; and that Phoenix Jackson is old, a fact so important Welty mentions it twice. In a lesser writer's hands, any of these details might be arbitrary, but in Welty's, everything matters.

December is vital because the story presents a seven-page microcosm of the whole Christmas season, its cold and warmth, its charities and cruelties.

December is a season of belief, and as Phoenix's story progresses, the reader comes to suspect that her ill grandson may no longer be alive. Yet still she carries out her errand, re-enacting the habits of love and hope.

Phoenix, too, might be no more than a backwoodsy southern name, but here it carries along allusive subcurrents: some underground fraction of the reader's mind is attaching death and rebirth to the woman, and consequently to the story.

And the pendulum! By the end of the passages, a reader feels Phoenix's slow progress not only along the trail but through *time*. We see heaviness balanced against lightness, death against life, shadow against light, and Welty gets all three cradles rocking in her first four sentences.

I believe a good writer is a generous writer. I believe a writer ought to be as unselfish and as magnanimous to her reader as she possibly can. The beauty of any good story is in the compression of so many days of work – two hundred afternoons of a writer thinking on things, wrestling with problems in her story, noticing, say, how a red headscarf seems to glow at a distance on a cold morning – compressing all of those thousands of hours into a space that can be experienced by a reader in thirty minutes.

Stories like 'A Worn Path' (or Joyce's 'The Dead', or Baldwin's 'Sonny's Blues', or Gogol's 'The Overcoat') seem to contain several lifetimes of fine, sharp observations, tested and probed and examined for years, then masoned into every paragraph. They are gifts.

Years ago, in a little private library in Rome, a librarian brought me a magnifying glass and three of Albrecht Dürer's etchings. When the library closed, hours later, she had to prise them out of my hands. It wasn't Dürer's precision or his choice of subjects that appealed to me as much as his breathtaking level of generosity. There's a tiny mountain goat in the upper right-hand corner of 'Adam and Eve', no bigger than the nail of my pinkie finger, and I stared at that goat through the magnifier and realized that Dürer had etched fur into its coat, cracks into its horns – that goat itself must have taken him 15 hours, and he made it in 1504, with handmade tools and without electric lights.

That's the kind of generosity we ought to bring to our work as short story writers. Every step along the path should matter; every centimetre should reward the closest inspection. If we're lucky enough to draw the reader down the first few paces of one of our stories, we ought to make those steps so clear, so sticky, so compelling – so *generous* – that she'll never want to turn around.

Voice
Vanessa Gebbie

Vanessa Gebbie is an award-winning short story writer, novelist and poet. She has published two collections of stories, *Words From a Glass Bubble* and *Storm Warning*, a novel, *The Coward's Tale*, and a poetry pamphlet, *The Half-Life of Fathers*, and edited *Short Circuit: A Guide to the Art of the Short Story*. She lives in Sussex.

Dance as if there's no one watching …

I read a lot of short fiction, and am asked to judge short fiction contests. What is the very first thing, in the first lines of any short story, to either make me engage with the piece or make me put it down and sigh? Voice. Voice makes a piece ring with honesty, tells me this writer is in charge, makes me trust them to deliver. But there is such confusion over what exactly 'voice' is.

Professor Wikipedia, echoing many other would-be gurus, tells us this: 'The writer's voice is the individual writing style of an author, a combination of idiotypical usage of syntax, diction, punctuation, character development, dialogue, etc.' – giving us a picture of writers sitting down making a conscious combination of choices purely in order to discover what their own voice is. Speaking as a writer of short stories (as well as many other forms equally dependent on voice), I don't think many of us would agree with that.

A more grounded professional, literary agent Rachelle Gardner, on her excellent blog, offers the best definition I have found: 'Voice is not style. It's not technique. It's not branding. It's not a decision to write in first or third person'; in her view, and I agree, 'Your writer's voice is the expression of YOU on the page'. Your voice is not 'you' trying to sound writerly. Or impressive. Or like any one of a hundred other writers you like and admire, or have been set to emulate for an exercise. It is not a coat 'you' slip on when you sit down to write, and take off when 'you' get up to do everything else.

Let's take the inverted commas from 'you' and shift them. Why? Because that, to me, is what you do when you've 'found' your voice. You write without inverted commas. You speak naturally through your writing. You are just you. And let's be honest. You don't 'find' it. Rather you clear away whatever you've hidden it behind. It's always there, waiting.

Here's a story from the Creative Writing staff at Columbia College, Chicago.

One student's work, read out in class, would send everyone to sleep. It was flat, expressionless, lacked colour. And yet he'd worked on it so hard. All students were asked to keep a daily journal in which they could write anything at all, anything that cropped up, thoughts about this and that, memories. Anything that asked to be written. These journals were scanned periodically, to check students were keeping them up. His journal was checked, and the penny dropped. He agreed to read a selected excerpt from it, instead of his homework, at the next class. He read a page or two, and when he stopped, his classmates begged him to go on. They were so taken with the story, they had to hear it to the end.

What was the difference? His voice. In doing his homework, the work to read out in class, he'd been REMOVING HIS VOICE, trying to make his work sound correct. Or acceptable. 'Like a writer.' Or whatever. He'd been trying not to sound like himself, when that is exactly what we all need to do. He'd been taking out what made his work sing, when everyone, tutors, agents, publishers, listeners and especially readers, all want to hear that song. HIS song. YOUR song.

Write as if only you will read it. Sing. As loud as you like. Dance as if no one's watching.

On short story endings

Tom Lee

Tom Lee is the author of the short story collection *Greenfly*. His short stories have appeared in the *Sunday Times* and *Esquire* and been broadcast on BBC Radio 4. He was born in Essex in 1974.

When my collection *Greenfly* came out, several friends who did not usually read short stories complained that, although they liked them, none of the stories had proper endings. They meant that scenarios and tensions were not resolved, outcomes and meanings were ambiguous, the big denouement the stories seemed to promise never quite happened. For example, we never discover if the greenfly of the title story is real or a figment of the unhappy narrator's imagination. In 'San Francisco', the story ends as the narrator awaits the conclusion of a possibly catastrophic drug deal. In 'The Good Guy', the main character, JP, collapses as he is on the verge of making a definitive statement about everything that has been happening to him.

I laughed and said I would try harder for the next collection. Inwardly, of course, I damned my friends as philistines. Life isn't like that, I thought. It doesn't come in conveniently self-contained episodes, with all loose ends tidied up and neatly put away – so why should fiction? A story that ended by saying something conclusive about its characters and life in general was inevitably full of false feeling, bad faith and bad art. If my friends were frustrated by this open ended-ness and ambiguity then they had missed the point of the stories entirely.

But their comments bugged me and made me wonder. Perhaps I had fallen into a habit, a convention, a Pavlovian reflex as to how to end a story, imitative of a million other stories written since Chekhov – climaxes aborted, meaning or moral refused, perhaps a sudden awkward leap for the obscurely profound or sublime. It was a formula of its own. This came home to me when someone remarked of a memoir I wrote: it ends just like one of your stories, ambiguously and uneasily. It was true and I hadn't noticed it. It seemed my writerly tics were taking over.

Ultimately, I stand by the endings of the stories in *Greenfly*: they are the only endings the stories could have had, and the shared flavour of them – and in my non-fiction, too – hopefully says as much about my voice or vision as it does about my laziness. But it is good to be aware of these things. Endings in stories carry proportionately more weight than they do in novels. You could say that for a reader a novel is a kind of process, an accumulation of pleasures, whereas the short story aims for a single effect. A novel will tolerate a few bum notes, some bad decisions, and still survive. In a story there is very little room for error, and none at all at the end. I am trying harder in my new collection.

On short stories
Toby Litt

Toby Litt is best known for writing his books – from the short story collection *Adventures in Capitalism* to (so far) *King Death* – in alphabetical order; he is currently working on *M*. His second short story collection, *I Play the Drums in a Band Called Okay*, was published in 2008. His stories have won the Manchester Fiction Prize and been shortlisted for the *Sunday Times* EFG Private Bank Short Story Award. Toby lectures in creative writing at Birkbeck, University of London.

I have thought of amusing-ish analogies, plenty of them, to make the distinction – when I'm asked *The Question*.

If the novel is a cake, the short story is a biscuit, and the poem is a sweet. If the novel's a marriage, the short story's an affair, and I leave to your imagination what a poem is. If the novel's an orchestra, short story's a string quartet, poem's solo. Novel = tour guide; short story = acrobat; poem = poltergeist.

What is the difference between ...?

The analogy that came closest was, embarrassingly, hearts. Hearts may not be different in kind, as are cakes and biscuits and sweets, but they vary vastly in size and rhythm. When an idea comes to me, it brings with it a sense of rhythm even when it gives no sense of scale. An idea is a big or tiny heart around which I have to build-a-beast. Wait long and listen hard. Fluttery-fast, it's a sparrow-verse; regularly rapid, it's the hare of a story; ten seconds between booms, it's Leviathan about to dive.

But recently I've come to a new and I hope better way of differentiating, and the difference no longer begins at the writing end.

Here it comes; see if it convinces.

Short stories are different from novels in this way: short stories have better readers.

Or, further from snappiness but closer to accuracy (at this stage), they *expect* their readers to be better – live in the possibility of it – and are written always in the glowing-growing space of that hope.

(Poems have for the moment gone off in a flap – your eye can follow their line of flight; but they haven't ceased to matter, and you can expect them to make a fairly devastating return.)

Shouldn't this distinction, then, be detectable in every line of a good novel and a good short story?

Yes, and I believe it is.

The sentences in short stories might look, cursorily, verbs, nouns, commas, full stops, the same as those in novels, but they are spaced more widely apart. Their readers expect to traverse Alaskas of implication, in between sense units.

In the completeness of each form, there is a big difference, too. Short story readers expect to make the meaning of the story themselves, never to have it laid out for them. If a story ends with self-explanation, and some do, you can be sure it's a misdirection. Go back, it will imply, re-read me again, against myself. I can't be that obvious, otherwise I'd have been created by a novelist for a novelist's exhausted or lazy or insecure readers.

The reason novels are written as joined-uply as they are is that they help exhausted or lazy or insecure readers along. Forgotten who that character is? I'll re-describe a bit of them, or refer back to the quirk I tagged them with in Chapter 2.

Worried about what happened between the Wednesday evening and the Sunday morning? I'll put in a little filler, just to reassure you the characters didn't cease to exist and have purpose.

Short story readers *never* require remedial paragraphs. Each word is beyond the foregoing.

Many novel readers, on their commute or in bed before lights-out, don't want the faff of restarting their brains every dozen pages.

I sympathize; it's far easier to have the same *dramatis personae* in mind, and a plot that re-energizes itself every dozen pages.

Easier, but not better.

(One thing we rarely consider, when discussing novels and short stories, is how they exist *most of the time* – which is not as they are while being read, but as they are when partially remembered. Perhaps this isn't your experience, but my memories of *War and Peace* don't bulk any more vastly than my memories of 'Lady With a Little Dog'. As many details of the latter have stayed with me, and its atmosphere of exultant melancholy is a value, a mind-presence, as weighty as Tolstoy's panoptic hurly-burly.)

Over the years, we short story writers have trained our readers to expect more of us, so we can expect more of them.

These readers should be celebrated, and praised, and rewarded with work that aspires to their excellence.

And here come the poems, like eagles, to rip our presumptuous guts to bits. Because the writers of poems will already have seen this argument through to its end. The experienced reader of John Donne or Paul Celan is, when compared to the average short story reader, supernatural in their adeptness. They can jump between universes.

If novel = tour guide, short story = acrobat, poem = poltergeist.

The question, now, with these brilliant readers of ours, awaiting – How to get to them?

Right now, we have a bewildering diversification of means. There are webzines, blogs, podcasts, online communities, open mic readings – all of these coming into existence alongside conventional print magazines, anthologies and single-author collections.

Sometimes money is exchanged for a story, though the economy is bizarre. Short story competitions exist for which the winning prize is many times what an average novelist will earn from a novel. But around these are dozens more whose gathered entry fees help finance literary organizations, magazines, university departments.

Articles are written about Alice Munro's Nobel Prize capping the Year of the Short Story.

It's all looking good, isn't it?

In ten years' time, we may think this age golden.

But sales figures.

Most editors at major publishing houses will say (watch their eyes) they *love* short stories, they *wish* (watch their blinking eyes) they could publish more of them, it's just …

The truth is, many of these maligned editors have been publishing them, in disguise. There's an un-named form around, between the short story and the novel – and, no, 'shovel' won't do for it. I have written a couple of them. It's a collection of loosely interlinked short stories. It's a form that is right for our virtualizing society. And I would argue that many of the defining books of the last 20 years have taken this form: Irvine Welsh's *Trainspotting*, David Mitchell's *Ghostwritten*, David Foster Wallace's *Infinite Jest*, Junot Diaz's *The Brief Wondrous Life of Oscar Wao*, Jennifer Egan's *A Visit from the Goon Squad* – I would claim all of these as books of interlinked short stories disguised as novels.

But sales figures.

No, none of these were mega-sellers.

(Give them time.)

Why aren't short stories more popular?

The question was answered earlier, I hope. Because although readers are getting better and better, there aren't *that* many exquisite ones out there. (Poets nod.) Because you can only sell short stories to short story readers. You can't simply expect a novel reader to turn magically into a short story reader. They're out of shape, dammit. They're *knackered*. We need to *train* them. We need to improve their diet. We need to show them that, in this miraculous form, they will have to make double the effort – but, as a reward, they will become more than half the author.

Tension in fiction
Alexander MacLeod

Alexander MacLeod's debut short story collection, *Light Lifting*, was shortlisted for Canada's 2010 Scotiabank Giller Prize and the 2010 Frank O'Connor International Short Story Award. He lives in Dartmouth, Nova Scotia.

If you have ever been attacked by a dog, you know what it's like. The raw fear, the pure pain, and the complete and shocking surprise. Nobody outside of those police trainers you see on TV – the ones whistling their commands and wearing those strange suits of soft protective armour – nobody ever *expects* to be bitten by a dog. Nobody sees it coming, nobody makes a plan. It just happens, a sequence of events unfurls in time. There is the chase: the dog sprinting from around the corner, panting hard, a thick gurgling from deep in its chest, claws ticking on the sidewalk. There is the attack: you trip and it is already there, gums pulled back, an animal driven only by anger and instinct. You see it and you actually feel it: the gaping jaws, the shaking head and the pressure of the teeth, white and perfect, tearing first into the denim of your jeans and then, amazingly, through your skin. A warm wetness leaks into your sock and a sound you do not recognize comes out of your mouth. Then there is the instant aftermath: all the things you do to the dog – with your good leg, your fingers in its eye sockets, the stick – and all the things the dog does to you before the benevolent stranger arrives. All of this is experienced on a purely physical and emotional level. There is no narrator. When you were attacked by the dog, you were not writing a story about being attacked by a dog. The event and its re-telling are two different things.

How does one become the other? Or, more accurately, how does the dog-attack *scene* make it onto the page as a vividly experienced reality? In my writing, I've found that tense short stories – narratives that actually envelop the reader – are built by paying careful attention to the element of timing: specifically, to the question of pacing. Learning how to strategically slow down the most shocking moments in a story allows writers to transform sharp physical sensations into detailed thoughts and reflections.

By shifting speeds, varying sentence lengths, incorporating the right visceral details at the right time, and by working carefully with punctuation, fiction writers, like good poets, can control the rhythm of their lines and actually manipulate the physical experience of reading. In my little canine story, for example – and no, I've never been attacked by a dog – I wanted to try and merge the abstract idea of fear or the experience of being afraid with an almost clinical description of the basic actions that the scene required. Again, in my experience: if a writer can make a reader *feel* raw sensations while simultaneously *thinking* about the broader consequences of those feelings, then that's usually a good sign. Also – and I can tell you this from 'real' first-hand experience – if you ever have to write a mini 500-word essay on tension in fiction, it's lots of fun to start by imagining a mean old dog and then sicking him on your unsuspecting readers.

On the life and afterlife of the short story
Alison MacLeod

Alison MacLeod's most recent novel, *Unexploded*, was longlisted for the 2013 Man Booker Prize. Her previous works include the novels *The Changeling* (1996) and *The Wave Theory of Angels* (2005) and the short story collection *Fifteen Modern Tales of Attraction* (2007).

Oddly perhaps for a short story lover, the moment I enjoy most in a story is the closing line. I read, waiting for the beautiful surge – or bite or kick or flash or hit – of a final image or phrase. A great story ending is a physical sensation. Comma Press publisher Ra Page once said: 'I want every story I read to go snap at the end, so fast it takes the skin off my fingers.' In that final instant, we're surprised – quietly, powerfully, comically or poignantly – by the truth, and *somehow* the story 'lifts' off the flat of the page into the reader's dimension.

The experience of that lift-off is exhilarating. For a moment, there it hovers: Raymond Carver's 'Cathedral' or Helen Dunmore's 'Lilac' or Katherine Mansfield's 'At the Bay'. A world vibrates in the space between the book and the reader's gaze: *that* cathedral, *those* two boys in a kiss by the lilac bush, *that* summer at the Bay. The story, briefly but intensely, outlives the story. It's a flare in the reader's mind. More than any other literary form I know, the short story has a strange, in-the-moment life. Somehow it leaps into *presence*.

James Joyce famously associated a story's revelatory action with 'the epiphanic', that unexpected experience when deity or spirit is somehow made manifest in the physical world. Joseph O'Connor describes the short story as a 'glance at the miraculous'. Writers from Katherine Mansfield to Kevin Barry have described short fiction as a sacred craft. Why? Mansfield, for one, was an atheist. Why was story-writing, in her words, her 'religion'?

A story is arguably bigger than we are. If it's good, it exceeds both its writers and its readers. It 'floats', water-lily-like, on a sense of mystery. It resists complete transparency. In the making of a story, I trust the discipline of short story craft and my writer's instincts, but I also go on blind faith. I follow the story. My job is to rest easy with 'unknowing', and to write onward, trusting in something I sense but can't fully see.

Perhaps, too, the short story summons up notions of the sacred because, as a form, it mirrors our sense of our own mortality. Great stories run inexorably towards their own endings, and it's no coincidence that many of our most enduring stories are, in their various ways, situated at the cusp of life and death. Joyce's 'The Dead', Chekhov's 'Ward 6', Mansfield's 'The Garden Party', Flannery O'Connor's 'A Good Man is Hard to Find' and Carver's 'What We Talk About When We Talk About Love' are just a few vivid examples.

I confess that as a reader I like to know the page-count before I begin a story. I'm not sure why. I suspect a part of me knows that the *passing* of the story is, paradoxically, the privilege of it. The detail of the story is heightened. Its world is charged with the reader's understanding that the vision is fleeting. Brevity, in turn, demands compression. Compression creates intensity. And perhaps intensity is the surfeit of energy that, in the final beats of a story, fuels a leap across realities.

Short stories — 'experimental' shorts
James Miller

James Miller is the author of the acclaimed novel *Lost Boys* (2008) and *Sunshine State* (2010). His short stories have appeared in a range of publications. He is currently senior lecturer in creative writing and English literature at Kingston University.

A short story is, by its very nature, short, so it represents a great opportunity to play with techniques or try out ideas that might not be sustainable in a longer piece. For example, I have recently published short stories that take the form of an argument on social media, a mock academic article complete with satirical footnotes, and a 'remix' story where the majority of sentences were lifted and scrambled from the translation of an avant-garde Argentinian novel and mixed with sentences and a plot of my own, creating an entirely new story that still contained the themes of the original. If dragged out over a longer narrative, such techniques could become contrived or tiresome, but compressed into the intensity of the short form I found they offered bold new ways to present character, channel a voice or approach a subject.

A short story is almost always a distillation of the elements we find in a novel: it intensifies character, location and event; it compresses time and narrative arc. The challenge is to find a form that does justice to these requirements. Linear realism and the sort of omniscient third-person narrator often found in the nineteenth-century novel require too much time, distance and detail to tell a story, demanding a leisurely unfolding of events and destinies across hundreds of pages and tens of thousands of words. Realism depends on a whole world, whereas the contemporary short story is almost always much more partial and fragmented (and, in a sense, closer to our lived experience). It is also mediated by other, currently more dominant discourses (digital media, technology, economics, pop music) and so uses a part to stand for the whole.

Structural or formal innovation is also a constraint, a way of limiting or excluding possibilities, but I have found that these constraints can have their own virtues. They can liberate the language we use from the burden of the 'literary', while also allowing us to acknowledge the way other styles and genres of language determine what we say and how we say it. Problematizing form in this way, by making the story about the problem of telling a story (even if the overt theme is about something quite different), can help us achieve all sorts of creative breakthroughs. For example, when I wrote sections of a short story about climate change called 'What is Left to See' in a form of futuristic 'twitter-speak', I was imposing a number of constraints on myself. I was using neither a proper first- nor third-person point of view, with all the 'action' reduced to a series of tweets between several 'tweeters'. It's obvious that social media has its own expressive resources (not least with # possibilities), particularly in terms of presenting voice and playing with different types of character interaction, as well as allowing for the coining of new slang and abbreviations. So rather than seeing this type of discourse as antithetical to literature, I turned it into literature. Embracing twitter-speak and an American teenage slang of my own invention (but based closely on present trends) allowed me to present the story and the near-future reality in which it was set in a way that was more vivid and immediate, I believe, than a linear, third-person 'realist' narrative would have allowed for. The technique also pushed the maxim of 'show don't tell' almost as far as it can go. The reader starts off disorientated, overwhelmed with the barrage of seemingly impenetrable slang between the characters; then gradually the scene becomes clearer, the twitter-speak developing its own clear logic through repetition and a vivid poetic-technological style suffused with branding, advertisements and self-conscious media-savvy. The technique enabled me to immerse the reader in my new world through the language of that world, showing again that there is 'nothing' outside the text.

So my advice would be to take a risk when writing short stories, to be bold and daring, have fun and try to push form, voice and character into directions that they might not normally go. You may be surprised at the results!

Other countries
Alison Moore

Alison Moore is the author of a short story collection, *The Pre-War House and Other Stories*, and two novels, *The Lighthouse* (winner of the McKittrick prize 2013 and shortlisted for the Man Booker Prize 2012), and *He Wants*. She lives in a village near Nottingham.

A few of my stories are set in foreign countries. 'Monsoon Puddles'* makes use of a diary I kept, details I noted down, during a trip to India: 'The train journey from Bombay to Surat takes about six hours. I sit on a hard bench, writing notes. Beside me is an Indian man who reads over my shoulder and stops me every now and again to correct my spelling of the names of the places we pass through. Beside him sits his mother who peels small oranges and includes me when she shares out the segments.' There is an element of autobiography in this story – it is fiction strengthened by first-hand experience.

I have another story, though, that takes place in a foreign country to which I have never been. In 'When the Door Closed, It Was Dark'**, the location is unnamed, but intended to be recognizable as an eastern European country; and I know that it is further east than the former Yugoslavia which is the furthest east I have been within mainland Europe, discounting airports. My unfamiliarity with the language and culture of this part of the world matches that of Tina, my au pair protagonist. I know that there are countries in eastern Europe that advertise online for British au pairs. However, having established this level of theoretical veracity, by keeping the location anonymous I could pick and choose the details of the physical setting and the cultural habits of my characters. The zigzag iron staircase which Tina has to climb to reach the top apartment is taken from a holiday in the Lake District. It rained all week, which meant that I was carrying a baby up and down several flights of wet metal steps, as Tina does. The pig fat Tina is given to eat ('Eat it') is something that my vegetarian husband was presented with in Ukraine. The taking of Tina's passport 'into safe keeping' is something that happened to my aunt when she was an au pair in Nassau.

There are benefits to putting my fictional characters into settings I know, sending them to places I've been to myself – I can be sure I've got the details right, especially if I've kept notes. But it is also highly satisfying to make a fictional place seem just as real. I know the country to which I sent Tina does not quite exist – I cannot unequivocally state its name or point decisively to it on a map – and yet I believe in it, as if it exists in a sliver of space between the borders of two very real countries, as if I could fly there, as if I could take a taxi from the airport and be delivered to a 'bruise-coloured and blistered' block of flats with a zigzag metal staircase up the side. I would keep my passport close, though.

* Published in *Quality Women's Fiction* in 2004.
** Published as a Nightjar Press chapbook in 2010 and reprinted in *Best British Short Stories 2011*.

The experimental short story or experimenting with the short story
Ryan O'Neill

Ryan O'Neill was born in Scotland in 1975. He worked as an English teacher in Rwanda, Lithuania and China, before finally settling in Australia. He is the author of three short story collections: *The Weight of a Human Heart*, which was shortlisted for the 2012 Queensland Premier's Literary Awards, *Six Tenses*, and *A Famine in Newcastle*. He lives in Newcastle, New South Wales and teaches at the University of Newcastle.

The British novelist and short story writer B. S. Johnson resented his work being described as experimental because, as he once explained, 'experimental' to most reviewers is almost always a synonym for 'unsuccessful'. Like all literary terms, from poetry to postmodernism, there are many ways to define the 'experimental' short story, but the simplest and, I think, the most useful is that it is a short story that attempts something new, whether in form, content or style. Of course, trying something new means being aware of the old, that is, the stories that have come before. What is considered experimental depends on what is considered conventional. A conventional short story is a realist one; it acknowledges an objective reality, tells a plot with a beginning, middle and end in which effect follows cause, has characters that act as real people might be considered to act, and reflects the writer's concern to make themselves invisible to the reader. An experimental short story, on the other hand, uncovers, abandons or destroys these conventions.

In experimental short fiction, old and new forms are adapted, or adopted, to tell stories. A short story can be an essay, a series of PowerPoint slides, tweets, a lecture, a letter to the parking bureau, or an index to a book that doesn't exist. A short story can be *anything*. In experimental short stories, rather than pretending that the characters in the story exist and the writer doesn't, the role of the writer is exposed and celebrated, and the artificiality of the characters is laid bare. Instead of the usual lines of sentences and blocks of paragraphs, typography explodes across the page. Why should a story have only one beginning and one ending? It can have several of both. In fact, why not let the reader write the ending?

In talking about experimental fiction, it is easy to fall into the trap of sounding too sombre. Even the term 'experimental' suggests seriousness; an antiseptic, bloodless, intellectual exercise. Some readers (and writers) still equate 'experimental' with pretentious (or 'unsuccessful', as Johnson complained), and it is true that there are experimental short stories that are affected, showy and hollow, just as there are conventional short stories that are predictable, drab and shallow. But the reason why I read so much experimental short fiction, and write it, is because it is so much *fun*. The best experimental short stories are hilarious, inventive, moving, surprising, confronting. Think, for a moment, about how many stories you have read about the break-up of a relationship. Dozens, at least. Perhaps even hundreds. Now imagine the break-up story told in a very different way; through graphs and charts, or lists, or perhaps the writer of the story losing control of it halfway through, so that the ending changes. The oldest, most threadbare plots and worn-out situations can be reinvigorated by an experimental approach.

The short story is the perfect laboratory for experimentation. Sometimes, perhaps even often, the experiment fails and all that's left is a mess of words to clean up. But, with perseverance, and a bit of luck, an experiment succeeds, and something new and strange and wonderful is created.

On short stories
Edith Pearlman

Edith Pearlman has published more than 250 works of short fiction and short non-fiction in national magazines, literary journals, anthologies and on-line publications, and won the 2011 PEN/Malamud award for short fiction. She is the author of four short story collections: *Vaquita, Love Among The Greats, How To Fall*, and *Binocular Vision: New and Selected Stories*, which won the National Book Critics Circle Award in the US. She lives in Brookline, Massachusetts.

I do short stories only. I've found the form's brevity usually requires few characters, few incidents, one theme, one crucial scene. In her headlong trip from beginning to end, carrying the reader with her, she hopes, the short story writer can dispense with things a novelist must include – motivation, say. She can make short work of setting – all she has to do is select a few essential details. (It can take a week to find 20 of those details in order to throw out 17.) As for a conclusive ending, a tying-up the loose threads – that's not necessary; it is often inadvisable. Enigmatic is our middle name.

The short story writer has been given special kind of freedom, first seized by the writers of fairy tales and passed on through the ages. She is free to do a Chekhovian vignette, free to do an Updike-like piece of a life, free to restrict her tale to a single afternoon in a New York park, like Grace Paley. Since she wants the story to suggest what is *not* said, she must offer hints, not posted up on the wall as in a declarative sentence, but instead slipped into a dependent clause or mounted on the back of a metaphoric verb or clinging to a noun she has been pursuing since the last equinox. We trust our readers to take these hints. Some of them won't, and reject us. A few of them do, and become our fans.

Setting

Jane Rogers

Jane Rogers is the author of one story collection, *Hitting Trees With Sticks*, whose title story was shortlisted for the 2009 BBC National Short Story Award. She has written eight novels, one of which, *The Testament of Jessie Lamb*, was longlisted for the 2011 Man Booker Prize. She also writes drama for TV and radio, and is a professor of creative writing at Sheffield Hallam University. Jane lives in Banbury.

I find setting is often the way into writing a story. Sometimes the whole story is sparked off by seeing a new place. It might be a different country, or it might just be someone else's house, but the strangeness of it means you look at it with fresh eyes. I once stayed in an empty B&B where abandoned children's toys littered the house and pets stared plaintively from cages, as if the family who lived there had been abducted in the night. Our host told us his wife had just left him and taken the children with her. The ruptured domesticity was shocking, and once I started to write a description, it grew surprisingly easily into the story 'Conception'. Another story that happened like that is 'Birds of American River', where a lagoon, caged birds and free birds on an Australian island provided a setting that was a story.

The eye-opening jolt that comes from a new place is a very satisfactory way into a story. But it is not always available. I was once commissioned to write a story about Alan Turing's theory of Morphogenesis, which I found so hard to grasp that I can still only understand it intermittently. I'd read an excellent biography, but I had no idea how to craft the vague 'sense of a story' that I had in my head into anything on paper. There was an idea there, but I couldn't have said it in words – I knew I would have to find it by writing my way towards it.

I must have made more than a dozen stabs at that story before I found an opening I could work with. It lets us in on Turing as a boy on summer holiday, on a Scottish moor, mapping bees in sunshine. His point of view. Conjuring the world through his senses, one detail at a time. This start, once

I realized it would work, pointed the way to other scenes from his life. The final version of the story takes place in four settings: the sunny moor, the school library, the dormitory at night, and his untidy living room by firelight. The way into the character was through those settings, through building the world he inhabited. Focusing on being exact in the physical description of those settings made a space for the difficult idea to unravel itself, or maybe simply distracted me from the anxiety I was feeling about attempting to write the idea; and once the anxiety was forgotten, and the physical world of the story was in place, the rest of what needed doing became clear. Flannery O'Connor told students: 'The first and most obvious characteristic of fiction is that it deals with reality through what can be seen, heard, smelt, tasted and touched.' I find that focusing on trying to create that reality, that setting, precisely, and leaving the rest of the story to take care of itself, can sometimes be a good way in.

Lost stories
Henrietta Rose-Innes

Henrietta Rose-Innes is a South African writer based in Cape Town. She is the author of a short story collection, _Homing_, and three novels, _Shark's Egg_, _The Rock Alphabet_ and _Nineveh_. Her story 'Sanctuary' won second place in the BBC International Short Story Award in 2012, and she won the South African PEN Literary Award in 2007 and the 2008 Caine Prize for African Writing.

There was that one about the body of a green giant, washed up on a beach. And the one about the blue birds, who made you happy if you stroked their feathers. The brother and sister, wandering through an infinite graveyard. A man, erotically instructed in a train carriage as it crossed a dark plain on a foreign planet, lit by stars ...

These pictures are all from short stories, 30 years old or more. Maybe you read them too; maybe you remember a different set of pictures.

Most of them are science fiction stories, I think, because that was what I was reading age 12, 13, when these images pressed themselves into my receptive brain. Crouched between the shelves in the Cape Town Central Library, lost in the sci-fi compendiums. I don't recall their titles or the names of the authors. Back then I wasn't concerned with provenance, just greedy for raw images.

The pictures remain as bright as postage stamps, steamed free from the letters they came on. I've lost the envelopes, lost the addresses. Lost the letters, too: I don't remember plots, characters, the beginnings or endings of any of those stories. Just: the green giant, the blue birds, the gravestones, the train. And others. Each image has its own particular synaesthetic taste, sharp or bittersweet. Mystery, longing, adventure, a touch of grief.

These lucid moments are, for me, the unique gift of the short story. (The sense memory of a novel is different: less concentrated, a more complex accretion.) And this is what I grope after in my own writing. Each story I have ever written has been an attempt to print a vivid postage stamp and mail it to the reader: the bust of a queen, a national bird ... I'd love to know that some bright image, peeled off one of my stories, has found a place in someone's collection.

It is harder to have that purity of experience now. The sensations don't arrive so cleanly. These days, my reading – and my writing – is more selective, cautious, tangled up in awareness of canon and context. I take note of authors' names. My books are bought not borrowed. If I need to, I can lay my hand on a particular story, I can cross-check. I may never lose a story again – and perhaps I'll never find one again in quite the same way, with that same serendipitous magic.

Over the years I've thought of those stories often. Replayed so frequently, the images become fixed, and no doubt distorted. By now they are probably unrecognizable facsimiles of the original. I've often wanted to track them down. Recently, after a couple of tries, I successfully googled that green giant; I thought he might be one of Ray Bradbury's monsters. Turns out the story was, of course, Ballard's 'The Drowned Giant' – and the giant was never green, but 'pearl-coloured'. I think I'll let the other stories stay lost. I rather like my pictures as they are.

Katherine Mansfield
Elspeth Sandys

Elspeth Sandys lives in New Zealand. She is the author of two collections of short stories, *Best Friends* and *Standing in Line*, which won the 2004 Elena Garro Prize, and eight novels, as well as plays and adaptations for radio.

As a teacher of creative writing, it's always struck me as curious that so many of my students choose to test the waters not with scenes from a drama, or a chapter from a possible novel, but with a fully realized short story, in my view one of the hardest things to pull off. Short stories are not condensed novels, they don't take kindly to plot, nor are they prose poems, though they sometimes come close.

So what are they? And why is it so hard to write a good short story? The answer, I think, lies in what is not said, in what is left out. Which is why the novice writer so often fails in his or her attempt to produce a piece of writing that is 'finished'. Katherine Mansfield, one of the greatest short story writers of all time, wanted her stories to be 'swords pointed at the heart of experience'. Growing up in the same country as KM, I absorbed her stories long before I could understand them. They were as richly satisfying as a novel, perhaps more so, because so much was left to the reader. Her stories are full of unfulfilled longings, of lives glimpsed as if from behind a fluttering lace curtain. In 'The Doll's House' a whole society, with its subtle gradations of class, is conveyed through the eyes of children – the privileged Burnells and the working-class Kelveys. Mansfield makes no judgement about this, but so exquisite is her depiction of the youngest Kelvey's awe at the sight of the doll's house, the reader is left in no doubt as to where her sympathies lie.

I have published two collections of short stories, and I can truthfully say all but one of those stories required numerous rewrites. Some of the rewriting took place months, even years, after the first draft was written. The reason for all this reworking is that, as in poetry, every word has to tell, every image must be shaped and polished till you are satisfied it is doing the work you need it to do – drawing out the emotions, feeding the imagination. Because behind the story you are telling is a much larger story which you can only hint at. In other words, events outside the narrative lie submerged in the text. The only story that came to me all but fully formed was about the death of my father when I was 14, an event which shaped the rest of my life. It seems I had been writing that story in my head for decades, so that when I came to put the words down they were already there, waiting to give life to that experience. But such easy births are rare. Far more common is the struggle to find the right word, the right phrase, the right voice, to conjure up a whole world in a few pages, pointing that sword directly at the 'heart of experience'.

The short story
Olive Senior

Olive Senior is the author of 13 books of poetry, non-fiction and fiction including the short story collections *Summer Lightning*, which won the Commonwealth Writers Prize, *Arrival of the Snake Woman* and *Discerner of Hearts*. She lives in Toronto, Canada and Montego Bay, Jamaica and conducts writing workshops internationally.

If the novel is a string of pearls, as has often been said, then the short story can be considered one perfect pearl. Like an attractive but flawed string of pearls, a flawed novel might even become a best-seller, but it is nearly impossible to get a bad short story published. The literary short story is much more demanding of craft and, I might add, demanding of both writer and reader. As writer you have to get it right from the start or you have no reader. You have to draw the scene, setting and characters in swift strokes and squeeze the action into one single, potent conflict that must be resolved by the end.

But, unlike the novel, resolution does not necessarily mean 'ending'. The story should suggest and tease out potential meanings and possible solutions. And this, I think, is at the heart of the short form. Not the presentation of a world that might take us away from our own, as many novels do, but one that requires a personal engagement on the part of the reader. We might not identify with the character, but we must identify with the dilemma.

The main characteristic of the short story form for me, then, is collaboration between writer and reader. While the sweeping canvas of the conventional novel requires completeness and a satisfying conclusion that ties up loose endings, invoking the spirit of the author as deity, the short story by its very nature proposes a single idea or event for scrutiny, and then offers the reader a share in the decision-making.

This, at any rate, is how I have always conceptualized my stories. I was shaped by an oral culture with a strong storytelling tradition, which implanted in my mind the idea of consensus and collaboration to bring a story to fruition. 'Crick!' goes the storyteller. 'Crack!' the listeners must respond before the storytelling can start. And it is the short story that is closest to the oral tale, giving the listener the freedom to interrupt, comment, reject or applaud as the action unfolds.

However, unlike the oral account, which is allowed to meander, the written form has to cut swiftly to the central conflict with no room for superfluity or indulgence. And this is where it tests the writer's skill. The finished product has to look like a perfect pearl – seamless and inviting, but the reader needs to sense beneath the glistening surface the grit from which it is born, the uncertainties lurking within, and the dangerous dive of its creator to bring this little world to the surface and proffer its gloss as lure.

Judging the BBC National Short Story Award
Di Speirs

Di Speirs is the Editor of Books at BBC Radio and Music Production. She is the founder and one of the judges of the BBC National Short Story Award.

Almost ten years ago when we launched the BBC National Short Story Award, the landscape for the short story was looking bleak. Gone were the many magazines, literary and glossy, which published short stories, few were the collections that made it into print. Young authors were being told, by publishers and on prestigious writing courses, to try to write a novel if they possibly could, and there was a general level of despair about the state of an endangered literary species.

What a difference a decade makes. How that landscape has changed. There is now a plethora of high-value and publicity-attracting prizes. Indeed I am sometimes asked if I mind that the BBC Award, with its £15,000 for the winner, has been trumped financially by rivals, but I don't. For one thing, it's still a significant sum, and the exposure all five shortlisted authors are offered is of enormous value. As importantly, the point was to help revitalize the story and get writers writing. The eruption of prizes and the celebration of short stories in all their forms mean that writers can look seriously again at what short form fiction can do. How wonderful.

Judging the BBC Award each year, I have learnt an enormous amount about both the craft and the power of the short story. I've been impressed by the writers who take risks as much with what they leave out as what they say – writers like Kate Clanchy, Sarah Hall or Lavinia Greenlaw, who understand the art of economy and trust that the reader will have sufficient confidence to travel with them. I've seen the value of plot, and that plot alone is not enough. I've understood that the best stories are honed and reworked, edited to their hard-won perfection. I remain amazed at the numbers of entries that come in with errors, from plot points to typos and simply 'sloppy' writing; and I've become increasingly aware of stories that go through the pre-planned motions adroitly enough but fail to reach a truth – or often a decent conclusion! I know how hard it is to pull off.

I've also learnt that every judging panel is different – an obvious point, but the truth is that however far we go in analysing exactly what works and where a story falters, there is also an element of subjective response that differs from one individual to another. And so I can't offer a formula for a successful story now, any more than I could a decade ago.

However, I do see what judges respond to year after year. A whole world captured in a moment, a sense of a life lived before and continuing after, economic prose or lyrical exploration – but never an extraneous word or superfluous subplot; a voice or a perspective that resonates long after reading, a moment of drama or quiet which illuminates a wider truth.

The great Irish short story writer Bernard MacLaverty recently compared the novel to a pint supped convivially in the pub with friends, while the short story was a dram, savoured quietly and intensely. Like the best whiskey, great stories stand the test of time and call you back for another shot. So, to all short story writers and readers, Sláinte and Happy Reading!

Tips and tales
Adam Thorpe

Adam Thorpe was born in Paris in 1956 and started his professional career as a mime artist. He is the author of two collections of stories – *Shifts* and *Is This The Way You Said?* – ten novels and six books of poetry, a stage play performed almost entirely in Berkshire dialect, and numerous radio plays and broadcasts, including two BBC documentaries. In 2007 he was shortlisted for prizes in three genres: the Forward Poetry Prize, the BBC National Short Story Award and the South Bank Show Award for the year's best novel. Adam currently lives in France.

BEGINNING

I loved English composition at school: a few decades back, this meant writing stories, and that was it. It was all I was any good at. One day when I was about nine, we had to describe a pirate attack. I laboured over my first paragraph for ages, trying to reproduce in words what I could see vividly in my head. I handed it to nice Mr Webb, somewhat sheepishly: the others had written around two pages to my five lines. It came back a few days later: I had to write *I must write more* a hundred times.

Now I tend to write too much, but I remain grateful to Mr Webb for unblocking me. I was snarled up in my own sense of imperfection. How did James Joyce put it, when a friend was stuck? 'In the writing the good things will come.'

So when I want to start a story, assuming I have no idea what it's about (which isn't always the case), I write down the first phrase that comes into my head. It might be a snatch of dialogue. I'll do it now.

'Ted says the lawn mower's snarled up in wet grass', Elaine shouted from the living room.

I have a number of healthy challenges with this one: place, character (there are more than two), tone, weather, and so on. The fun is unravelling it, taking the imagination for a walk (no, it takes you).

If no phrase pops up, or you keep censoring it as not good enough or, fatally, as too dull (really unforgivable – glad your life is so exciting), then open a thick dictionary at random and plonk your finger down on the page, without looking. Imagine a little circle drawn around your fingertip, like a ripple: use any word in that circle (two or three, at most). I'll do that now, too.

trans-Siberian

Incredible, almost like the *I-Ching*: I've recently returned from a 21-hour train trip, Moscow to Perm, on the trans-Siberian route. Well well. Let's add another word in our opening sentence, using the same method.

Lyre

Youch. OK, here goes:

He never thought it would be easy, looking after his lyre on the trans-Siberian railway in peak season.

There you have it: someone with a problem (good), an exotic setting, an extended metaphor (train journey), and a puzzle: what's he doing with a lyre? Of course, it's Apollo. Or someone who thinks he is. Maybe his dog's called Hermes. And maybe the friendly uniformed female attendant looking after the carriage is called Daphne. Or maybe he's just a geeky music student called Neil setting out to busk in Vladivostok, but the lovely Olga will distract him on the way. Or maybe the lyre gets stolen and he chases it and ends up stranded in a woebegone village on the steppe straight out of *Dr Zhivago*.

There's no excuse for being stuck. It's all out there, and in there too. It's only you looking over your own shoulder, after all. Forget that burning issue you want to address and go for the wild card.

A paranoid vision
David Vann

David Vann is the author of the short story collection *Legend of a Suicide*, winner of 11 prizes; three novels, *Goat Mountain*, *Dirt* and *Caribou Island*; and two books of non-fiction, *Last Day On Earth*, and *A Mile Down*. Born in Alaska, he teaches at the University of Warwick, England, and is honorary professor at the University of Franche-Comté in France.

The short story is a paranoid world. In 'Signs and Symbols' by Vladimir Nabokov, the boy has 'referential mania'. He believes that everything in the world refers to him. Even the clouds are speaking about him. This story is metafiction (a story about fiction and how it works), and Nabokov is showing us that in fiction, everything relates to the protagonist. So that's the first rule of a short story (though of course there are really no rules):

1 There's no room in a short story for anything which is not referring in some way to the protagonist and, more specifically, to the problem that the protagonist has.

   Every protagonist has a problem. Without this problem, there is no story, and in the best stories, the protagonist is deeply divided by the problem. Julian, for instance, in Flannery O'Connor's 'Everything That Rises Must Converge', can never speak of the old family mansion (or the Old South) without contempt, nor think of it without longing. This interior divide drives his exterior conflict with his mother and creates everything that happens in the story. So here we can see several more rules for the short story:

2 Every protagonist has a problem.

3 This problem divides the protagonist, who is conflicted and ambivalent.

4 The protagonist fights about this problem with someone else, who is the antagonist.

5 What happens in a story is a result of this fight (not determined by outside factors, such as the author's ideas about cool plots).

The antagonist is a mirror of the protagonist. He or she has the same problem, in other words, but manifested differently, often oppositely. Julian's mother, for instance, is constantly reminding herself, Julian and us that she's a 'Godhigh' and hasn't really fallen. She pretends they still have that old family mansion, in other words, and by extension that they still have the Old South and still are a kind of aristocracy, despite their current 'reduced circumstances'. This denial drives Julian into a rage because he so desperately wants the old mansion, though he's unable to admit this and speaks of it, and her, only with contempt.

6 The antagonist has the same problem as the protagonist, expressed in a way which antagonizes the protagonist.

7 The antagonist is not a stranger. The antagonist is close to the protagonist, and the two usually love each other. They often even want the best for each other.

The fight between the protagonist and antagonist never ends well, at least in tragedy. This is called the crisis. But things come to a head gradually, often with the use of other people, who act as pawns. The protagonist and antagonist can also fight over physical objects, which become charged with significance because of this fight, and these are called symbols. In the O'Connor story, a large black woman on the bus is wearing the same hat that Julian's mother can barely afford. And when Julian's mother tries to condescend to this woman by giving her cute little black boy a penny, she knocks Julian's mother to the ground.

8 The protagonist and antagonist, like angry gods, use the people and things of the world as weapons in their battle. These are the minor characters and symbols.

9 This fight has at least a few rounds before we can get to the crisis (in the O'Connor story, there's a black man on the bus Julian tries to befriend, for instance, and a white woman who makes comments, and Julian and his mother spar using several objects of clothing, including gloves and a tie as well as the hat).

Once Julian's mother is knocked to the ground, Julian has won. But actually, he's lost everything. As he loses her, he calls her 'Momma, sweetheart, dearest', in contrast to all the nasty stuff he's called her earlier.

10 The protagonist can never win the fight in a short story. As in Greek tragedy, no choice comes without a price.

Julian, deprived of his mother, must now enter the adult world.

11 A short story changes the protagonist's life forever. She or he can no longer be quite the same. His or her life before the story represented a kind of stasis, and the story details the change.

12 The very end, called the denouement, gives us some sense of how the protagonist will go on into the rest of her/his life (if he/she lives).

This ending is really about vision (how the protagonist views herself/himself, the antagonist, and the world, and how that has shifted throughout the story). We write short stories for this shift in vision, for a clearer view.

Absence
Clare Wigfall

Clare Wigfall won the inaugural BBC National Short Story Award in 2008. She is the author of the short story collection *The Loudest Sound and Nothing*. Born in London, she now lives in Berlin.

Absence is definitely a quality that characterizes my stories, and certainly there are several of them that rely on the narrative being sustained by what is unsaid, by what lies beneath, between the lines of the story. But then I think that absence is in itself a quality that the short story form invites. Within the space of only a few pages, a short story must create a world, a mood, a plot, wholly real characters, as well as exploring life and its complexities. Economy is therefore an absolute necessity and presents a very specific challenge to the writing. And of course what you leave out becomes as important as what you leave in.

For me, there's something almost beautifully mathematical and precise about this, and I suppose that perhaps it's the reason why people say writing a short story is more difficult than writing a novel. I feel in a way that your safety net is taken away, because when you write a short story you're relying on an unknown quantity: your reader. With a novel you have the space to fill in all the gaps; with a short story you're forced to leave these for your reader to complete and you have to be able to trust in their intelligence and engagement. I believe, though, that this is why the very best short stories can haunt you long after you've read the concluding line, because so much of the experience is not just about the words on the page, but is individual to you and the way your own brain interprets and digests what you've read. There's something magical about that.

Getting the balance perfectly right, though, can be very difficult, because you want to create something that will invite a personal interpretation from the reader, but won't be so obscure or unsatisfying as to alienate them. When it works, I believe it can make the story more powerful. My story 'Night After Night', for example, is narrated by a woman whose husband has committed a horrific crime, but I deliberately chose not to name that crime. Leaving it absent allows the reader to fill the gap with whatever might be for them, personally, the worst crime they can imagine, and I think that this lends the story more force, allowing it to touch a nerve.

To be honest, though, learning to utilize absence was only something I came to recognize the power of through practice and experimentation. And often it only comes in the editing. It might be that for your own understanding of the story you need all the information there on the page when you begin, and only then can you identify what you might be able to withhold from your reader.

I can give you a concrete example of this from my own experience. In 'Free', the story pivots on the answer to an uncomfortable question that one character asks the other. In the first draft of the story (a draft that only one other person besides myself has ever read), the answer was there in the story. In the final draft, I chose to cut it:

After a minute she turned finally and stared straight at him with her strange sand-coloured eyes. 'What was the worst thing she ever did to you?' He frowned, taken off guard by the question. 'Your mother,' she continued, 'what was the worst thing?'

He shook his head to the side then looked back to her with a sort of laugh. 'That's not a thing to ask a stranger.'

She shrugged but didn't smile.

He stared at her for a moment, then sighed slightly and sat back in his seat. His hand reached to unhook the swatter from the wall, but he held it limply in his lap. Only after a few moments did he tell her, quietly without turning her way.

'Why was that the worst thing?' she said eventually.

'I don't know,' he said, shaking his head with a slight laugh. 'I don't know why I even said it. I never told anyone about that before.'

'Did she look happy?' she said quietly.

'She looked ...' he said, then paused, 'she looked free.'

When I was reworking the story, I realized that leaving the answer absent would create an intimacy between the two characters that we weren't privy to, and in turn would force the reader to ask questions. What was it that the mother had done? Why does the woman ask if she looked happy? Why does the man consider this the worst thing and why might he have shared this information with a stranger when he's never told anyone else about it before? Why would the woman be asking this question of a stranger in the first place?

In the answer to these questions lies the story. But had I published the first draft, with the man's answer there for all to see, it's likely that as a piece of writing it would have fallen flat. There would have been little room for personal engagement from the reader, little chance that they would have cared enough to be even asking those questions. As a writer, you also always hope that your work will cause the reader to somehow reflect on their own life. I'd hope that some readers of that story, after pondering what it was that the man's mother might have done to him, might even be compelled to turn the question on themselves. What was the worst thing your mother ever did to you?

Part 3

A note on craft and critique: writing is not a democracy

Tania

I don't like the word 'craft'. It makes me think of Arts & Crafts, of basket-weaving or crochet, which is all very well, but for me it doesn't fit with the notion of writing short stories. If you haven't heard the word, there's a load of jargon that comes along with writing workshops, and 'craft' is a major part of the vocab. It refers to the different technical aspects of a story: character, voice, point of view (first person, second person, third person, singular, plural), tense (past, present, future), dialogue, structure, etc. ... It is common in workshops and books on writing to separate these out, to say, 'Let's look at point of view'. And it is a very useful exercise to see what another writer has done, the choice she's made, for example, to have it told by the boy's best friend, rather than the boy, or to tell it in the present tense rather than the past.

But for me this is something that comes after the fact, after the writing. As Ron Carlson says in *Ron Carlson Writes a Story*, 'Taking all these craft considerations separate from story is artificial ... Rarely does a writer sit up straighter in her chair, shake her hands above the keyboard while she says, "Now the dialogue!" and dive back into her story.'

But – a second but – these things are vital and, as you can see from my section in Part 1 on the evolution of my story 'Under the Tree', when a story isn't working, it may be that changing any one or more of these aspects will get you to the story you want to write. Nothing is sacred; everything is up for grabs; everything is changeable.

TOP TIP

Nothing is sacred; everything is up for grabs; everything is changeable.

However, it may be that you end up with the same tense and point of view you started with, after trying a load of other things, or it may be that you hit on the right elements in your first draft. There are no rules here, and there are definitely no quick fixes. These are suggestions of things to be aware of, questions to ask yourself if you are not happy with your own story yet. It's all about the story you want to tell in the way you want to tell it. As I saw over and over again in writing workshops I was taking part in, there's always someone who says, Why don't you do it this way? because if it was their story they'd tell it from the point of view of the wife's first cousin, who only gets a brief mention in your story, or they'd start the whole thing 20 years earlier, when the kid was born. But it's your story. Even the teacher or whoever is running the workshop might be wrong. As Israeli short story writer Etgar Keret said in an interview with *The New Yorker* about running writing classes: 'I have to admit that talking authoritatively about my students' stories can make me feel, at times, like an astronaut who has just landed on a new planet and insists on giving guided tours to its inhabitants.'

This reminds me of a question someone asked me at a reading focused around one of my earliest flash stories, 'Plaits', about a married couple, told from the wife's point of view. The questioner asked why I didn't give the husband's side, and I said it's because it had never crossed my mind. That wasn't the story I wanted to/was compelled to tell, but I told him he was welcome to go off and write that himself! Maybe he did.

So, this is all by way of introduction to our practical sections in which we are taking elements separately just to give some attention to each one. But everything is connected. Also, Courttia and I have intentionally duplicated several sections here because we wanted you to have at least two opinions, if not more (you have our wonderful guest authors' thoughts too). We sometimes disagree. That doesn't mean one of us is wrong. That means we've each found our own way, and Part 3 is here to help you find yours.

Further reading

Carlson, Ron *Ron Carlson Writes a Story* (Greywolf Press, 2007).

Hershman, Tania, 'Plaits', *The White Road and Other Stories* (Salt Publishing, 2008).

From beginning to end

Courttia

One of the most common complaints I hear when I teach creative writing is: 'I want to write, but I don't have a story.' This is sometimes swiftly followed by: 'I don't know where to begin.' For the first statement, there are only two answers, or reasons. One, you haven't thought about it for long enough. You haven't allowed yourself the time and space to let the story develop inside you. You haven't devoted enough time, or done the necessary work in order to grow your idea from that precious kernel, the urge, into something more tangible, something that has flesh and bones. The second answer or reason is far more brutal. I hesitate to say it even now, because a part of me simply refuses to believe it's possible. It might, just might be that you are not a writer. I don't say this to be harsh. I might want to put up shelves, or go out into my garden and plant tomatoes. Unless the talent has evaded me until now, no matter how good my efforts in each area might be, I will never be a skilled carpenter or a gardener. My creativity (and I do believe very much that these are creative endeavours) just doesn't stretch in that direction. I have to accept that, as much as it pains me – and probably my wife too. Although I do believe we all have stories within us, and some of us might even be quite skilful verbal raconteurs, it doesn't always follow that this necessarily means you can put pen to paper, or even fingers to keys, and turn what you have in your head into a story.

Only you can find that out. Prove me wrong. I sincerely hope you do. We can always use another good storyteller. So if you're in the first camp, those who haven't been struck by the desperate urge to say something, but want more than anything to write, there are a few things you can do that can help free up your imagination.

I've alluded to some of those methods of generating ideas in Reflections One, but let me be clearer; I believe the best stories come from *you*; your lives, loves and wants. They come from the things that interest you, that make you feel things passionately. They are your deepest, darkest fears, your secrets, things that make your skin crawl. They are your desires, cravings, lusts and needs, which are vastly different from wants. They are the places you've been, the people you've known, your mundane thoughts and observations. They are the very things that make you, you. If writing stories is about the articulation of what it means to be human, then it naturally follows that the human beings we know most about are ourselves. So like Joyce when he wrote *Dubliners*, or Carver writing 'What We Talk About When We Talk About Love', a dissection of ourselves, a literary turn from inside to out, is paramount to writing fiction. This is because fiction is actually a deep form of self-analysis – it infuriates me when I hear people say 'this is creative writing, not therapy' – because writing *should* make you, the author and afterwards the reader, feel good. Anything that makes you feel good can be deemed as therapeutic. Therefore, the best fiction serves two aims: to work as a coherent piece of art, and make you feel better, or at least more aware about yourself. Sigmund Freud, known to be an avid reader and writer of prose, is quoted by the critic Lionel Trilling as saying: 'The poets and philosophers before me discovered the unconscious. What I discovered was the scientific method by which the unconscious can be studied' (Trilling, 1971). Even a deeply imaginative writer like J. R. R. Tolkien couldn't help but analyse his own life while writing *Lord of the Rings*; not only are the landscape of The Shires and that of the Lancashire countryside where he stayed during the 1940s almost identical, but some locations and characters are said to be inspired by his Birmingham upbringing, such as the name 'Underhill'. His great work, the second-bestselling novel ever written, was also heavily influenced by what Tolkien had seen during his military service in World War I. He even fought at the Battle of the Somme, where post-traumatic stress was first diagnosed as 'shell-shock'.

This doesn't mean you should write identikit copies of yourself. I'm suggesting that as an artist, you can give yourself permission to delve into your own psyche and uncover the things that make you tick, even if those things may be deep inside you, never uncovered or admitted even to yourself. The most interesting things about you could be the parts that nobody else knows.

A very important part of being a writer when we come to this point is to tell ourselves there must be *no censorship*. You cannot allow yourself to be stifled by the internal voice. We all have one – and unfortunately for most writers they do not go away. I can see mine even now; heavily influenced by the Warner Bros cartoons I watched as a child, they burst into existence from a cloud of ether and dust, one perched on each of my shoulders. The figure on my right has a pitchfork and red toga – in fact, he is red all over – and devil's horns. The figure on my left wears an all-white toga and holds a harp. This one has a glowing gold halo and large wings. Unnervingly, they are both me. The Devil jabs me with his pitchfork, saying that I'm fooling no one. I'll never be a real writer, I'm doomed to failure and obscurity. The Angel strums its harp, singing of success, and the notoriety I'll achieve if I can just get to the end. That's all I have to do; get to the end. Freud would have had a field day.

Whatever form your inner critic takes, even if it's not as animated as mine (or heaven forbid, even more so), the important thing is to grow practised in the art of tuning them out. Both can be dangerous if listened to unreservedly, for different reasons. If overly heeded, the Devil will grant you the deadly gift of writer's block. The Angel, the gift of ego. When you can tune both out and fall into the world of the story, the rest will take care of itself. The more you accomplish on the page, the quieter those voices will get. I promise that. You need not drown them out entirely. What you're looking for is a perfect equilibrium between both parties. Soon you'll hardly hear them at all unless you really need them. I tend to use the Angel's generosity most when I'm at the ideas stage, or hammering out a first draft. I listen to the Devil's harsh critique when I'm at editing stage, or if I'm writing story outlines.

IDEAS FROM OBSESSIONS

Ideas usually stem from some form of obsession for:

- A theme
- A genre

- An archetype
- A region
- A class of people or community
- A place of work
- Anything at all

EXERCISE

Describe yourself in the third person, no more than 500 words minimum, or however much you can write in 15 minutes. No rules, other than the stipulation of perspective.

Who are you? What's your family history? Where you have been in life? Whom you have loved? Where you are going?

Write in any manner you choose. Abstract, realist, delving into your past, using a scene that you feel illustrates a particular characteristic. Write without stopping to think about it.

Now write about someone or something that you love. Use the same amount of words, or time. Try to concentrate of the details of the person or thing, without spending much time telling us what it is.

Afterwards, look at the piece of work and underline anything that strikes you as interesting, whether it's a word or turn of phrase, an image or line of dialogue. Anything.

Keep the work, put it away for two weeks, then take it out and look at it again. Mark what jumps out at you once more. Are there any themes that resonate? Do the original lines you marked still work? What would you change? What images immediately spring to mind?

Of course, this is pretty simple. Anyone can do it. But if you can write uncon-sciously in this way, even if you are well practised, you can almost always uncover something new that might give a fresh insight to some untapped realm of your psyche. If you're lucky, it might even lead to an idea.

Mining memory

Writing these things, which I've heard described as 'small documents', are often a prelude to the real story. Again, if you already have a real story then you don't need this. I would go off and write. But if you don't, or you'd like to uncover something new, then it's good to do these exercises. They can help to find things about the story you didn't know, especially if you write from the point of view of your protagonist. Ask them to describe themselves in the third person. What do they love? If they can't answer that, and they love nothing, then what do they hate? Write from the point of view of the character and you might be surprised by the results. They might be seeds of bigger ideas hidden in sentences. Viewed in this way exercises can work as tiny blueprints that might form the basis for larger works. Uncompleted line sketches, if you will. They are especially good for formulating short stories.

EXERCISE

This exercise is particularly good for tutors in a workshop setting:

Ask the class to write about a location that meant a great deal to them when they were eight years old. They must write in present tense and use all the senses to make the piece come alive, and feel as real as it did then.

After they have shared their work, ask the group to partner up with the person to their left and pen another short piece, using *their partner's* location in any way

---

they like. So they can use the actual location itself, or use it as a jumping off point to write about a similar location, prompted by their partner's writing. Read the results.

It's important even for writers who consider themselves to be practised or established not to turn their noses up at exercises. As the ancient hunter-gatherers no doubt used to say millennia ago, 'You never know'. Of course, what often takes the place of exercises once you have got into a pattern of writing regularly, is reading. A good passage or story might stimulate you to think of another way to do some semblance of the same thing, or to go somewhere else entirely. Or an idea might come from the world beyond our doors. I do think that a vital part of the process, however it happens, is to find a place to be still.

Finding the voice

- Contemplate. Allow the voice of the character, or the world, or the story, or the theme to drown out your own.

- Who knows what will happen? Certainly not you. It may be too early for that.

- Begin with the idea of *what would you like to say?* Will it be tragic or redemptive? A single moment of time without any structural middle or end, or a deeply resonate point of clarity? Are you speaking of Love, Religion, Man's Inhumanity to Man, the Environment, or Race, or Bullying, or the Fear of Dark Places, or Misunderstanding? Try to work out know what you want to the story to do on a basic human level.

In *Creative Writing: A Practical Guide,* Julia Casterton has some great advice for writers at this stage. She says: 'What do you want your hero or heroine to come back with? Empty your mind and consider this. Breathe deeply again for over five minutes and allow the story to begin to come to you. Remember it only needs to come a little at a time. You don't need to know the whole thing. Indeed, it may be better if you don't, because then you too, like your reader, can be open to the wonder of the story as it unfolds' (Casterton, 2005a).

Plotting with holes

- Don't worry about the places that are unseen. If you answer all the questions then there will be no surprises, and your story may feel leaden and dull.
- Sometimes a beginning is all you need. Once you have an idea of who the character is, where they are in the world you've created and who is or is not around them, you might be able to see the first image, or scene.
- You can often start with a phrase. Write the words down, wait to see what the character or narrator says beyond those first utterings.
- Don't be afraid of the dark, or the unknown.

Casterton advises us to sit at our desks, even if we have no thoughts about where to go next. Because I'm a bit of a foodie I tend to call this, or any other point where you sit and wait, *marinating*. She tells us: 'Soon an image or phrase will come to you' (Casterton, 2005b). This image should be based at as point in the story where the plot is already in progress. A moment of action, or forward momentum. It should occur at the point of an inciting incident, or just after.

Write what you see

EXERCISE

Write a scene, or a story, told only in images. You should still be writing about people, but concentrate on what they do rather than what they think and say. Zoom in on the details of their actions, and the objects around them, think most about why the things we don't hear might cause them to act the way they do.

WHEN TO USE TELLING DETAILS AND WHEN NOT

● *At this point, at the beginning of your story, you should rely on pure showing.*

● *Omit as many overtly 'telling' details as possible – time, location, a description of character's personality or physicality to name a few, to go for something which conveys the information indirectly.*

● *Try to create a sense of intrigue for my reader. Be ambiguous, vague. Make the reader ask 'why?' What's going on? Hopefully these details will urge them to want to know more, and read on.*

● *This can be gone about in a variety of ways, and of course, you can use time, location, or a description of character to achieve this effect, providing you do this in a compelling way.*

● *Confusing? Yes it is. Basically, whatever you choose to write, especially in a short story, should create a question in the readers' minds. Not confuse them – that's something else. But give them a glimpse of an interesting subject without telling them what the subject is, where it's going and why it might interest you. That can all come later down the line. Or not.*

EXERCISE

Take control of your character by giving them a series of imperative commands; do this, do that, go here and there. Try to place them in situation of intense emotion; anger, sadness, lust, joy, etc. As always, concentrate on the mundane details of the situation. Write in the second person. This story or scene can be used to describe something you have already written. Experiment with the movement of time using this device.

My favourite story opening comes from Walter Moseley's *Gone Fishin'*. It's the first in Moseley's series of Eazy Rawlins crime fiction novels, claimed by ex-president Bill Clinton as his favourite read. The fact that it was about Eazy

Rawlins already made it pretty intriguing for me, as I'd devoured at least six of the titles over the course of five years. But when I read that first line, more than any of the others, I was immediately hooked. The line was: 'Mouse had changed.' And I was dumbstruck. Incredulous. I must have read it at least three times over. I couldn't believe a simple three words could contain such power. If you didn't know who Mouse was, you'd want to know more. If you knew who Mouse was, you'd be *dying* to know more. The sentence had all the brevity of a short story opening, all the unspoken questions that would make a reader want to read on. You almost can't help but go on to the next sentence.

TOP TIP

The story must strike a nerve – in me. My heart should start pounding when I hear the first line in my head. I start trembling at the risk.

Susan Sontag (As Consciousness Is Harnessed to Flesh:
Journals and Notebooks, *1964–80)*

Let's compare Mosley's line with this one: 'On the island of Crete there lived a Minotaur, a ferocious creature that was half man and half bull.' Now this is classic storytelling stuff that instantly makes me want to read on. The story of Daedalus and Icarus is one of the original surviving short stories of antiquity; I'm not about to suggest that it doesn't work – even the fact that I'm using an example that possibly dates as far back as 1,300 years before the birth of Jesus Christ is a testimony to its longevity. But in these modern times, the majority of that first line would be considered telling; mostly information, very little action. Consider the line that follows: 'The people of the island of Crete were terrified of the Minotaur; it loved nothing more than to eat human flesh.' This is far more compelling for me, and closer to the innovations that have taken place since the Ancient Greeks. Humans have arguably become more practised at paring our stories down so that today, if an author was to attempt to rewrite Daedalus and Icarus, they might say: 'The Minotaur loved human flesh.' Pretty obviously this tale is themed around hubris and failed ambition, but we begin far away from Icarus and his father, the sun and the glittering sea, to focus on the villain of the piece, a stark and memorable image of a monster that consumes human meat.

Endings

- Try to see the final image, almost like a portrait of a landscape picture, a freeze-framed Moment in Time that captures the mood of what you want to say. A 'projected ending'.

- Don't worry if it's vague, a little blurry. It might end up in the finished piece, or might not.

- Endings can sometimes come from theme – if you were to use academic language to describe your short story, the opening is an indirect abstract constructed of what you are attempting to say in relation to your theme, and the ending is your conclusion.

- Think about: what would you like to leave the reader with? What are you saying about people and their response to the point you are raising about the human condition? In Casterton's terms, what does your hero or heroine 'come back' with?

- Sometimes you just don't know exactly what you mean until you get there, which is why it's always good to get started even if you have no concrete ideas, to see where the characters take you.

- You can change your story at any time. Even when you've completed the final draft, when you think it's done and dusted, you will always have the opportunity to rewrite. Samuel Beckett is reputed to have written up to four versions of his short stories for differing publications, in English and French.

- When you've decided what will happen, try to 'seed' the plot, or 'lay bread-crumbs': important bits of action, dialogue or memory that trace a subtle line between where the characters start and where they end up. Be gentle with this!

- Remember nothing is set in stone.

How does viewpoint work?

Another of my stories, 'Beach Boy' from my collection *A Book of Blues*, had an extremely pessimistic ending at first draft, where a young British poet visits Lamu Island, Kenya, and is hounded to a death by drowning by some locals who have been antagonistic towards him during his entire stay. When my wife, who was with me on our actual trip to Lamu, a Canadian we'd met in our hostel, and another writer friend all read it, they were fine with the story, although a little disturbed by my ending. I tried to explain that I'd written it because I felt my protagonist's ignorance about the inhabitants of the island had caused him to leap into the sea, only to be swept to his death by a strong current. In my mind he'd been the author of his own demise. My Canadian friend and my fellow writer pointed out that the nature of my story's viewpoint, third person from my protagonist's sole perspective, meant we never heard the islanders' side of the story, which was a great deal more sympathetic than I'd made room for. My wife, to my horror, explained what I'd actually written made it seem like the islanders had killed my protagonist, inadvertently or otherwise. 'Is that what you intended?' she asked.

I read the story again and saw she was right. My intention was to show how a misunderstanding of cultures and my protagonist's inability to empathize had caused him to drown, but instead I'd made the islanders look like unwilling murderers. In academic terms, I'd strayed from the point of my conclusion. Immediately I rewrote the penultimate paragraph and the one that followed, giving the islanders a chance of redemption more in line with what I'd originally envisaged and my true experience of visiting Lamu. When it was done I breathed a sigh of relief. I would have been mortified if I had sent my flawed first draft into the world. I owe a huge debt of thanks to Sharmila, Gaetan and Koye for being honest enough to tell me the truth. It led me to my true ending.

Where to start – ideas and inspiration

Tania

Ways to find inspiration on your own

This is the question every writer gets asked. Where do we get inspiration from? I believe that contrary to popular mythology ('writing is easy, you just stare at a blank page and sweat blood') you never need to start with that often-terrifying blankness of either notebook or screen. That sight can be so daunting, it's a wonder anyone writes anything. Who wants to spoil the purity of an unwritten-on page with a mess of words which may not make anything at all? All that whiteness. Second: where to start anyway?

If you don't have anything in your head demanding to be set free, then go looking. Seek out inspiration. My first conscious source of inspiration was *New Scientist* magazine. I used something factual as a jumping-off point for the title story of my first collection, *The White Road*. The *New Scientist* article that got this story going was about a snow road in Antarctica that the Americans were creating in order to get supplies through to the South Pole when bad weather grounded flights. I read the article, and what eventually surfaced was a voice, a character. She was American and she ran a café on that white road. Of course: if there's a long road you need somewhere for people to stop and eat, right? Made perfect sense. I heard her voice clearly, from the opening line, and the rest of the story unfolded from there.

New Scientist is one fantastic place to look for ideas, remembering that you are writing fiction and are under absolutely no obligation to stick to any facts. I might have read the same article and started a story about someone working on the road who might have been there to sabotage the project. Or someone at the South Pole desperately waiting for the road to be finished. Or I might have written a story about a sand road through a desert. Inspiration is there to be taken, played with, altered, made your own. The main thing is to start.

Another way to get yourself going is to borrow words from somewhere else and use them as your first line. Best not to borrow the first line from someone else's short story but a line in the middle, or the last line? (There is a fine literary tradition of authors writing a sequel to someone else's work.) Or a line picked at random from a novel or a poem? I wouldn't use more than one sentence; you might only need part of a sentence. Write it down and already your page is blank no more. See where it takes you, and once you have your story, you can always take the borrowed words out. They got you there, but you might not need them in your story.

If you prefer visual stimulation, open a magazine and pick a picture. Or head to YouTube and choose a random video.

You could collide two different types of inspiration and see what your head makes of them. For example, read two books at the same time, one fiction and one non-fiction. Read a page of one, then a page of the other, then back to the first. This will produce sparks!

The point is: there is inspiration everywhere. You just need to train yourself to see it. One way is to carry a small notebook, which has philo-sophical importance too – it makes you feel like a writer.

I prefer a plain, unlined notebook, so that I can write notes diagonally, or in any shape I want. That makes me feel as if this is creative work rather than, say, journalism. It encourages me to play, and playing is something I take very seriously as a writer. At first, I wrote down snippets of conversation I overheard, as well as observations. I would sit in a café and watch. I love doing this, because you see how little other people notice, as they rush in and rush out, or as they sit and chat. You feel you're the only one in the world who has seen certain things, who is paying attention. This is a great skill to have. Attention. Noticing. After taking notes for a while, beginnings of stories would arrive.

Once you get into the swing of doing this, the notebook can become a sort of Pavlovian device, getting it out switches you into Story mode. I have a way to perpetuate this: my very first notebook was a present and had a lovely removable cloth cover. When I filled it, I found a notebook of the same size which would fit into that cover, and now I have six or so already filled. It's a bit like having the same notebook that keeps filling up and then emptying again.

Keep a notebook by your bed, too. I find last thing at night and first thing in the morning are fertile times for story beginnings to arise. You might think you will remember them later, but, especially with the night-time ones, it's generally not a good plan to rely on your memory.

Two other things to try is to keep a list of a specific topic — for me it's unusual occupations I come across (so far I have used the UN special advisor on summary executions, and a diver for the city council, for example; I have dozens more). What I then might do to get a story started is find my list, pick an occupation and 'collide' it with a completely different idea or observation that I've noted down. Smash them together in some way and see what happens. I did this with the two occupations above, in two different stories: I collided the special advisor with an article I'd read about how clever octopuses are; and I combined the diver for the city council with Beatles' songs, which happened to be preoccupying me. I had no clue what might happen and had a wonderful time finding out.

TOP TIP

There is inspiration everywhere — you just need to train yourself to notice it.

Always have a notebook to hand, in the house and outside — don't trust your memory.

EXERCISE

Next time you are out, note down three things in your notebook that you overhear three different people saying, making sure to use exactly the words they use, in their voice. When you get to a place you can write in, look back at what you noted down and invent jobs for the three people. Then begin writing a scene with these three people in a waiting room (you don't need to know what they are waiting for), and have one of them complain to one of the others about how long they've been waiting. Keep writing and find out what happens.

Ways to find inspiration with others

Something that also helped me enormously was the inspiration provided by other people. First, a writing group, which may be online or face-to-face. I was a member of two online writing groups for several years which helped me generate over 100 short short stories. How? Well, these groups focused on flash fiction and every week, someone in the group would set a challenge, something like: Write a 500-word short story in which someone dies in the first line. Or, write a story under 750 words which uses the words 'orange', 'seaside' and 'promises'. Or, write a story of exactly 200 words in which every line starts with the letter 'L'.

Another excellent online writing group introduced me to the idea of using sets of prompts: someone would pick lines from five or six different sources and then the challenge was to sit and write for half an hour, getting as many of the prompts into the story as possible. This is like the section above – you already have some words to get you going, and if the prompts are chosen at random, they can take you in very interesting directions! Someone else providing the prompt works extremely well for me, as do deadlines. Constraint can be liberating.

Online writing with friends

You can do this in your face-to-face writing groups too, or with a writing buddy, online or IRL (in real life). Make a date with a writing friend for a certain time period, say three hours, during which you will both be online. Then prepare three sets of prompts – which might be words, images, videos, anything at all – and every half an hour one of you emails a prompt to the other and you both write. It takes practice, this kind of very fast writing – it's a muscle that needs to be warmed up – but it can be enormously fun and invigorating and somehow you feel the other person is there writing with you, even if you are in different countries!

The guiding principle here is that anything that gets you going is a good thing. There is nothing, in my opinion, that 'shouldn't' be used as inspiration. I get asked this when I give readings or run workshops. 'Is it okay to write about (fill in the blank)?' Of course it is. You are the writer, write about whatever you want to write about.

Further reading

Hershman, Tania, 'The White Road', *New Scientist* http://www.newscientist.com/article/dn15029-short-story-the-white-road-by-tania-hershman.html (October, 2008).

Where to start: titles, beginnings and endings

Tania

Once you have an idea, where and how do you start? As with everything in this book, there are no rules. There are always many places to start and this is one of the choices you have to make as a writer. Don't worry about this when you are writing your first draft. Don't even think about it. Sometimes the place you begin writing the story will turn out not to be exactly the place the story wants to begin. I often need a run-up until I find the meat of the story, start to hear the voices of my characters or narrator – a bit like the high-jump. Once you've got your first draft, go back, get rid of the run-up and start where the story lifts off.

> **TOP TIP**
>
> *Where you start writing the story may not end up being where the finished short story begins; it may be where you need to write from to find out what happens, and once you've found out, you can get rid of the 'run-up' and start where the story takes off.*

Something I often see in stories I critique is that the writer has 'forgotten' to get rid of the run-up. And it's easy to see, in someone else's story, where it takes off. But there is always more than one place where a story could start. If you're not happy with your story-in-progress, try starting it in a different place. Even if you end up with the beginning you first started with, you'll have refreshed it in your mind by allowing yourself to see that nothing is sacred.

Another thing I see often is the writer giving away too much in the opening paragraph. This is a tough balance to maintain: create enough mystery so your reader wants to read on, but not too much that they are still confused by the bottom of page one. If you reveal everything, summing up what the story is going to be, e.g. 'This was the day I learned that Tina never loved me and that we had to break up' (a clunky, made-up example), there's no reason for you to carry on writing or us to carry on reading. You're telling the reader what the story is, instead of trusting them to figure it out for themselves. Readers are clever, let them do the work.

Openings

1 With short stories, you have to seize the reader with your opening and not let them go.
2 Whoever starts reading your story – the editor of a publication you've submitted it to, the judge of a short story competition, or a reader – will never, ever, be under any obligation to finish reading it (unless you are paying them to). You have to make them want to.
3 Published short stories rarely appear in isolation, they are either in a magazine, collection or anthology, so your story is competing with others for the reader's attention. That's a good thing to keep in mind – I know that as a reader I approach short stories differently from the way I approach other pieces of writing, be they poems, non-fiction books or novels. I say to the short story: 'Give me a reason to keep reading you'. And I don't give it much time to do that.
4 There is a widely quoted 'rule' that says a short story 'should' begin in media res, which means, roughly, 'in the middle of the action'. The short story has no time for preamble, for any introduction. Well, perhaps. Let's see. This approach is exciting – if you are thrown straight in you want to read on to find out what the hell is going on. But if not done well, the reader might get confused because too much is unexplained.

Take a look at a piece of writing that recently grabbed you, something you felt compelled to keep reading — it might be a short story, a novel, a magazine article or blog post. Read the opening paragraph and make notes on what it did that made you want to read on. Pay close attention to a few points:

- The language the writer uses — is it chatty or formal? Simple words or more complex terms?

- Do you get a sense of a strong voice, either the writer's voice or a character?

- Does the writer spend a lot of time setting things up or are you thrown straight in?

- Remember back to when you read it the first time. Did you know everything that was going on or where you a little confused or very confused?

- Did it remind you of anything you'd read before, either the subject or the style?

Then jot down a few different ways the writer could have begun this short story, novel, article or blog post, and how that would have changed the finished piece.

Let's take a look at examples of openings to stories I happen to love:

Memory Wall
Tall Man in the Yard
Seventy-four-year old Alma Konachek lives in Vredehoek, a suburb above Cape Town: a place of warm rains, big-windowed lofts and silent, predatory automobiles.

('Memory Wall' by Anthony Doerr, from *Memory Wall*, Scribner, 2010)

The first thing most readers will look at is the story title. This story is called 'Memory Wall'. What does that tell us? It is fairly intriguing because a 'memory wall' is not a concept we're familiar with. But it doesn't give much away. The second thing you see is a subtitle: 'Tall Man in the Yard'. Five words that are imbued with not only intrigue but menace. Not simply a man in a yard, but a tall man in a specific yard. Anthony Doerr makes each word work here.

The opening line, at first glance, seems simply to be description. But look how much is packed in here! We are introduced to a character, her gender, her age, where she lives, in detail. But it is not an objective, clinical description: the rains are warm, which sound pleasant, as do the lofts' big windows – but then Doerr hits us with those two words 'silent' and 'predatory'. What an effect they have, combined with the thought already in our minds of the tall man in the yard. He is signalling to us that this may be a suburb but this is not a place of safety.

So, while this opening might appear not to throw us into the action, to be preamble or introduction, in fact it sets us up perfectly for a story about memory, intrusion, predators and ageing.

Let's take a look at another:

Grandma

Grandma used to be a woman of action. She wore tights. She had big boobs, but a teeny-weeny bra. Her waist used to be twenty-four inches. Before she got so hunched over she could do way more than a hundred of everything, pushups, situps, chinning ...

('Grandma' by Carol Emshwiller, *Fantasy and Science Fiction*, 2002)

The title and the first word are the same here, and then instantly the reader's possible expectations of a story about a grandmother are subverted. A grandma described by words such as 'action', 'tights', 'big boobs', 'teeny-weeny bra' and in terms of how many pushups she could do? Carol Emshwiller is letting us know from the start that this is no ordinary grandmother. We aren't starting in the middle of any action here, but we instantly have two characters – the grandma and the grandchild who is telling us about her – although no setting, enough about her to intrigue the kind of reader that wants to read about slightly extraordinary grandmothers. There is humour here, giving us the hint of what kind of story this could be, setting a possible genre as a kind of comic/action hero, and an interesting use of time from the outset with 'Grandma used to be', piquing our interest about what might have happened, what Grandma is like now.

Here's another:

Bullet in the Brain

Anders couldn't get to the bank until just before it closed, so of course the line was endless and he got stuck behind two women whose loud, stupid conversation put him in a murderous temper.

('Bullet in the Brain' by Tobias Woolf, *The New Yorker*, 1995)

In this Tobias Woolf story, a favourite of writing workshops, there is an enormous amount going on in the title and first line. We have 'bullet' and 'murderous' and a character we are immediately so intimate with that we are on first-name terms. We know where he is, and, because most readers over a certain age know how it feels to be in an endless bank line; Woolf doesn't have to explain. We feel it. We know it.

We learn a lot about Anders's character from his reaction to the situation he is in. This opening is stuffed full. We are in the 'close third person' point of view here, because 'loud, stupid conversation' sounds like Anders's voice rather than an omniscient, god-like narrator. This is definitely throwing us straight into the action – but being stuck in a bank queue sounds like an incredibly boring story were it not for the title, 'bullet', 'murderous' and Anders's strong and distinctive voice.

It's interesting to think where else this story could have started. With Anders walking to the bank? Or that morning, or when he's at the front of the queue? All these would result in a slightly different story – with any other opening we would lose the women's stupid conversation which puts him in a foul temper, which, clearly, is going to be important. Oh yes.

Another one:

The Redemption of Galen Pike

They'd all seen Sheriff Nye bringing Pike into town: the two shapes snaking down the path off the mountain through the patches of melting snow and over the green showing beneath, each of them growing bigger as they moved across the rocky pasture and came down into North Street to the jailhouse – Nye on his horse, the tall gaunt figure of Galen Pike following behind on the rope.

('The Redemption of Galen Pike', Carys Davies, from *The Redemption of Galen Pike*, Salt, 2014)

First, the title tells us a great deal – we have the name of a character and we know he is going to be redeemed, unless the author is lying to us, which we have no reason to suspect. His name is unusual, especially to a British audience, which is where the story was published, so that's already intriguing. And of course, his surname is 'pike', which for me conjures up both the fish (slippery) and is almost 'spike'.

Then we do start in media res. This opening paragraph is one long sentence, filled both with evocative action words ('bringing', 'snaking', 'growing', 'moved', 'came', 'following'), and already a whole host of characters, the immensely powerful and somewhat menacing 'They', which, when swiftly followed by 'Sheriff' we might assume were the townsfolk, probably somewhere in America. We also have the Sheriff ('Nye' – his name almost a denial, a negation), and Galen Pike himself. There's little doubt what is going on here, who appears to be the Good Guy and who the Bad. But it's not a tale of the Sheriff and Pike because Carys Davies, the author, has chosen to tell it from the point of view of the townsfolk; right from the start it's not what's happening but what they see happening, which may be something entirely different. So she sets us up here with both a fairly traditional story, but with that twist that what is seen may not be what is.

And one more:

Butcher's Perfume

Later, when I knew her better, Manda told me how she'd beaten two girls at once outside the Cranemakers Arms in Carlisle. She said all you had to do was keep hold of one, keep hold of one and keep hitting her.

('Butcher's Perfume', Sarah Hall, from *The Beautiful Indifference*, Faber & Faber, 2012)

What a title! Those two words, in a combination that I imagine most readers will never have seen, are so evocative, engaging your senses: sight, smell. They do so much work here, implying savagery, flesh, destruction, but also something feminine, something at odds with this. A clash. The first two lines of the story – the opening story of Sarah Hall's collection, so it also sets the tone of the book – reinforce that first impression. They introduce us to our main character and the other important person in the story, as well as our location.

Hall also does something interesting with time here – she begins with the word 'Later', bold given that we are not told what this is later than. You can imagine all the different choices that Hall faced here – this story could have started when Manda and our narrator first met, say. That 'later' implies a whole world of events, a depth. The repetition of 'keep' three times, including 'keep hold of one' twice, is violently poetic. Once again, a dissonance. These two lines give us such a strong picture of their relationship – one in charge, giving instructions, and one who may or may not follow them. What on earth is going to happen? That's exactly what you want a reader to think.

Grasping for clues

What it's worth remembering is that the reader is reading your opening knowing nothing about your story, grasping for clues or answers to at least some of the following:

- What kind of story is this going to be? (e.g. humour, mystery, science fiction, tragedy)
- Whose story is this/who should I be interested in? (main character/characters or narrator)
- Where is the story taking place? (geographical location or specific setting, like a kitchen)
- How is this story going to be told? (traditional or experimental, realist or surreal)

Don't give away too much, otherwise the reader doesn't need to carry on. But also be careful of over-mystifying, which can result in confusion. It's difficult. Sometimes, if you're lucky, your story will tell you exactly where it needs to start and you don't have to over-analyse. As you will see in my analysis of my own story, 'Under the Tree', in early drafts I introduced characters in the opening paragraph that would never come back again, and it took a long time to realize I didn't need them.

Endings

Endings are intimately tied to beginnings. It would be unfair of me to give you the endings of any of the stories above – or of any short story you haven't read yet – but where you choose to start your story and where you end it are definitely linked. In many ways, short stories are all about their endings, about 'ending-ness', because the reader has in mind when they begin reading that the ending is imminent. I don't believe it is possible to have a great short story with a weak ending. However, no one else can tell you how to end your story. There's no formula for short story endings, but a good ending means you know, without having to turn the page to check, that the story has finished.

One thing to note is that twist-in-the-tale endings, the surprising kind where something happens that the reader couldn't possibly foresee, Roald Dahl's kind of endings, have mostly gone out of fashion. That doesn't mean you couldn't do it, if that's what your story needs.

Tension

What every story requires is tension – first, to compel you, the writer, to keep writing in order to find out what happens. Even if you think you know where your own story is going to end, you won't know for sure until you get there. If it is enough to keep you involved in writing it, the hope is it will do the same for a reader.

1 The first requirement of any ending is that it satisfies you, the writer. A physical sensation occurs when I 'get' the ending to a story I've been

working on. A kind of release, I can finally breathe out because I've done right by my characters, told their story as best I can, in something close to the way I'd hoped.

2 It is often an emotional experience for me when I finish and I know that the story is finished. After being in this game for over ten years, I now rarely know what my own story is about until I get to the end (and sometimes not even then). But when it's done, it's done, even if I can't explain why. (It has only happened once in more than 150 stories that a character from one of my stories demands to have more written about her.)

3 What an ending doesn't have to be is a neat tying-up. Something I came across in the writing of this book which might be useful here is the section on riddles in Paul March-Russell's *The Short Story: An Introduction*. He says: 'The riddle is arguably one of the most influential sub-genres in the history of short fiction – an early form of modernist short story emerges out of the riddle rather than in opposition.' He mentions the hoax and the conundrum too, to demonstrate how the short story lends itself to 'mystery, play and pastiche'.

4 With riddles, hoaxes and conundrums the reader needs to do some work trying to figure out what is going on, and the writer needs not to give it all away. So there is a push/pull going on. March-Russell points to something else important: 'Readers are increasingly made aware of the darkness that surrounds these narratives' – by darkness, I take him to mean a lack of explanation rather than existential gloom, but maybe both – 'a darkness to which they themselves are being made responsible by the weight of interpretation being transferred from the author'.

5 These kinds of stories don't spoon-feed you – you, the reader, are part of the process, not simply watching the story unfold.

6 If the short story is a species of riddle – the writer straddles the line between giving it all away and not providing enough hints – the ending to a great riddle solves it enough to leave you thinking. This fits with what I love about short stories: for me, they reflect our reality in which effects don't generally have direct causes. We don't necessarily know why we do the things we do, why we feel what we feel.

Perhaps later we see a bigger picture, or we try and create a pattern from events because that's what we humans tend to do: we are pattern-creators.

7   My personal preference is for stories that reflect this uncertainty, whether they be short stories, films, novels, or TV shows. I find these kinds of stories reassuring, telling me that yes, life is difficult, it's not me imagining it. If the story ties everything up neatly, that, paradoxically, leaves me feeling less satisfied – the story has until this point felt true to me (and 'true' does not mean 'realistic' – it could still be set on another planet, or involve flying pigs). Also, a tying-up of loose ends doesn't leave your reader any more to think about.

Good endings

One of the 'truths' I did absorb from writing workshops that I do think is valuable to think about is that a great ending 'should' be both surprising and inevitable. This fits with the riddle theory. It's a hard balance to achieve. For example, in my story 'Under the Tree', it wouldn't have been a surprise if the mother had actually managed to achieve what she wanted, which was to get her son to get up and come back into the house. But if the ending is too surprising – say the mother runs off to the circus, but her desire to do this was never mentioned – the reader might have either felt stupid for having missed some clue that would hint at this, or annoyed that there were no clues. When I read someone else's short story that gets this balance just right, it once again causes a physical sensation, a combination of joy – even if the ending is tragic, if it feels like the 'right' ending – and sadness at leaving this world in which I had been so completely immersed, even for just a few minutes.

TOP TIP

Fighting the urge to solve all issues at the end is hard. Assume you've overwritten and try chopping off the last line, paragraph, or sometimes the whole of the last page!

What will help you develop your own story sense, hone your instincts regarding beginnings and endings, is to read as many short stories as possible. Read them first for enjoyment, the sheer pleasure of it, and then, when you find a story you love, read it again and make some notes about how it does the thing it does to you. This is reading as a writer, and it's enormously useful. We will do some of this later.

Further reading

Davies, Carys, 'The Redemption of Galen Pike', winner, 2011 V. S. Pritchett Prize, *Prospect* magazine http://www.prospectmagazine.co.uk/magazine/fiction/the-redemption-of-galen-pike/#.Uup8LqHh-mg, and in *The Redemption of Galen Pike* (Salt, 2014).

Doerr, Anthony, 'Memory Wall', *Memory Wall* (Scribner, 2010).

Emshwiller, Carol, 'Grandma' (*Fantasy and Science Fiction* magazine, 2002).

Hall, Sarah, 'Butcher's Perfume', *The Beautiful Indifference* (Faber and Faber, 2012).

Wolff, Tobias, 'Bullet in the Brain' (*The New Yorker*, September 1995).

Movement and syncopation in fiction: writing the long short story

Courttia

Taking the journey

I've only just returned from a trip out of the United Kingdom, halfway across the world to Kerala, South India. I say this not to brag, but because the experience is fresh in my mind and it began a train of thought that's grown in size and volume since I shut the front door behind me and left for the airport. It's strange what travelling does to you. I felt it from the very moment I first left the country as an adult, alone, possibly a little afraid, clutching the few items that kept me tethered to the world I thought I'd known; passport, house keys, phone, suitcase, and a battered rucksack containing my laptop. It's an opening of the senses. The fear of loss becomes as visible as exhaled breath on a winter morning. I'm aware of just how much I've taken for granted in this nominal world now laden with expectation, charged with the familiar. That first time I made the journey to the airport by myself, long before I left the soil I called my own, my eyes dilated far beyond their normal capacity. In Jamaica, the religion of Rastafarianism has invented a term for this way of seeing. They call it 'overstanding'. I owned that profound knowledge when I looked from car windows to witness the world I thought of as solid slip away, as though I was gripping seaweed. I 'overstood' my place in a manner fast becoming common in those early days of finding the new me – a writer, no less. I embraced the humming rush of that tear in the fabric of the tangible, the known.

Picking moments

Back then I would immerse myself in the buzz of the encounter, like inhaling a first cigarette, or getting really drunk, or having sex, or really losing yourself in music. It's overwhelming, that primary meeting with experiential feeling, and for the most part the majority of us can do nothing more but let it wash over us, take us where it may. It's only after you've tried it out again, and again, repeating the process until it becomes as commonplace as riding a bike or tying your shoes, that you can switch off and allow the more analytical side of your brain take over. You can talk yourself through it as it were, picking moments and feelings that merge to form an emotional by-product, like or dislike. Those by-products produce anticipation, or its antonym, doubt or even dread. This, in turn, can go some way to creating a response, internally or otherwise.

The difference between looking and seeing

By the time I was making my journey to India I was used to, and even relished, the idea of viewing the world I'd thought I known in this way. It was a cold Boxing Day morning. There was frost on the car windows. Our flight was scheduled for 11 that morning, and we were travelling from East London to Gatwick, and so when we left it was dark; no lights in the houses in our street, everybody asleep, or at least in bed. We dragged our suitcases into the boot, climbed in and left. Mostly I slept, but there were some moments when I peered out of the misty windows and took time to look at the things I saw every day. And yet something different was happening. I was *seeing*. That might sound strange to some people at first — what difference is there between looking and seeing?

I define it as the difference between listening, and *hearing*. Understanding, or *overstanding*. Instead of letting the scenery outside my window wash over me like low tide, tickling my toes, giving me a taste of its substance and troubling me none, as much as I could given my limited proximity, located in a travelling vehicle behind glass, I tried to immerse myself in what I saw. To take in all the details, grab anything of note and store it for later thought, or if I was really lucky, for fictional use. I tried to examine what leaving felt like for me and what staying looked like for the people, places and even the animals outside my window. I was a pocket of air floating, serene and graceful, within a thickened substance that conducted a continuous mass of experiential force. Movement had created anticipation. That anticipation caused me to see.

An interesting fact; in music, anticipation serves a slightly different purpose than in fiction. The Berklee College of Music defines the word as a technique of melodic or rhythmic alteration, changing a note that is performed on-the-beat, causing it to be played early. The result is syncopation.

A delayed attack, on the other hand, is a technique of said alteration which changes a note that occurs on-the-beat to be played either one-half beat late (an 8th note delayed attack or hesitation), a quarter of a beat late (a 16th note delayed attack), one-third of a beat late (a triplet delayed attack), or one full beat late. Delayed attacks are the opposite of anticipations, and are also called 'hesitations'. The result is syncopation.

Movement creates anticipation, or delayed attacks

The interesting part is not the technical aspects of written sheet music, which I find baffling at best, but the idea that anticipation, whether disrupted as in the case of the first example, or enforced as in the case of the second, creates syncopation – a placement of stresses and rhythms where they would not normally occur – either way. If we were to leave music and apply this to lived human experience and its interpretation via prose (for our purposes the creation of characters in short fiction) we could take the above as an example that it doesn't really matter if an anticipatory moment is relished or feared. The result will always be syncopation. In fictional terms, in most cases, this syncopation will be felt or experienced via the page, rather than translated from the page to be heard aloud. Of course, there are some exceptions to this rule – in live fiction readings for example, or the work of traditional storytellers.

In fiction, syncopation occurs in a number of forms. The short story and its narrative by-product hinges on that transition from the protagonist's normal state of being into a new state, informed or otherwise, producing stresses and rhythms where they might not normally occur. Simply put, stories dramatize change. Events might cause to the character to do or say things out of the ordinary, behave contrary to their normal manner. They might internalize the transition and simply act out, throwing minor characters in their orbit out of synch, thus producing more change. Those changes create a new way to visualize the world, in the best stories, for everyone who plays a part in the narrative. It is the transition, wherever it takes place in the story that creates forward momentum. And as we have seen, anticipation for character, reader and author alike, stems from that transitional movement.

Movement as communication

The word movement has myriad uses in the English language.

- It can be used to refer to clockwork, or the inner mechanisms of a timepiece.
- It can also refer to sign language, where it defines the nature of the hands when signing.
- It can mean a political, artistic or social group gathered together for a shared cause, the passage of food through the body, or the actual passage of the body itself through space and time.

If there is no movement, anticipation is dulled, or even lost. We become bored, restless. That feeling of boredom comes from being made to feel, or actually being static. What's even more interesting here is that in each of these definitions it can be argued that the word movement is highly associated with time, transition and communication in some form or another.

TOP TIP

'Leave the door open for the unknown. That's where the most important things come from, where you yourself come from, and where you will go.'

Rebecca Solnit's A Field Guide to Getting Lost

Rebecca Solnit's work is a treatise on the idea of movement for writers, a concept more often known as a journey. Yes, it's true. As prose writers we work at our very best when we are travelling through time and space much as we expect our characters to. How else will we know how it feels? How might we discover, as they must? Solnit tells a story about teaching a workshop in the Rockies. A student enters bearing a quote from the pre-Socratic philosopher Meno. The quote reads: 'How will you go about finding the thing the nature of which is totally unknown to you?' Solnit copied the words down, and they've stayed with her ever since. For her, even more important than the journey itself, is the venture into the unknowable. The ability to find comfort moving forwards without quite knowing where you are going. The possibility of not seeing at all, finding yourself lost. For myself, journeying in a car towards a country I had never been to *and* the prospect of being surrounded by unknown food, currency, religion, land, language and dialect, a whole way of *being* that would result – if only for 14 days – in me being *lost*, made me look at my known world in a whole new way.

EXERCISE

Here's another exercise to use in a workshop setting.

Split the writers into two equal groups, the Blind and the Leaders. Give the Blind aeroplane blindfolds, and have them spend 15 minutes wandering around being led, or guided by the Leaders.

They stop, and for ten minutes each writer pens their relative experiences. Afterwards they swap; the Leaders becoming the Blind.

They wander around for another 15 minutes and do the same thing again, writing about how it felt to have their situations reversed.

Read the results.

Why?

There are two reasons for doing this exercise:

- The first is practical and strips the writers of their most commonplace sense, sight, forces them to rely on the remaining senses. Hopefully this will stimulate an awareness that might be kept in subsequent writing.

- The second is more abstract. When the writers are blind they can equate their experience with that of a reader. They don't know the location they are being led around. They have been stripped of their most prominent sense, the one which has ensured the survival of the race from primeval human being until modern man and woman. They are reliant on the skills, guidance and benevolence of the Leader, who, in my version of this exercise, represents the writer. These burgeoning writers can be made to think about each role carefully and be made aware of their workings.

- The feeling of losing our bearings, of movement, and benign guidance are all essential fictional attributes. Nowhere more than in the short story.

Working it out

Often in the work of new writers, the urge to convey information is powerful. So much has been learned, whether through research or from their own life experiences, and they are desperate to get these things down on the page. The reader is sometimes stifled by the weight of information. There are few or no points in which she is made to wonder, to build her own mental picture. Instead of trusting her instincts and allowing her to find her way through the story of her own volition – to become lost in the world of the author's creation – these writers rely on signposts, and oftentimes GPS roadmaps in the form of detailed exposition and character descriptions, chunks of dialogue that inform us exactly how their characters are feeling, but also strip them of their humanity. This is generous, and demonstrates great care, but it is also overbearing. As writers we must trust in our ability to be a tough guide, willing to show our readers the way, but also to step back and watch them figure things out for themselves, so they might feel as clever as we perceive ourselves to be. We might even feel as though we have worked things out together.

The push and pull – character vs plot

It is this act of actually withholding information that makes the longer story so compelling to read. It is the not-knowing that makes us want to find out more. It is the forward momentum that makes us see what we did not know. The push and pull between these actions, interior and exterior, mirror the actions of what I believe constitute a good narrative: character (interior, inward mental action) and plot (exterior, outward physical action). For Aristotle, plot is the 'soul' of tragedy and character is secondary, but this doesn't mean all short stories must have narrative momentum as a primary driving force. It is possible to assert inversion. Neither do I share Forster's vague contempt when he claimed that even the lowliest bus driver could show an interest in suspense, or a sequence of events. Both plot and character are worthy devices, and can produce astounding results. Some stories demand to be told weighted towards narrative drive (Edna O'Brien's 'Black Flower'). In others, the pendulum swings in the opposite direction, demanding the story be weighted towards characterization (Stephen Millhauser's 'Beneath the Cellars of our Town'). I do believe, generally anyway, that plot-based stories with a devastating climax and denouement demand a shorter word count than character stories, which have more room to meander and therefore might produce greater length. Obviously this is not always the case; one good example I can think of that immediately breaks my 'rule' is Raymond

Carver's 'Errand'. The real point is, either choice benefits from the act of losing the reader, immersing them in the world the author has created without signposting where they might be, or how they might find their way towards the exit; and then carefully, gently, ushering them in that direction.

TOP TIP

'The imitation [of life] is not just of a complete action, but also events that evoke fear and pity. The effects occur above all when things come about contrary to expectation but because of one another.'

Aristotle

Getting lost, for character, reader and author alike, becomes essential to building a story that develops contrary to the expectations of all involved, and certainly in the creation a long form story. Screenwriters use the metaphor of 'doorways' to traverse the traditional three-act structure of film. In long form stories, the character should be made to negotiate a maze of twisting, dizzying doorways, moving forwards, sometimes even seemingly turning back on themselves, before their characters find the exit, or remain trapped.

Although you as the author, the audience as the reader, or the character as a fictional being have no need to know where any of you are going in terms of a journey, I do think it's imperative that the writer knows that essential thing I always come back to; what they are trying to say. It's not enough to detail a series of events, as well as they may be written, without there being some focus, some drive, some point. Think about your theme, what the story is about. This will help you traverse the story, and shape your conclusion. How you feel about the world, your character's place in it, and how those things come together via the events you have set into motion intellectually or instinctively, all play a part in the stories outcome, which must feel organic and true to the verisimilitude you have created.

The more we can do this, the more complex the movement of the story becomes. This intricacy gives rise to a story with many twists and turns.

There will be discovery, and the possibility of dead ends which may or may not come to pass. We will evoke pity or fear, and sometimes both, as the reader roots for our characters, cheers them on to the very end. This can sometimes lead to the most cherished tales, the story that lives on after the tale is told. If the reader can imagine the characters and the world of the story after the final page, then they can possibly be content with the feeling of anticipation that has been created enough to conjure their own forward momentum, perhaps indefinitely.

EXERCISE

Split your story into three basic acts; beginning, middle and end. Try to keep it simple, focused on the main crux of the story.

Lengthen these three acts into eight plot points, or moments:

1 Set-up
2 Inciting incident
3 Conflict
4 Progressive complications
5 Ordeals
6 Crises
7 Climax
8 Resolution

Try to see how many of the points you can have your character go through, again in simple bullet point style.

Write 50 words on these plot turns, detailing how they would work in each scene throughout the story. When you are done, look at the shape of the story. Are there places that are too long? Too short? What would happen if you moved them around? Practise prolonging the conflict and complications, thus causing the tension to rise. After one day, revise if necessary.

Plot versus story – where's the tension?

Tania

This is a very very common issue: what is plot and what is story? They are not the same thing but one is often confused with the other. I am going to use the word 'plot' to mean: an event or series of events, the 'what happens'. 'Story' will refer to the 'why'of these events, the part that includes feelings, emotions. It is 'story' that creates the tension that keeps you writing to find out what happens and keeps the reader reading.

For example:

Girl goes into a sweet shop every day and buys a bag of sweets.

This is plot.

Girl goes into a sweet shop every day because she is in love with the guy behind the counter, but doesn't have the courage to talk to him so she buys a bag of Jelly Babies.

This is one of many possible stories that can wrap around this simple sequence of events. Here are some more:

Girl goes into a sweet shop every day and buys a bag of Jelly Babies because they were her sister's favourite sweets but her sister disappeared five years ago and no one but the girl believes she is still alive.

and

Girl goes into a sweet shop every day even though she is diabetic,
  and she buys a bag of Jelly Babies because she loves the way they
  smell, but she doesn't eat them, she gets them out at lunchtime in
  a corner of the playground and whispers to them.

and

Girl goes into a sweet shop every day because she is being
  followed by an invisible creature which is allergic to sugar so she
  buys a different bag of sweets each day to keep it away.

I don't think it's an exaggeration to say that there are almost an infinite number of stories that can be woven around just this one sequence of events, this one plot. The story could be a romance, a mystery, science fiction, a comedy.

Because a short story has to be short, there might not be room for a great deal of plot, but this doesn't mean there can't be a complex story. For example, in Tobias Woolf's 'Bullet in the Brain', the plot is simple to explain: man gets shot during bank robbery. But the story encompasses life, death, art, beauty, childhood, adulthoood, desire and disappointment.

I often see stories in which the writer has confused plot with story and tried to ramp up tension by having the fictional equivalent of one car chase after another. This would be like Woolf's main character not only being shot but then being kidnapped and flown to a foreign country, where he is kept in captivity. Well, that's a different story entirely. Second, it doesn't necessarily increase the tension − if what the main character really wants, and what we read on to find out whether he gets, is to stay alive, then putting him in a second dangerous situation might actually serve to dilute the tension, because first you, the writer, have to get your head around all the plot points, figure out who is doing what and where they are going, and then your reader has to follow all of this too.

If you want to write one of these multi-car-chase short stories, then please do, it sounds rather fun! Write whatever story you want to write. What I am trying to say is: don't feel the need to add in more events because you're not sure there's enough tension. More plot doesn't necessarily equal more story.

I sometimes get asked whether by definition a short story can't go off on tangents, whether, to continue with the movie analogy, it has to zoom in and focus, like one of those miniature portraits. I don't think so. There aren't any rules, there isn't a formula: short story = 1 tangent + 3 plot points + 2 characters + 1 flashback.

The main thing, though, is to create the condition which British author Neil Gaiman sums up, in his introduction to the short story anthology *Stories: All New Tales*, edited by Gaiman and Al Sarrantonio, as 'and then what happened?' If you are not gripped by this while you write, where is the tension in your story? It's going to be unlikely your reader will need to know what happens next.

For there to be tension, someone has to want something. It's really that simple. Take one of Roald Dahl's stories in *Kiss Kiss*, where the wife kills the husband with a leg of lamb which (spoiler alert) she then cooks and serves to the policemen who come to investigate his death. What does she want? To get away with it. And we read on to find out if, mouthful after mouthful, the police are going to eat the murder weapon and she's going to get off scot-free. Romeo and Juliet? They want to be together. Easy.

If your main character doesn't want anything, why are you interested in her story, unless her not-wanting-anything-ness is the story and you're writing it to find out if there's anything she does want? (I was a little sneaky there ...)

There is another common saying, that there are only seven basic plots. Boy meets girl, etc ... Well, that might be true, but as we saw from our girl-buys-sweets example, there are possibly infinite stories to weave around these plots. The thing is to make it your story, that only you could write, given everything you've done, seen, read and thought about up to the point of writing this story. Then it will be unique.

Further reading

Dahl, Roald, *Kiss Kiss* (Penguin, 1962).
Gaiman, Neil and Sarrantonio, Al, 'Stories: All New Tales' (HarperCollins, 2010).

Editing and revising

Courttia

Here we are, at the point most writers loathe. Editing and revising. When I say most writers, I mean to say those at the beginning of their careers, as I've yet to meet a published or practising writer who doesn't believe that this is where the 'magic' happens. I use inverted commas because we all know the truth – although this stage of the process can invoke massive changes in your draft, and lead to revelations that make the difference between failure and success, it's also the part where we do most hard work. Analysing your story to the very last word, if that's what's necessary, is a daunting task for new writers, but sometimes it's the very thing that saves your writing.

And sometimes it's not. Confusing? Yes, very. It's actually happened rarely, but I have had those occasions where I hardly changed a word after the end of my first draft. Sometimes this happened with stories, and even once with a whole novel. I'm not even sure why. Some writers would put it down to experience, but my only near-perfect story (in as much as it turned out the way I imagined it in my head) was published over ten years ago, and I've written plenty of failures after that. Even after the novel, which was finished more recently, I've turned out first draft stories I couldn't quite make work. Again, whether they worked or not is by my own estimations. Some stories never felt right even after they were published; I think others are pitch-perfect that haven't yet seen the light of day. Go figure. The point is that for a writer, we learn and unlearn, often in succession. It's often said the completion of one story doesn't necessarily carry over into the next. We start again, trying to make the words fit in the right way, for the right sentence, to create the right scene, which expresses the right perspective for our characters, and on and on ad infinitum.

When to edit

So what purpose does editing serve then, if we are constantly made crawling infants at the feet of our art? Well, to my mind it gives us a method. And this method can extract a large part of the uncertainty from the act of devising a piece of work *during the first and second stages of writing.* I stress this because while I tend to believe you do need to be creative while writing your first draft and analytical in the second, this is only to stop yourself over-thinking. A lot of writers are critical of their work, believing that their writing should emulate any of the long-dead, largely of European descent, often male writers who make up the literary canon. I won't name names. And so they write to reach that end point of their literary forebears' published work, without realizing those writers spent hour upon hour writing endless drafts (probably in longhand) in order to get to that stage. The easiest thing in my mind is to cast doubt aside, disallow editorial thoughts for the most part. I suppose this is where the experience comes in, with the thought that *I can fix that.* Hours of doing intense line-by-line work at least gives that much assurance. I always think that more than anything else at first draft stage, I like to get to the end. That's it. Still, I don't believe particularly in being prescriptive. As Tania says, there's not one way of writing your story – only *your* way. So, as she has done, I'd like to share mine.

The sifting stage

Many people believe that editing is what you do after you begin writing, but these for the most part are people who think editing is not a creative endeavour. It is possible to be analytically creative, and that's what editing is. The truth is we are editing our stories from the moment we have our first idea. Do you write the ideas down in a notebook, or on computer? Do you make notes on that first paragraph of the story? Do either of these things change from one draft to the next? Then you have begun to edit your story.

I call this the sifting stage, and I find it very useful in the beginning to splurge ideas down onto the page, rough as you like, often filled with questions. Otherwise I work from a single sentence (usually, but not always, the opening), a line of dialogue, a theme or mood. Sometimes I take an existing piece of unfinished work and try to move it from that unformed stage into something more complete. There's no set method, but I'm more likely to start fresh with the first option, the splurge of ideas and thoughts. Then it's down to the task of trying to pull things out, the good stuff, the stuff that intrigues me and makes me want to move further down the line to the opening sentence. Often I try to imagine as much of the story as I can. I write things down; this is so I won't forget the images in my head, not so I can slavishly recreate a narrative arc. Anything that seems really important, some image or clothing or speech, or physical movement that's really compelling, I also put down. One of my main problems when I first started writing was structure, the not knowing how to get from one point to another. I worked out that scene-by-scene drafting helps, and if ever I feel like I can't 'see' the story, I plot in this way. Since then I've learnt I can hold smaller stories in my head for quite a long time, but anything large than around 3,000 words seems to dissipate like smoke, and so it's better for me to have these sifting notes. If I'm a long time between note taking and writing, I find it comforting to return to my notes and find my imagery intact. I refine, move scenes around, make additions. Of course, this is editing too.

TOP TIP

'How do I work? I grope.'

Albert Einstein

The writing

Einstein's words are true of the first draft writer too. We are trying to see the images in our mind, and record them onto the page. If these are coming to me in a rush, then it's a good day. If they are slower and I have to think about them, that's not bad by default, but it is a slightly different type of day and I take that into account. Maybe I do more reading, or listen to music.

Maybe I just write through it. One thing I'm not is hard on myself. I often find that if I've had a good writing day, the next doesn't come as well as before. So I treat it as part of the cycle, shrug my shoulders and get on.

The editorial process is happening in a limited form at this point, because I am already looking at the sentences and seeing if I can make them work better. I do this by moving the words around. Generally, I tend to try and make my word quota before I do this, but if things are going well and I'm flowing to my satisfaction, I do this any time. And so I attempt to try out every possible sentence construction to find the optimum choice, which also suits my protagonist's manner of speech and doesn't jar. It's important for me to know I have the best possible sentence to get my point across. In *Politics and the English Language*, George Orwell said the writer must ask themselves four questions in order to achieve this task.

---

1   *What am I trying to say?*

2   *What words will express it?*

3   *What image or idiom will make it clearer?*

4   *Is this image fresh enough to have an effect?*

He goes on to pose a further two:

5   *Could I put it more shortly?*

6   *Have I said anything that is unavoidably ugly?*

My notes should have taken care of the first four questions, so it is five and six that trouble me most. One of the things I do to help is to keep my PC open at all times (terrible for the environment I know – environmentalists out there, it does go into a power-saving sleep mode). The American novelist Colson Whitehead also does this. Up until then I'd thought I was the only one who damaged my green credentials in this way. Still, that way the line-by-line editing process becomes an organic part of my day; I can walk past my computer, read through a sentence, change it completely or give it a slight tweak and then continue what I was doing. This is surplus to my daily writing quota, but it quiets that nagging sense of unease I feel when I'm away from my desk during a project.

Another thing I try to do is start from the previous day's writing, working down the page reading and tidying, and then I continue from where I stopped writing the day before. This helps me get back into the word and mood of the writing I was doing, and also gives me a chance to tidy as I go. This allows me to really go all-out in terms of what I write on the day, and also contributes to the draft being as close to finished as I can get it at the end of the first run. Hopefully any of the major problems in the work will have been ironed out by then. Whatever the results after I'm done with the story as a whole, I tend to look at my completed first draft with a more critical creative gaze.

The revision funnel

At this stage I turn to a process very similar to what MA creative writing tutor Tessa McWatt calls the 'revision funnel': a series of set tasks that compartmentalize the editing process, so you're not just mindlessly hacking away at your work.

There are six stages of the funnel, ranging from macro to micro, each one tackling a separate aspect of your work:

- **RE-WRITE:** hand-written to word-processed? Printed out and scribbled all over? Consider flow, themes, cast of characters – get rid of excess.
- **REVISE THE BIG PICTURE:** plot, pace, timing, characters, setting, POV, voice, tone, humour. If any of these things don't gel right, or jump out at you as wrong, now is the time for a fix.
- **ACTION SECTION BY ACTION SECTION:** Does one follow another smoothly? Do transitions work? What's in the way?
- **PARAGRAPH BY PARAGRAPH:** Ideas/actions in each paragraph; tension/voice; dialogue; description.
- **LINE BY LINE:** Clear, polished sentences, punctuation, repetitiveness, cliché, clarity.
- **WORD BY WORD:** Spelling; is each word the RIGHT word?

While you are free to look at any of these points during the writing process, it might be best to work at them one at a time after a first draft – something I call a 'pass'. So my first pass will be focused on the Rewrite. Second on the Big Picture, third on Action Section by Action Section and so on. This makes it easier to concentrate on that particular aspect without being sidetracked and results in the draft being finished much faster. Think of this stage of the editorial process as your production line and you're preparing your finely tuned literary machine to go out into the showroom, to await the buying (and reading) public.

EXERCISE

Useful creative questions to ask yourself after a first draft are:

Does your story begin well?

Does your POV help or hinder?

Is the language working?

Are you using physical details effectively?

Do the characters feel real?

Does the structure work?

How is the story paced?

Does it end where it should?

Tenses

Tania

This is worth stressing again: nothing in your story-in-progress is sacred. Just because your first draft is in the past tense, this doesn't mean that the past tense is the best for your story. There are pros and cons of using each different tense. Let's take a look.

It is quite traditional to tell a short story in the 'close' past tense, as if it has only just happened. Here is the opening paragraph of Ali Smith's wonderful short story, 'The Child' online in Blithe House Quarterly (http://www.blithe.com/bhq9.1/9.1.01.html) or in her collection, *The First Person & Other Stories*, (Hamish Hamilton, 2008).

> I went to Waitrose as usual in my lunchbreak to get the weekly stuff. I left my trolley by the vegetables and went to find bouquet garni for the soup. But when I came back to the vegetables again I couldn't find my trolley. It seemed to have been moved. In its place was someone else's shopping trolley, with a child sitting in its little child seat, its fat little legs through the leg-places.

The close past tense, combined with the way Smith describes the events, gives us the strong impression that our narrator is telling us this just after it has happened; there isn't the sense of great distance from events.

What happens if we put it in the present tense?

> I go to Waitrose as usual in my lunchbreak to get the weekly stuff. I leave my trolley by the vegetables and go to find bouquet garni for the soup. But when I come back to the vegetables again I can't find my trolley. It seems to have been moved. In its place is someone

else's shopping trolley, with a child sitting in its little child seat, its fat
little legs through the leg-places.

The difference is subtle. With the published story, the past tense can
reassure us that nothing terrible is going to happen because it's sort-of-
already-happened. If this was told in a more distant past tense (e.g. 'I
remember that day years ago that I went to Waitrose ...') we would feel even
'safer', even if that was not at all justified as we read on.

But with the present tense, we have no reassurance at all. Nothing is
safe. Not for the writer as you write it, not for the narrator of the story, not
for the reader. Anything could happen next, no one knows what's coming,
certainly not the narrator. It adds immediacy. It makes us feel like it's
happening RIGHT NOW.

What if we put it in the future tense?

I will go to Waitrose as usual in my lunchbreak to get the weekly
stuff. I will leave my trolley by the vegetables and go to find bouquet
garni for the soup. But when I come back to the vegetables again I
won't be able to find my trolley. It will seem to have been moved. In
its place will be someone else's shopping trolley, with a child sitting
in its little child seat, its fat little legs through the leg-places.

Instantly, this adds a dash of weirdness, right? We are writing/reading about
something that hasn't happened yet. If the whole story was written like this,
the reader would get used to it, though.

You can move from one tense to another and back again, especially if
you are moving around in time, of course. Your 'now' might be in the present
tense, and flashbacks in the past tense. Or as with the above permutation,
your 'now' could be in the future tense and your flashbacks in the present.
Tenses do provide signposts to help ground the reader. If you want to deliberately create a confusing story, mess with them. Let's try this:

I went to Waitrose as usual in my lunchbreak to get the weekly
stuff. I leave my trolley by the vegetables and go to find bouquet

garni for the soup. But when I came back to the vegetables again I couldn't find my trolley. It seems to have been moved. In its place is someone else's shopping trolley, with a child sitting in its little child seat, its fat little legs through the leg-places.

What effect does this have? It's hard to get a grip on the story, it seems to be a little slippery ... It definitely makes the reader think, and you might not want your reader thinking too much yet, in this opening paragraph. You might want them to settle down into your story, and then later on, when it's a bit more established, when you've 'got' them, then mess with things a little. Or you might not want these structural elements to get in the way of the words, to become part of the story. It's your choice.

Now that I have whetted your appetite, go off and read the rest of Ali Smith's short story! Online in Blithe House Quarterly (http://www.blithe.com/bhq9.1/9.1.01.html) or in her collection, *The First Person & Other Stories* (Hamish Hamilton, 2008).

Step into a world – thoughts on structure

Courttia

The realistic representation of time in fiction is one of the most obscure, and yet fundamental aspects of storytelling. As human beings, our perception of time is that it flows in a series of onward steps, a continuous movement in one sure direction. At its most fundamental, this consciousness permeates our very existence.

> We are conscious of existing in time, moving from a past that we recall very patchily, and into a future that is unknown and unknowable.
>
> Milan Kundera

Dawn becomes early morning, and mid-morning, which morphs into afternoon. Afternoon becomes late afternoon, and dusk. Dusk becomes evening, and evening descends into night. Night becomes dawn, and the cycle repeats. This, for us as for most beings on this planet, helps to form our ideas of linear time, influenced for the most part by the movement of the sun across our skies, interpreted by humans as hours and days. The phases of the moon aid our ability to track larger time periods, and have become known as months and years. It's easy to imagine our ancestors watching shadows move across bare earth and begin to construct machines that would help them chart the passage of time. Over the course of history, sundials, watches and clocks have all served the purpose of tracking our temporal journeys from one moment to the next, while reinforcing our notion of its limitations.

Time is a bridge that leads in one direction. We should not try to
cross it twice.

Valerie Bloom

And yet fiction writers, particularly the writers of short stories, routinely
disturb any direct passage over that never-ending bridge, sometimes making
great leaps so as to cover great distances, sometimes moving forwards,
backwards, forwards again, sometimes even halting in the middle as if to
say, 'Here I will rest. Why? Because it's the best place.' Sometimes they drift
away into the obscure distance, where nothing can be seen but a haze of
possibility.

The story (real time)

- Narrative time: the time period the story takes place in.

Plot (rearranged time)

- The order in which we rearrange those events so that we can shape narrative
  and tell that story *in a relatively small space.*

This is key. Short stories demand brevity, and with that brevity comes a
price. We won't be able to fit everything in, or certainly nowhere near as
much as long-form fiction, the novel. But the good thing for us short story
writers is that the events we do include, if we choose carefully and hone
them for optimum effect, can become concentrated with mood, emotion
and thematic resonance, so much so that a single moment can be made to
sparkle, and dazzle the eye.

How do graphic novels use time?

- Pick moments carefully.
- Capture the *optimum moment of attack* with which to convey necessary
  information.

EXERCISE

Break your story down into bullet points, or beats, which trace the beginning, middle and end. Don't concentrate on the messy details. Just write the optimum moment of attack for each beat and see how many you have in your story. Confine yourself to the major plot movements of your story. Once you have written these, try to gauge whether you have too many, or too few.

TOP TIP

We should not see the mechanics of the story over and above character, place and narrative voice. If those elements are strong, then you will hold the reader.

When does structure work best?

- In most cases the author will hop around the narrative, much like our imaginary writer traversing their time bridge.

- They begin the story at a Moment in Time that has the optimum point of attack.

- How is this chosen? By thinking about the theme. What do you want to say, and how do you want to say it?

- Are you being tragic? Comic? Do you want to begin with tragedy and end in hope? The reverse maybe? Does the story have a topic? If so, what?

- Once you can answer the questions you can decide the moment in time, or your point of attack.

Think about is the span of time in your story. Is it five minutes? An hour? A day? Six months, or 20 years? It's inevitable that your chosen time span will determine the length of your story. Too many or too few scenes and you run the risk of a story that is unsatisfying as it overruns your time span, or falls short. Some might plough ahead at this stage and begin to write. This can be useful, but it can also help to have even the most basic idea of the scenes that comprise your story; either plotted section by section, in bullet points, or note form, or even just in your head. Use the last choice only when you're writing a story that spans no more than a few days, possibly a week at most. For anything longer, write it down. Visualise the scenes and how they sit against each other. When you imagine them in your head, they're often perfect in every way. Writing them down makes it easier to see the flaws and how you might make the story better.

TOP TIP

Do not have strict formula for writing stories. If you have a formula, there's a chance you might become formulaic.

Character and plot — the basic components of scenes

If you're not concerned with one of these two points: developing the character (usually the principal one), or moving the story forwards in order to reach your conclusion (which in some way should be a rumination on your chosen theme) – then you're digressing, which means you're not really telling a story. These points can be reversed if you like. Plot can precede character, and that creates a different style of story. But these are the only two points you should be thinking of.

Writer's tools

These two points, character and plot, can be broken down into even smaller pieces. Tools, if you like, at the writer's disposal. These are:

- Scenes
- Exposition

- Summary
- Flashback
- Flashforward
- Jumpcut

How these are used, and in particular when they are used, determines how well a story is told.

Building a scene

Dramaturge and playwright Will Dunne asks the writer to consider seven points before writing a scene. He uses this method to map, or structure the opening of a story, and also as a means of developing backstory. For Dunne's purposes, the story he's talking about is a play, but I believe these points are true whatever form of dramatic writing we have chosen. It's also good to be able to answer these questions in reference to any scene, wherever it takes place in the narrative. They are:

1 What is your character doing now?
2 Where is your character doing this?
3 When is your character doing this?
4 Who else, if anyone is here and what are they doing?
5 How does your character feel now?
6 What is your character thinking about now?
7 What is the next thing your character says?

If you can answer all seven questions for every scene in the story, there's a strong chance you have worked out the structure. Don't be afraid to tweak if necessary, or in some cases, if it's not working, scrap the whole thing and start again, either with that story or something new. The point is that this is a road map; it's supposed to lead you someplace. If it doesn't, then it's useless, and it needs to be revised or scrapped. Revision or its unfortunate counterpart, dismissal, are as much as part of the job as the actual writing of words. Don't be afraid of either. Treat them as your friend. If you can learn to love both equally, they can be invaluable at the plotting stage.

TOP TIP

Just because you might have structured what seems like the ideal story does not necessarily mean it should be set in stone. Your structure is a skeleton, nothing more.

If you plot too rigidly, it will move like one: all bones, no muscle, blood and sinew, what's more no *flesh*. This will reflect on your characters and story. They will become marionettes, mere robots dancing to the whims of their creator. They will not mimic the life and free-flowing movements of humankind. Allowing your subjects (in the topical, not royal sense of the word) room to breathe and think for themselves means they will reward you by doing things you never imagined they could, far outside the realms or your original insights. Some writers scoff at this idea. They claim the author is in complete control 100 per cent of the time, that there is no such thing as free will for a fictional character who has been invented by real human being. While I understand where those authors are coming from somewhat, I do not want to read their books. Their opinion undermines the sheer *magic* that must take place at every level of a story's evolution: the planning, the creation, and the reading. If you can allow just a touch of that magic to become infused in your structure from the very beginning, there's a strong chance it will remain, and even grow.

Structure and how to use it

Tania

Finding the right structure was the key to finishing writing my story *Under the Tree* in the way I wanted to tell it. 'Structure' can mean several things. To go back to my building analogy, the structure of a house is both external (the shape of the house, type of brick, where the windows and doors are, etc. ...) and internal (the layout of the rooms, the furniture within the rooms, etc. ...). The internal structure of your story is how the parts of your story come together, which refers to everything we're talking about in this section: time (linear or non-linear), point of view, tense, where you choose to begin and end, etc. ... What's left to talk about here then is the external structure, the shape of your house, and how this works with the content.

> **TOP TIP**
>
> *Altering how your story looks on the page can help you see it with fresh eyes, notice things you haven't noticed before.*

Stories often look the same as each other on the page – text is traditionally aligned to the left margin, with frequent paragraph breaks and indented scenes of dialogue, perhaps with 'white space', a blank line denoting a larger break in time or change of location. But as with poems, the way the story looks on the page, the way the words are arranged, can play a part in the story, both the writing of it and, then, the reading of it.

I was recently given an unpublished story which was several pages long and had not one paragraph break. I found the endless block of text unappealing, even before I'd looked at the first word. Something about it seemed suffocating. Now, this could be enormously useful if you want to create this effect. My philosophy is: you can do anything, as long as you know why you might be doing it. While I am all for letting go of 'rules', to write a story with no paragraph breaks will suggest to me that the writer might never have read any fiction and doesn't know what a page of fiction 'usually' looks like. This won't fill me with confidence and the writer will then have to work harder to win me over.

Use of breaks in text

- Breaks in the text are there first of all to allow us – the writer and the reader – to breathe. There are different strengths of breath.
- Commas, semi-colons, colons all give us pause.
- Full stops slightly greater, paragraph breaks greater still, and white space, or a section break, the strongest pause.
- They can be useful to change the pacing of a story, speed up or slow down. A paragraph that is one single sentence which runs on for four lines has a different pace from the same paragraph separated into three sentences.
- I've read wonderful flash fictions that have no full stops at all, conveying a breathless pace that served the story beautifully, for example.

Sections

- Dividing your short story into sections is something that is becoming more common.
- The sections might simply be separated by white space – a single blank line – or may have subheadings, numbers, or both, or something else.
- This can help you write the story, giving you something akin to a map to navigate through it a little easier.
- And it can help a reader too, as we saw with the opening to the Anthony Doerr story, which has subheadings, the first coming immediately below the title.

Examples of experimental structure

You can try something more experimental with external structure, such as aligning your text to the right margin instead of the left, or leaving large sections of the page blank. You could split the page and lay your story out in columns – for example, the opening paragraph from Alexandra Chasin's 'They Came From Mars':

```
Then they walk pour flow ooze down town rows upon rows flow
folk from Mars rows upon rows like ants Dont obey when City
Hall says dont Then wewe spec they want fear they want TAKE
OVER TAKE OVER Wewe spec fear that what they want they want
from usus Come from Mars this flow ants that want what wewe
have rite here What Dont Mars have nice down town nice life
```

The story is tough to read, but the effort pays off, and the layout is so important that it's almost a character in the story.

TOP TIP

As with houses, there are many shapes a short story can take. Trying out some different structures can help you see your own story-in-progress with fresh eyes, notice something you hadn't noticed, help you tell it the way you want to tell it.

Further reading

Chasin, Alexandra, 'They Came From Mars', *Kissed By* (FC2, 2007).

What gets left out and minimalism

Tania

Short stories are almost more about what is not on the page than what is. The short story is the only form (together with the novella, similarly length-restricted, but at both ends) that has to be below a certain number of words. A poem can be book-length, a film might be ten hours long, a novel part of a trilogy. But a short story is short, which means as a writer you can't include everything.

Traditional short stories

Questions

- What do you need to write the story?
- What do you need to know about your characters, for example?

There are writing exercises which have you interview your character before you start writing to find out their favourite colour, say, and their views on world peace. This is too cerebral for me; I prefer to dive in and get to know them through the story. I think of my characters as friends: you don't tend to become friends after knowing someone for ages and finding out a lot of information about them. It often happens quickly, a click, a feeling. You might meet someone only once, at a party, and they say something that stays with you for years, but you never see them again. I don't expect them to be my best friends, my spouses. I am dipping into their lives and I try and tell their story as best I can.

EXERCISE

Write a scene in which two people who are going to become good friends meet for the first time. Is there an instant click or are they shy and tentative? Remember that people don't often say exactly what they mean and that we learn a lot through body language.

TOP TIP

A piece of writing can never include everything, especially fiction, where the aim is to engage your reader's imagination. If you give them every detail, what is left for them to imagine?

American writer Adam Peterson said in an interview with online journal Smokelong Quarterly *of his flash story, 'When You Look For Us, I'll Be Here': 'I didn't really want to say too much about these people. That ambiguity – which I imagine some find obnoxious – is maybe my favourite thing about short pieces. I feel like I get to openly not care about things I don't care about ... I'd rather focus on that feeling and that voice and leave the specifics...'*

So, if there's something you don't care about, why are you putting it in your story?

What readers already know

Let's start with a simple example of what you might not need to include. Your character is making tea. You can assume most readers know how to do this, so there's no need to say 'He switched on the kettle, put a teabag in the mug, and when the kettle boiled he poured hot water over the teabag. He then took out the teabag and put in milk and a spoonful of sugar'. A reader will infer all of this from just 'He made tea'.

However, if your character makes tea in a specific or odd way that tells us something about him that we need to know for this story, include it. For example: 'He flicked the switch on the kettle with the little finger of his left hand and when it had boiled, poured the water into the mug very slowly, drop by drop, until it began to spill over the brim. He sipped at the boiling water, wincing as his lips burned, until there was enough room in the mug for the teabag, which he left in for fifteen minutes, just as his father and grandfather had done.'

What readers don't need to know but you do

The bizarre tea-making ritual does tell us something about that character, but there are often things you need to know about your character that don't have to be on the page. The first thing that springs to mind is what your character looks like. Describing exactly what you think your character looks like can be risky because your reader may have imagined the character you see as tall, skinny and red-headed as squat and dark, and are thrown by your description.

What readers need to know about in fantastical stories

If you are writing a fantastical story set in a world that is not the one we know, you might need to know much more about how that world works to write the story than the reader needs to know to read it. Experienced short story readers already expect not to be given everything, to suspend disbelief for the length of a short story in a way they might not with a longer work – for example, one of my favourite very short stories, 'When We Lived Inside the Alligator' by Robert Kloss (published in *Fractured West*, issue 2). His first line is: 'Then I, without regard for the teeth and humidity, the mist and the blood, the birds clawing and staring and screaming, moved my family into the alligator.' Not just 'an alligator', but 'the alligator'. He never explains anything, just carries on as if it is completely normal to move into an animal. He trusts his readers – if they decide to read on past this opening line, which signposts the kind of story this is – to fill in the gaps themselves, each in their own way.

Pre-empt and explain

Another common pitfall is to pre-empt what is about to happen, and then explain what has just happened. Here's a made-up example:

> She looked at him furiously.
>   'How could you do that!' she screamed. She couldn't believe what he'd just done.

This can be achieved with:

> 'How could you do that!' she screamed.

When you're writing your story, you might not know that she's about to scream, so you need that sentence before, but then, later, you can take it out. And you don't necessarily need to explain why she's screamed – trust that we've got that she's angry and disbelieving.

TOP TIP

Leaving things out doesn't mean foregoing description, letting go of any particular element of story, like dialogue, number of characters or backstory. It means having a sense of what the story you want to tell needs and doesn't need.

Show not tell

Be wary of telling the reader too much instead of leaving him to figure it out himself.

> **TOP TIP**
>
> *Every story has its own needs.*

Minimalist short stories

Minimalism is the most extreme end of 'what to leave out'. A minimalist story is one designed to make the reader work hard. Not every reader wants to do this. But it can be fun to write minimalist stories, which verge on the absurd or surreal. You can let go of knowing exactly what you're writing. This happened to me with one of my very short stories/prose poems, 'Like Owls'. After I'd written it, I was puzzled. It felt complete, but I didn't know what it was about. After it was broadcast on Radio 4 and provoked a very positive reaction, I began to see that that was okay, that many listeners/readers liked being allowed to figure it out for themselves.

These kinds of stories are even closer to the riddle or conundrum I mentioned earlier. Readers work hard to understand what is going on – but with the minimalist story as opposed to a riddle, there often isn't one right answer that the reader has to 'get'.

> **TOP TIP**
>
> *Minimalist stories leave room for each reader to come to his or her own conclusion. An example of minimalism is a story that gives you only one side of a conversation, say. Or provides no details about the characters or setting, leave you to assign gender, place, etc. in whatever way feels right to you as you read.*

EXERCISE

Write a story that is only one side of a conversation. Write it first as a 'normal' conversation between two characters, and then delete all the questions and responses from one character. Now take a look and see whether a reader would get enough about what is going on here. It will be hard to resist the urge to tweak it a little to explain more, but don't do it. Leave room for your smart reader to not only figure it out, but to get involved in your story.

Further reading

Peterson, Adam, 'When You Look For Us, I'll Be Here', *Smokelong Quarterly*, http://smokelong.com/flash/adampeterson42q.asp

Speaking their minds – character and voice

Courttia

It's impossible to know how to give voice to a character without first knowing who they are. This is not to say that inspiration cannot happen on the page, at the moment the story is being written. Whether your knowledge comes in a flash of inspiration, or whether it is laid out in meticulous notes that take years to plot and plan, the result is still the same. You know, and so you move forwards. If you can't answer those questions, stop and think about them. Don't put a limit on your thinking time. The awareness that you need to fill in gaps, however or whenever you do this, marks the difference between a writer at work and one who believes they have failed because they can't write.

TOP TIP

'With literature, everything depends on the tone of voice.'

Al Alvarez

EXERCISE

Have one character from your story write a letter to another in the same story; either your protagonist to another character, or that character to your protagonist. Be sure to give the letter an impetus spurred on by a particular emotion: love, lust, anger or jealousy. The author of this letter never sends it, and so you can be as honest as you like in the writing; they hold nothing back. If it also helps, treat the letter as an exercise in building backstory.

What the character knows and feels

Try to discover the truth of what a character feels, even if you know better than they. Have them act according to what they hold within the deepest wellsprings of their being, and bring that into conflict with how they see themselves in the world. That first initial battle of emotions gives rise to internal chaos that, if handled correctly, can paint a picture of who they are far better than you can by telling, or reporting character traits to us. We will believe what we see, but only if you show us. If you are forthright in your observations, and bold, then we as readers will feel we are being dictated to.

TOP TIP

'As he thinketh in his heart, so he is.'

Proverbs, 23.7

Empathy and respect for your characters

Respect your characters and grant them empathy. Most people in the world feel that they are good people, or that even if they are bad, there are reasons why they behave that way. Don't typecast your characters, even if they do bad things. Give them a moment of kindness, or reflection, even if this occurs when they're alone. No one is evil 24 hours a day, 365 days of the year. If they are an essentially good character, have them do something bad.

THE SECRET LIFE

- *Everyone has one secret thing they've done that they never told anyone, for better or for worse, one secret deed no one will ever know.*
- *What's your protagonist's?*
- *Even if it doesn't take place within the confines of the story, how has is shaped their lives? Does it lurk in the forgotten corner of their memory, only to surface against their will?*
- *If you can make it work for or against that belief of who they are, what they hold in their heart, you've got your internal chaos.*
- *How does that cause them to view the world, what does that make them say or do?*

The components of characters

Think about five aspects of their protagonists at the beginning of their stories:

1 Personality
2 Physicality
3 Mannerisms
4 Speech
5 Their flaw

Write what you know about these components of your characters in as much detail as you like. It can be done in bullet point fashion, a selection of random words, sentences, or even scene fragments. These are the basic building blocks of a character, easily defined, and some of them are known either before or during my writing. It's not something I do as a hard-and-fast rule, but a quick exercise I use if I'm ever stuck about who my character is, and what they might look or sound like.

Now draw up a summary of your character's life, describing them in 50 words. Write down their likes or dislikes; create scenes a day before the story starts, or a week, or a month, or a year. Anything that helps you know you character better is a good thing.

It's essential that the writer can move seamlessly between authorial voice, narrative voice and character voice. Most often these techniques become fused — for instance, the narrator is often the main character, as in first person perspective. Or there are fragments of narration told in the character's voice during third person, if the author is using free indirect style. A steady movement from one technique to the next gives rise to an uninterrupted flow, and the reader is less likely to become bored by repetition. Here is the categorization of different ways to present the character's thoughts, which are much the same as the presentation of dialogue:

Is she angry with me? (free direct thought)
He wondered, 'Is she angry with me?' (direct thought)
Was she angry with him? (free indirect thought)
He wondered if she was angry with him. (indirect thought)
He wondered about her anger towards him. (narrative report of a thought)

Direct thought highlights the fact that the character is thinking, either by speech marks, or italics, or saying 'he thought', and is largely authorial. Indirect thought reports without speech marks, yet still anchors what is written to the voice of the narrator, by placing the character under their observation ('he wondered'). Free indirect thought has no reporting word, italics, or speech marks; the thought is untethered, and so it allows us to see the character's point of view using their own words. Here there is an allowance for dialect, slang or colloquialisms which are particular to the character's manner of speech. It is a way of shaping text around a subject, so that the prose is injected with subconscious thought.

TOP TIP

See James Wood's How Fiction Works for a detailed explanation of the history and use of this invaluable tool.

- Think about who is telling the story (it's not always who the story is about).
- What is your narrator's relationship to the story, or its characters?

Answering these questions should make it clear what the character will sound like and what they will say. Spend time on this. It will make the writing much easier, and is likely to produce great results.

Writing flash fiction, liberation through constraint

Tania

Flash fiction is a narrative of extreme brevity – also called short-short stories, microfiction, nanofiction, ultra-short stories and many other names. Exactly how short is a question for debate: Americans go for 1,000 words and under, whereas in the UK we limit ourselves further, to under 500 words. There is no real lower limit; there is a current trend for six-word short stories such as Ernest Hemingway's: 'For Sale. Baby shoes. Never worn.'

Is it only about word length? Not exactly.

Hint from Robert Shapard

Robert Shapard, who edits a wonderful series of Sudden Fiction and Flash Fiction anthologies, was quoted in an article on FlashFiction.net, saying: 'I love hearing some people talk about flash. One of my favourites is Luisa Valenzuela, who says, "I usually compare the novel to a mammal, be it wild as a tiger or tame as a cow; the short story to a bird or a fish; the microstory to an insect (iridescent in the best cases)."'

Hint from David Gaffney

British writer David Gaffney, who has written four collections of tiny stories, said in the *Guardian* on the UK's first National Flash Fiction Day in 2012: 'The story could live much more cheaply than I'd realised, with little deterioration in lifestyle. Sure, it had been severely downsized, but it was all the better for it. There was more room to think, more space for the original idea to resonate, fewer unnecessary words to wade through. The story had become a nimble, nippy little thing that could turn on a sixpence and accelerate quickly away. And any tendencies to go all purple were almost completely eliminated. Adjectives were anthrax.'

Definition from Tara Masih

In *The Field Guide to Writing Flash Fiction* (Rose Metal Press, 2009), editor Tara L. Masih defines a flash as 'simply a story in miniature, a work of art carved on a grain of rice'.

Flash fiction is an iridescent insect, carved onto a grain of rice, which can turn on a sixpence. Is that clear? Let's not worry too much about definitions. Why do I love writing flash fiction? First, if I am setting out in advance to write a very short story, I can now – after several years of practice, of limbering up that writing muscle – write a first draft very fast, the process being as 'flash' as the end product. Which means that I can write several first drafts of flash stories in one day.

Advantages of writing flash fiction

- I can use up quite a few of my ideas, the things I've been thinking about, consciously and subconsciously, and wanting to explore in fiction.
- As opposed to a longer story I might work on for months or years, I am less 'precious' about each flash story I write. If I write four in one afternoon and three don't work for me, then a 25 per cent hit rate is pretty good, right?
- I don't have to grip each story so tightly, take it so seriously.

TOP TIP

If short stories are like long-haul flights – you take off, reach cruising altitude, cruise for a while, then land – flash fiction is like a short domestic flight, where just as you've reached cruising altitude, you already begin to prepare for landing.

As with all short stories, a flash story can be about anything, in any style, genre, form. Just because they are very short, does not mean they are easier to write. Almost as soon as you begin a flash story, you are already starting to end it, to narrow it in rather than send out tendrils to widen out. I find this image helpful when I'm writing. It doesn't mean flash fictions aren't complex, can't encompass worlds. They can, and do.

Effect of flash fiction on readers

As a reader, the flash fictions I enjoy most have a hint of the magical, the otherworldly. This may be because it is easier for the writer to step into more surreal situations for such a short time, being 'allowed' to let go of explaining how these worlds work. But there is realist flash fiction, flash crime fiction, a great deal of flash science fiction – and humour, too. Take a look at Dan Rhodes's collection, *Anthropology*, of 101 stories, each 101 words long! As well as the delights of writing it, there is an ever-increasing number of publications that publish flash fiction of every stripe and flavour, and competitions specifically for very short stories.

Liberation through constraint

As Leonardo da Vinci apparently said: 'Art breathes from containment and suffocates from freedom'. Poets know this well – the sonnet must be 14 lines long; the sestina has six stanzas of six lines each and then a three-line 'envoi', and the words that end each line of the first stanza are used as line endings in the next; the villanelle is five stanzas of three lines and one stanza of four lines, and various lines have to alternate in certain ways; the haiku has 17 syllables arranged in three lines of 5–7–5. The constraints are both a challenge and a preset structure for your words, a frame.

We can do the same in short stories. The first restriction you will experience is length. Decide in advance you are going to write a piece of flash fiction in under 300 words, say. Or take it further and aim for a drabble, exactly 100 words (not including the title), or a dribble, exactly 50 words. No, I haven't made these up, they are recognized terms, and there are plenty of places that publish them! I often set students in workshops the task of writing a drabble, and I give them longer to do it; less takes more time – and there's much counting involved. I find – in my own work and in theirs – that writing drabbles emphasizes the weight of every single word, and can also bring out something quite magical in the writing, when, as I mentioned, you are 'allowed' not to explain anything because you have so little space.

EXERCISE

Open a magazine and pick the first picture you see, or go onto the internet and do a search for 'picture'. Don't think before choosing. Then write a drabble — a story of exactly 100 words — inspired in some way by the picture. Remember: the title is not included in the 100 words so make good use of it!

TOP TIP

Constraints come in all flavours, some physical, some to do with language, or content. Different kinds of constraint will work for different writers. (There is a whole movement, called Oulipo and founded in France in 1960, within which writers set themselves constraints, such as writing a whole novel without the letter 'e' ['A Void' by Georges Perec].)

Exercises using constraints

Pick a letter and write a story where each sentence starts with that letter; draw a shape on a piece of paper and write your story within that shape; make a list of all the words used in someone else's poem and set that as your vocabulary; you can use only words from the list in your story; decide in advance if your story is going to cover five minutes or a whole life. Come up with your own and see what works for you!

Further reading

Gaffney, David, 'How to Write Flash Fiction', *Guardian*, May 2012, http://www.theguardian.com/books/2012/may/14/how-to-write-flash-fiction

Masih, Tara (ed.), *The Field Guide to Writing Flash Fiction* (Rose Metal Press, 2009).

Shapard, Robert, 'What is Flash Fiction?', Flashfiction.net, February 2013 http://flashfiction.net/2013/02/what-is-flash-fiction-robert-shapard-james-thomas.php

A brief history of time in the short story

Tania

You can do anything with time in a short story – brevity has no bearing on how much, or how little, time a story can cover. Peter Orner's story 'Initials Etched on a Dining Room Table, Lockeport, Nova Scotia' covers a period of around 30 years in two-and-a-half pages. Tobias Woolf's story 'Bullet in the Brain' is 1,900 words long and the main story takes place over about an hour, and includes a flashback to the main character's childhood. Alice Munro is well known for enormous time jumps in her short stories; turn a page and 40 years have passed without explanation.

TOP TIP

Your story might move along a timeline in a linear fashion, with the next thing that happens in the story being the next thing that happens chronologically. Or it may skip around in time.

Flashbacks

I have heard some teachers forbid the use of the flashback in short stories, but you won't find any prohibitions in this book. What is a flashback? It's when you move from the present 'now' of your story into the past. Here's an example from one of my own stories, 'Self-Raising':

> I make them out of flour, sugar, eggs, like you would any cake. But they're not any cake, they're lab coats and test tubes, DNA and petri

dishes, just like in Science at school, when I used to get things right and the teacher would say, Excellent, Madeleine, that's exactly what happens when magnesium oxidises, and he'd smile at me and I'd grin at him, and the rest of them'd laugh and throw things and call me Swot. But I didn't mind about the names they called me; I knew what I knew and I wasn't going to pretend I didn't.

We moved from the present (our narrator making cakes) to the past (her time at school) within one sentence, and there are signals to alert us to what is happening to the timeline. The first is the phrase 'used to', which tells us we are not in the present. The second is that we have moved from present tense, 'I make' to 'I didn't mind', past tense. This helps the reader figure out 'when' we are, especially if it happens in the middle of a sentence.

There is also the cousin of the flashback, the flashforward, when the story takes a peek into the future. We saw a flashforward in the opening paragraph to Sarah Hall's story, 'Butcher's Perfume', in the section on beginnings and endings:

> Later, when I knew her better, Manda told me how she'd beaten
> two girls at once outside the Cranemakers Arms in Carlisle. She said
> all you had to do was keep hold of one, keep hold of one and
> keep hitting her.

The signal time-word here is 'later', so we know that this is not happening in the 'now' of this story. Unless your aim is to confuse your reader, these words are the most useful ways to hint at where we are, even if your story is linear – and especially if you are moving backwards or forwards. They help you while you're writing, too, so you don't get lost in when your story's 'now' is.

A flashback or flashforward can last as long as you want. It can all happen at once, or you can insert part of a flashback or flashforward, then return to the 'now' of your story, then a little bit more of the past scene, say, then back to the now, drip-feeding information, either through exposition or through a scene. Here's an example I just wrote:

She was looking at him as if he had something all over his face.
  She started doing this the week after they moved in together.
    'Why are you staring like that?' he had said and she hadn't
  answered. Now she was doing it again, saying nothing. That first
  time, he had held himself in, since their relationship was so new, he
  hadn't asked again, and, after a few minutes, she had looked away,
  sighed, gone off to do something else.
    She sighed again now.
    'What?' he said.

Here, the flashback is woven into the present scene, and the scene from the
past illuminates what is happening in the 'now' of the story. Some of the
time-words here are 'now' versus 'that first time'. The 'now' of this story is in
the past tense already, so the flashback is in the past perfect, 'he had said'.
  And example of a flashforward in this same situation, changing the
tenses, might be:

  She is looking at him as if he has something all over his face. She
  will do the same thing several years later and he will remember this
  first time.
    'Why are you staring like that?' he will say and she won't answer.
  She is saying nothing now, and he is holding himself in, since their
  relationship is so new. He won't ask the next time either, and, after
  a few minutes, she will look away, sigh, and go off to do something
  else.
    She sighs now.

This could be that same couple but the 'now' of this version has moved to
what was the past in the first, and the flashforward is showing us a glimpse
into the future, which is the 'now' of the first story. Flashforwards change
the tone of a story, they give the reader knowledge that the characters don't
have – unless one of them has the gift of prophecy, of course.
  So, altering the time aspect of your story will change the story itself, and,
as ever, it depends on how you want to tell your story. Time also, of course,

refers to the point at which your story starts, which might be anywhere from when your main character is born – or even before! Another thing you can do is tell your whole story backwards in time, as I talk about in the section on experimental short stories. If a story you are working on isn't working, playing with some time-related aspect can give you a fresh perspective. Each choice you make will subtly alter the story.

EXERCISE

Take a short story by someone else that you have read and enjoyed and read it again, making notes on how time works in this story. Sketch out a time line: where is the 'now' of this story? How many flashbacks and flashforwards are there? Are they woven into the 'now' or do they come as a separate section? How do you think the way this story uses time affects your reading experience?

Further reading

Hall, Sarah, 'Butcher's Perfume', *The Beautiful Indifference* (Faber and Faber, 2012).

Another perspective – point of view in the story

Courttia

Key question 1

'Who is telling this story, and why?'

Not knowing the answer is a constant barrier to finding a way 'in' to the story, and makes all the difference as to whether the author is excited about what they are writing, or simply sitting on the sidelines, bored. Even if that occurs, you can change your mind along with your perspective. Novelist Brian Chikwava, author of *Harare North*, told me that he started the novel in the third person and struggled to make it work, until he chose to write in the first person. That simple act caused the character to come alive. The narrator's voice spoke with strength and clarity, and Chikwava could continue. It became relatively easy to finish the book once a right and true perspective became apparent.

Key question 2

Another way of looking at this question might be: 'Who has the clearest view?' By this I mean which of your characters can narrate the action from a perspective that sheds light on the things you as an author want to say? Edna O'Brien's 'Black Flower' illustrates this by using the observer-narrator, an innocent bystander who watches and reflects on the events, but plays no real part. Sometimes we hear the story from the point of view of an unseen narrator. Shirley Jackson uses this in 'The Lottery', an omniscient narrator's voice that allows a lofty overview, speaking as numerous characters gathered in one location. There is the close third person of Percival Everett's

'The Appropriation of Cultures', a narration that sits tight on protagonist Daniel Barkley's shoulder, allowing us to see only what he sees, know what he knows. The first person pronoun of the collective 'we' at play in Stephen Millhauser's 'Beneath the Cellars of Our Town', or the wandering, restless perspective of Rachid Mimouni's 'The Escapee', a story that successfully breaks an unspoken rule by shifting between three points of view in a mere ten pages, finally coming to rest on the central protagonist for the denouement – the escapee himself.

Choosing your view

Imagine your story as a place on a map, Google if you will, but if you're technophobic an ordinary paper map will suffice. The choice the author has is this – whether they want to zoom out for a wider view and lose clarity, or zoom in, limiting the overall picture, but gaining precision. There are benefits and restrictions with each choice. No point of view is going to award the reader with boundless insight, no matter how well wrought it may be. We are searching for the best view, not the one that's perfect, and often this is the simplest choice, uncluttered by complications that get in the way and cause confusion for everyone involved.

Ursula Le Guin, the award-winning author of eight collections of short stories, outlines what she calls 'The Principal Points of View' in *Steering the Craft*. These are:

- First Person Narration
  The viewpoint character is 'I'.

- Limited Third Person
  The viewpoint character is 'He' or 'She'.

- Involved or Omniscient Author
  The story is not told from any single character; there may be numerous viewpoint characters.

- Detached Author 'Fly On The Wall', 'Camera Eye', 'Objective Narrator'
  There is no viewpoint character; the narrator can only say what a neutral observer might infer from characters' behaviour or speech.

- Observer-Narrator in First Person
  The narrator is present, but not a major actor in events.

- Observer-Narrator in Third Person
  The viewpoint character is a limited third person narrator who witnesses events.

There are a few aforementioned points of view not mentioned by Le Guin, which I would define as:

- Observer-Narrator in Second Person
  The viewpoint character witnesses events, but addresses the story to another character, or even sometimes the reader, i.e. 'you'.

- First Person Pronoun
  The viewpoint character is actually a social group or family, some collective unit by which the story is being told.

- Interior-Narrator in First Person
  Inward limited first person otherwise known as 'stream of consciousness'.

- Interior-Narrator in Third Person
  *Inward limited third person, where the character is still 'He' or 'She', but we also hear their conscious thoughts, usually in free indirect style (see **Character and Voice**).*

The important thing to remember when deciding on a perspective is *why* you have chosen to tell the story from this point of view. You must have a reason for doing so. That reason should not be random. You should genuinely be able to see a clear way into the narrative by using your chosen angle, and that way must shed light or convey information that is useful to your characters, the reader and yourself. If you chose a character whose vision is somewhat obscured in some way (the two-year-old brother of the protagonist, perhaps, who spends most of his time crawling under the table) you won't get a clear picture of the action. This is an exaggerated example of course, but it's important to track your chosen character's journey through the story, physically and emotionally. Are they present throughout? If not, why not? It might be that this hindrance of vision is necessary to the narrative – they might become unintentionally unreliable – or better still, intentionally reliable, if they have chosen not to be present in some way, for reasons of their own. This might sound contradictory but that's because the choice is yours. You can do whatever you like. If you can make a decision and know why you're doing so, it will strengthen your story no end. The driving force of fiction is intent.

EXERCISE

Find the perspective you have chosen for your story from those listed above, and then find two more, either from my list or a story you have read. Make sure your chosen two allow the insights detailed above.

Now write from these two different perspectives and see how this changes the story.

You might decide that your original choice was best. That's no bad thing, as you can move forwards assured you've made a wise decision.

You may also find that you've discovered a new way of seeing your story, which opens up all sorts of possibilities. That is also good.

TOP TIP

As always with the short story, being pliable and open to new ideas allows the gift of insight. That probably means that you'll have fun, and having fun is one of the best things about writing.

Voice and dialogue, using scenes

Tania

Why use dialogue?

Dialogue is where your characters are speaking, in their own voices, without you mediating at all, without you explaining what they've said, their intentions, their motivation. It's direct communication. And it may be the best way for you, the writer, to start to hear their voices when you are in the beginning stages of finding out what your story is about.

Tania's experience

With my first published story, 'The White Road', the first two lines came into my head pretty much fully formed:

> Today is one of them really and truly cold days. You're probably thinking cold is cold is cold, either everything's frosty or you're sipping margaritas by the pool in Florida, but let me tell you, there are degrees of freezing.

There she was. She was talking to me, she even says 'let me tell you'. Already from the opening sentence I could tell she had an odd way of speaking that was unlike the way I speak. I wouldn't say 'them really and truly cold days'. In fact, when this story was published online in New Scientist magazine, a reader left a comment criticizing the writer of the story for her bad grammar. They had confused me with my character, they didn't understand that what was on the page was a direct transcription of the way Mags, my character, talked. I forgave them, since New Scientist doesn't

---

usually publish fiction, and it was an interesting lesson for me about what voice is in fiction.

Frankly, it's a pretty weird thing for a new writer to get used to, the voices in your head! But this is a common part of fiction-writing; my writer friends and I feel we know our characters, and, more importantly, we want our characters to feel real not just to us, but to a reader too. Hearing their voice is one way to achieve that.

EXERCISE

Take a short story that you are currently working on and write a scene in which two of the characters — who might be main characters or lesser characters — talk to each other. One character is trying to say something to the other but can't refer to it directly, and the other character isn't really listening. What happens during this conversation?

Using a narrator

Your story may not be told by any of the characters at all but by a narrator who is watching it all unfold – but voice may be important in this situation too. Your narrator might be disdainful, making witty comments on the action, or warmer and sympathetic, say.

Even after you've got your character or narrator's voice, writing a scene where your character is talking to someone can be enormously useful in finding out what is happening in your story. It can feel like you are listening in, transcribing, rather than writing it yourself. So, if you are unsure what might happen next, or what your character wants, get her to talk to someone – or write an email, text message. You might learn not just from what she says, or writes, but from what she doesn't say, what she can't bring herself to say aloud or include in the email. All this can help you get the story written – you may later decide it doesn't belong in the story itself, but it got you to where you needed to get.

What's wonderful about human conversations is how much we say without saying it directly. In 'real life' conversations, we rarely reply directly, often half-listening and half-preparing what we want to say. A lot can be conveyed in how a conversation proceeds: how much interruption, for example; how many pauses and silences.

Scenes also help break up paragraphs of 'exposition' – describing what has happened without showing it to us – which can be a refreshing change after several paragraphs or pages of exposition. A change of pace – it's action. It can also jazz up the way the page looks. So instead of:

xxxxxxxxxxxxxxxxxxxxxxxx
xxxxxxxxxxxxxxxxxxxxxxxx
xxxxxxxxxxxxxxxxxxxxxxxx
xxxxxxxxxxxxxxxxxxxxxxxx
xxxxxxxxxxxxxxxxxxxxxxxx
xxxxxxxxxxxxxxxxxxxxxxxx
xxxxxxxxxxxxxxxxxxxxxxxx

your page looks like this

xxxxxxxxxxxxxxxxxxxxxxxx
xxxxx
xxxxxxxxxxxxxxxxxxxxxxx
xxxxxxxxxx
xxxxxxxxxxxxxx
xxxxx
xxxxxxxxxxxxxxxxxxxxxxx

There are a number of ways to format speech inside your text. The traditional way is like this:

> 'It was never going to happen,' she said, shaking out the towel.
> 'Look!' he said.
> 'I knew it,' she said.
> 'Where did you put the tea?'

You could do this without the speech marks, for example.

> It was never going to happen, she said, shaking out the towel.
> Look! he said.
> I knew it, she said.
> Where did you put the tea?

Or

> – It was never going to happen, she said, shaking out the towel.
> – Look! he said.
> – I knew it, she said.
> – Where did you put the tea?

These latter two formats are slightly less clear – there is nothing definite separating what she says and the description of her shaking out the towel, but you might like how this looks in your story. An even less clear way of using dialogue is without the line breaks:

> It was never going to happen, she said, shaking out the towel. Look! he said. I knew it, she said. Where did you put the tea?

You may choose to do this when you don't want the page's flow to be broken up, the pacing to change, or you're so immersed in writing the story that you don't want to stop to put in line breaks. Your reader might not quite know who is saying what, but this confusion may be exactly what you want to imply, an essential part of your story.

There are stories told entirely in dialogue, perhaps with some description, a little like a play with stage directions, which means your reader will probably have to work hard. This can be a fun exercise to do, telling it all in dialogue. There are stories that take this even further, giving you only one side of a conversation! And then, on the flipside, there are stories with no dialogue at all, when the writer doesn't want you, the reader, to necessarily hear anyone voices. How do you want to tell your story?

Experimenting and experimental short stories

Tania

The meaning of 'experiment' and 'experimental'

What does 'experiment' mean? Various dictionaries have it as 'a test, trial, or tentative procedure; an act or operation for the purpose of discovering something unknown or of testing a principle, a chemical experiment; a teaching experiment; an experiment in living'. And 'experimental'? 'Using a new way of doing or thinking about something.' So, the crux of experimentation seems to be newness, novelty. And surely, something is only new if it hasn't been done before, right?

In fiction and poetry, 'experimental' tends to be used these days as a synonym for 'weird' rather than 'innovative'. But it's about fashion, isn't it? If the majority is doing it, then it can't be 'innovative'. Something that was once experimental might well become mainstream. Chekhov was considered innovative in his day for his stories' lack of 'proper' beginning-middle-and-end-ness. Metafiction – a short story that comments on itself from within the story – was once highly experimental, as were stories in the form of lists, etc. ...

Examples of journals and presses specially for experimental fiction

- *FC2* in the US, 'an author-run, not-for-profit publisher of artistically adventurous, non-traditional fiction'.

- *Conjunctions*, a US-based print and web journal of innovative writing, says of itself: 'For over three decades, *Conjunctions* has challenged accepted forms and styles, with equal emphasis on groundbreaking experimentation and rigorous quality. We are committed to launching and supporting the careers of unknown authors while providing a space for better-known voices to work outside audience expectations ... we strive to provide a forum for unconventional work.'

It seems like a case of 'We know it when we see it' ... and since being unconventional depends on what the conventions happen to be at the time, perhaps 'experimenting' – as opposed to 'experimental fiction' – is more about the writer trying something she has never done before, testing things out, taking risks. For me, everything I write is an experiment in some way. It must be if it's not paint-by-numbers or formulaic.

Why experiment in short stories?

The short story is a great place to experiment – first, because if it doesn't work, you probably haven't spent years of your life on it. Second, a short story already demands that things be left out; it's easier to innovate if you know you don't have to explain too much of it, either to yourself or to a potential reader, who is already primed to do some of the work. As a reader, I am far more prepared to enter into a world whose rules I don't quite get for a few pages than for an entire book-length work, say.

TOP TIP

If you'd like to get experimental – or if a story-in-progress isn't quite working – why not first see what it is that you tend to do and then turn that upside down, or inside out?

EXERCISE

Find your comfort zone, and take a step outside it. Take a look at some of your recent pieces and make some notes:

- How long do they tend to be?

- How many characters?

- Which point of view, which tense?

- How much time passes?

- Are there words you tend to repeat that you weren't repeating consciously? (We all do this.)

Then try something else. Try:

- Writing in second person ('You were sitting on that bench when the sky fell').

- Writing in the first person plural ('We decided to confront him the following night').

Both of these are still considered fairly unusual, and add a different spin to a story.

Try something new with tenses:

- Write a short story in the future tense ('He will wake up and yawn') or some permutation ('He will have woken up and yawned'). This could be construed as messing with the reader's head — or your head, first!

- Try writing your story backwards, for example. It certainly creates mystery. Both stories I have done this with are about memory, and so the structure seems to add to the content. My stories were still linear, there was a timeline, but it was reversed.

Experiments with linear structure

I've read stories that were in parts that could have gone in various orders – once you've finished your draft, you could print it out, cut it into sections, and move them around. There's nothing more fun than playing with paper, scissors and glue!

- Try different forms. Write your story as bullet points or a numbered list. Write it as a letter, a recipe, an email, text messages, FedEx delivery notes.

I want to emphasize the concept of 'play'. I looked this up in the dictionary and among the myriad definitions found one I like: 'Movement or space for movement'. I play in my writing in order to find new ways to move, new spaces to move in.

Playing with language

- Experiment with using words to mean something other than their accepted meaning.

- Look up a glossary of words in a subject area you're completely unfamiliar with (fox hunting, particle physics, dressmaking), or rifle through a very large dictionary, making a list of words you've never heard of, preferably without looking at definitions.

- Write them down on slips of paper, then start writing your story and pick out a 'weird word' to throw in every now and then, assigning your own meaning.

The suggestions I've made above are ideas I and others have already tried, but if they are only being done by the few, they are not yet traditional or conventional.

Close reading of 'Between My Father and the King' by Janet Frame

Tania

This is the section where I take a short story that I love and dismantle it to see how it ticks, reading it closely to understand why and how it does what it does to me and learn from it.

TOP TIP

It is much easier to do this with someone else's story than your own, but if you put your own story aside for weeks, preferably months, that can help.

The story is 'Between My Father and the King', by New Zealand short story writer, novelist and poet Janet Frame (1924–2004). I was first smitten by Frame's stories when I read her collection, *The Daylight and the Dust*. The story I am going to examine is the title story from a volume of new and uncollected short stories, published posthumously in 2012 (the book is called *Gorse Is Not People* in the UK). Here is the story for you to read first.

Between My Father and the King

by Janet Frame

My father fought in the First World War that used to be called 'Great' until the truth of its greatness was questioned and the denial of its greatness accepted. My father came home from the war with a piece of shrapnel in his back, remnants of gas in his lungs, a soldier's pay book, an identity disc, a gas mask, and a very important document which gave details of my father's debt to the King and his promise before witnesses to repay the King the fifty pounds borrowed to buy furniture: a bed to sleep in with his new wife, a dining table to dine at, linoleum and a hearthrug to lay on the floor, two fireside chairs for man and wife to sit in when he wasn't working and she wasn't polishing the King's linoleum and shaking the King's hearthrug free of dust; and a wooden fireside kerb to protect the hearthrug, the linoleum and my father and his wife from sparks when they sat by the fire. All this furniture, the document said, cost fifty pounds, which had to be paid to the King in agreed instalments.

I found this document the other day, and the accompanying note of discharge from debt; and it was the first time I had known of my father's dreadful responsibility. For besides promising to repay the loan he had sworn to keep the bed and mattress and fireside kerb and hearthrug and linoleum and dining table and chairs and fireside chairs in good order and on no account sell or exchange them and to be prepared at any time to allow the King's Representative to inspect them.

If only I had known!

In our conscienceless childhood days we ripped the backs from the kitchen chairs and made sledges from them; we drove nails into the wooden kerb – the King's Kerb! We pencilled and crayoned the dining table, scuffed the linoleum, bounced on the bed, split open and explored the mattress and the two fireside chairs, looking for money. Finally, the tomcat peed on and permanently impaired the hearthrug. And all this was the King's property on gracious loan to my father and we never knew!

It is all so far away now. I have no means of discovering what my parents thought or talked about when they lay in the King's bed and ate at his table and sat in his chairs and walked on his linoleum. When a knock sounded on the door did my father glance quickly around at the fifty pounds' worth to make sure it was in good condition in case the King's Representative happened to be passing?

'I'm the King's Representative. I happened to be passing through Richardson Street, Dunedin, and I thought I'd inspect your bed and mattress and chairs and linoleum and hearthrug and wooden fireside kerb.'

'Do come in,' I imagined my mother saying rather timidly.

And with my father leading the way and my mother following they conducted the King's Representative on a tour of the far-flung colonial furniture. My mother nervously explained that there were young children in the house, and babies, and a certain amount of wear and tear ...

'Yes yes, of course,' the King's Representative said, taking out his notebook and writing, for example: wooden kerb, two dents in; linoleum, brown stain on; while my mother's apprehension grew and my father looked more worried and when the Representative left my mother burst into tears.

Or so I imagined.

'He'll go straight to the King. I know he will!'

My father tried to comfort her. He glanced with hate at the King's furniture. He wished he had never borrowed the fifty pounds.

And then perhaps he had one of his bright ideas and that evening as he and my mother sat in the King's armchairs with their feet on the King's cat-stained hearthrug and protected from sparks by the King's wooden kerb, my father took out his own small notebook and pencil and carefully studying the Great War in all its Greatness and himself in it with his fellow soldiers in the trenches, he wrote, inspecting deeply the life and the death and the time and the torture,

Back, shrapnel in; lungs, remains of gas in; nights, nightmares in; days, memories in.

Dear King, the corresponding dents and stains and wear and tear in my life surely atone for the wear and tear of your precious kerb and hearthrug etc. Please wipe out the debt of fifty pounds or passing by Buckingham Palace I shall drop in to inspect you and claim settlement for your debt to me.

What did you think? Whether it did to you what it did to me, pulling it to pieces is, I hope, going to be useful.

Let's start with the title. 'Between My Father and the King' is almost a story in itself. It has several potential layers of meaning that I can see, perhaps more. It could refer to the distance between a father and a king in terms of physical space and hierarchy/status. It could refer to communication between them, already implying an argument of some kind. It also has a hint of fathers being like kings and kings being paternal. The 'my' immediately tells us that the main character of our story is going to be the child of the father, which is useful. And it tells us this takes place somewhere that has a king – although 'king' could refer to the king of car insurance salespeople, for example!

The next thing is to take a quick glance at how this story sits on the page. It looks pretty 'traditional' in that there are paragraph breaks. There are paragraphs broken up by dialogue and the dialogue is contained in speech marks. The structure has nothing that immediately grabs the eye. No surprises here.

Next, the content. This story is 770 words long and here in the first line are 29 words, or just under 5 per cent of the story. 'My father fought in the First World War that used to be called "Great" until the truth of its greatness was questioned and the denial of its greatness accepted.' This line pretty much sums up the story. This is not a short story where you have to puzzle through to find a hidden message – Frame gives it to you. The repetitions of the word 'great' is mesmerizing. You have to do a little work to take in the questioning of truth and then the acceptance of denial, so this first line also implies complexity. This is not going to be a straightforward, easy story.

The next sentence, the second sentence of the opening paragraph, is 140 words long, or almost 20 per cent of the entire story. Rhythm is very important in Frame's work (she was also a poet), and here we have a wonderful example. The second line starts with the same two words as the first line, emphasizing both who is narrating this story and who the story is about, as well as setting up a rhythm:

My father came home from the war with a piece of shrapnel in his back, remnants of gas in his lungs, a soldier's pay book, an identity disc, a gas mask, and a very important document which

gave details of my father's debt to the King and his promise before
   witnesses to repay the King the fifty pounds borrowed to buy
   furniture: a bed to sleep in with his new wife, a dining table to dine
   at, linoleum and a hearthrug to lay on the floor, two fireside chairs
   for man and wife to sit in when he wasn't working and she wasn't
   polishing the King's linoleum and shaking the King's hearthrug free
   of dust; and a wooden fireside kerb to protect the hearthrug, the
   linoleum and my father and his wife from sparks when they sat by
   the fire.

At first glance, this long, long line looks like a list, yet it is so much more than that. It is list turned into story, list-to-evoke-emotion, something I have rarely seen done so well. It reminds me of Tim O'Brien's stunning short story, 'The Things They Carried', a Vietnam war story told through what the soldiers have with them (first published in 1986 in *Esquire* magazine). Both stories demonstrate the power of well-chosen items to evoke entire worlds. Frame chose very carefully here – slipping in between tangibles the 'remnants of gas in his lungs' to devastating effect, you almost miss it there, but you don't, you can't. This is a list within a list too: the final item is a promise, and what is promised is then a further catalogue.

Before I get to that, the major thing I notice here is that Frame is getting straight to what underpins this story: 'My father came home from the war' – this is a cause for joy, for celebration, and yet it is swiftly followed by his 'debt to the King', and not just that, such an important debt that he promised 'before witnesses'. Before we even reach the details of this promise, what has Frame got us to think without her actually having to say anything directly? Wait a minute, surely this man fought for the King, surely the King owes him? Already, in paragraph two, Frame sets up the tension, the reason for us to keep reading.

Talking about tension, it doesn't quite fit the who-wants-what model of story. It is more complicated, in great part because it is being told by the father's child (we don't know if it is a son or a daughter; we haven't been told, but for reasons of simplicity here I am going to assume it is semi-autobiographical and say 'she' from now on).

Frame might have chosen to tell this from a different point of view: the father's, his wife's, or an omniscient, disinterested narrator who is simply presenting the 'facts', but she chose the father's child for a reason. It implies, without it having to be stated, that she was aware of the insult to her father, to his service, the indignity of this 'debt'; it was something that permeated the family and continued down the generations. Tension is immediately created around the question of whether, of course, the debt will be paid. This one word – 'debt' – is an excellent tension-creator.

The catalogue of what he is in debt for conjures not just his whole life, but his family too. You may think, especially in a story this short, that adding on to 'a bed' the words 'to sleep in with his new wife', and to 'a dining table' adding 'to dine at' may be an indulgence, but Frame needs these descriptions for her purpose, which is to tell us that the things he bought became instantly so much more than just objects. They became part of everyday actions by real people. Are they not the foundations of a life – sleeping, eating, working, cleaning, being with your spouse – the opposite of the war he had just come back from, grounded, settled, safe? But not, in fact, completely safe. Because of the debt.

Now, in paragraph three, one-third of the way through the story, the tone shifts.

I found this document the other day, and the accompanying note of discharge from debt; and it was the first time I had known of my father's dreadful responsibility. For besides promising to repay the loan he had sworn to keep the bed and mattress and fireside kerb and hearthrug and linoleum and dining table and chairs and fireside chairs in good order and on no account sell or exchange them and to be prepared at any time to allow the King's Representative to inspect them.

Two interesting things happen here. We hear directly from our narrator, who tells us straight away that the debt was paid, 'discharged'. So that source of tension, that 'reason' to keep reading, has gone. Something else needs to keep the reader going forward. Now what might do that is our interest in our narrator, and what she makes of the discovery. It's not a new plot – child discovers something about parent a long time after it happened – but what use will Frame make of it here and what story will she weave around it?

Frame also advances the story by bringing in something she's held back about the debt, a twist: the debt incurred was not in fact a loan he was required to repay for furniture he bought. He didn't actually own the furniture. It still belonged to the King such that this wonderfully ridiculous figure, the 'King's Representative', might need to inspect the state of it.

Bringing this fact in here heightens the tension again and adds a new dimension, perhaps the one that enabled her to finish writing this story. Frame could have stated this at the start, but there was a good reason for the story why she didn't. What this twist does is it involves the father's family in the debt in a very tangible way; it gives the debt an enduring power throughout their lives, which our narrator finds out retroactively. 'If only I had known!' she says next, hinting that this whole story may be about, among other things, what is known and not known in families, and about the very things we took for granted all those years.

Our narrator then tells us, with no small amount of dark humour, what they did as children:

> In our conscienceless childhood days we ripped the backs from the kitchen chairs and made sledges from them; we drove nails into the wooden kerb – the King's Kerb! We pencilled and crayoned the dining table, scuffed the linoleum, bounced on the bed, split open and explored the mattress and the two fireside chairs, looking for money. Finally, the tomcat peed on and permanently impaired the hearthrug. And all this was the King's property on gracious loan to my father and we never knew!

This is no minor wear and tear! The words Frame chose here are strong, physical, active ones: 'ripped', 'drove', 'scuffed', 'bounced', 'split', 'explored'. And if that wasn't visceral enough, if we couldn't quite see, hear and feel all of this, the peeing of the tomcat (not just a cat, but a tomcat, a hint of wildness) bursts open our senses, adding smell into the equation. Here we have children running wild; there was not a great deal of discipline in this household. Frame doesn't have to tell us this; she doesn't tell us much directly at all.

Once again she ends this paragraph with 'and we never knew!', echoing the 'If only I'd known!' from the previous paragraph, both with exclamation marks which heighten the knowing and unknowing, tipping it almost into farce, but not quite. This, for me, is the exquisiteness of this story. It could have been out-and-out humour, but Frame wants to do more.

This next paragraph is the half-way point of the story:

> It is all so far away now. I have no means of discovering what my parents thought or talked about when they lay in the King's bed and ate at his table and sat in his chairs and walked on his linoleum. When a knock sounded on the door did my father glance quickly around at the fifty pounds' worth to make sure it was in good condition in case the King's Representative happened to be passing?

Frame grounds us in the 'now' of this story, that the daughter is looking back from much farther in the future. Then she does something else interesting: she has her narrator tell us she can't possibly know what the parents thought about all this, but then swiftly has her narrator imagine exactly this:

> "I'm the King's Representative. I happened to be passing through Richardson Street, Dunedin, and I thought I'd inspect your bed and mattress and chairs and linoleum and hearthrug and wooden fireside kerb."
>
> "Do come in," I imagined my mother saying rather timidly.
>
> And with my father leading the way and my mother following they conducted the King's Representative on a tour of the far-flung colonial furniture. My mother nervously explained that there were young children in the house, and babies, and a certain amount of wear and tear ...
>
> "Yes yes, of course," the King's Representative said, taking out his notebook and writing, for example: wooden kerb, two dents in;

linoleum, brown stain on; while my mother's apprehension grew
and my father looked more worried and when the Representative
left my mother burst into tears.

First, this tells us more about our narrator, the father's child, and her imaginative talents. Frame is taking a risk with this scene, which could descend
into farce, but she has built up the story in such a way that I suspect
most readers may smile but not laugh out loud; she stirs in just enough
poignancy. 'Far-flung colonial furniture' is worth noting, because until here
there has been no reference to the fact that (if this story is autobiographical),
the father is in New Zealand and the King is in Great Britain. This serves to
heighten the silliness of the King sending a Representative all this way –
which, of course, he didn't. But it also heightens the injustice of the debt, too.

The words 'timidly' and 'nervously' – the second and third adverbs she
has used so far (the first is in the previous paragraph, 'glance quickly') – do
a lot of work here, showing us the mother, who is the only one who seems
to speak to this fictional King's Representative. She is also the only voice we
hear directly in the entire story, apart from our narrator.

Once again, we have repetition and rhythm with the list of items, which,
to the King's Representative, do not, of course, have the associations Frame
gave us earlier ('a bed to sleep in with his new wife, a dining table to dine
at', etc. ...) To the King's Representative, they are simply objects, and he is
clearly uninterested in the facts of life, which include young children and
babies.

The last line of this paragraph above is another long one, with a colon
and a semicolon, and this conveys something of the mother's apprehension
growing. She can't breathe, until the final release: tears.

Frame then grounds us for a moment with 'Or so I imagined', which
reminds us who this story is affecting now, but then we are back into the
story-within-a-story, getting towards the climax, and the ending.

"He'll go straight to the King. I know he will!"
My father tried to comfort her. He glanced with hate at the King's
furniture. He wished he had never borrowed the fifty pounds.

'He wished he had never borrowed the fifty pounds' is the climax here. It's what we have been subconsciously waiting for from the opening line. How could he not regret it? But the climax of the story is not the ending. We need something more. Here it comes, in another paragraph-long sentence. I am going to pull it apart slowly:

> And then perhaps he had one of his bright ideas

'And then' leads us gently into it, with a qualifying 'perhaps' which seems not so much to indicate hesitation as the hope of our narrator, who knows her father was a man of bright ideas.

> and that evening as he and my mother sat in the King's armchairs
> with their feet on the King's cat-stained hearthrug and protected
> from sparks by the King's wooden kerb

This hammers it all home once again, the list of items once more, but altered, subtly, physically and metaphysically, following the visit of the King's Rep. The image of their feet 'on the King's cat-stained hearthrug' is a strong one, because it makes the King look bad – his hearthrug is no longer immaculate – and gives the mother and father power: they have their feet on it, they are acting on it rather than it on them. And they are 'protected from sparks'. They have turned the situation around.

> my father took out his own small notebook and pencil

The emphasis here on 'his own', not the King's. Everything is about to change.

> and carefully studying the Great War in all its Greatness and himself
> in it with his fellow soldiers in the trenches, he wrote, inspecting
> deeply the life and the death and the time and the torture,

The resonance here is with the opening of the story: we have come full circle, but something fundamental has changed. At the beginning he 'fought in' the war and now he himself is 'in it', and it is not just about him, this is bigger than him. '[T]he life and the death and the time and the torture' pulls no punches. Here is the meat of the story.

> Back, shrapnel in; lungs, remains of gas in; nights, nightmares in; days, memories in.

Frame delivers the beginning of her ending in a topsy-turvy way that keeps us on our toes. She's not letting us rest yet, no release. Another list, but what a list. Everything backwards, and all the more horrific for that because it creates the awful repetition of 'in', 'in', 'in', 'in'.

And then, finally, it comes.

> Dear King, the corresponding dents and stains and wear and tear in my life surely atone for the wear and tear of your precious kerb and hearthrug etc. Please wipe out the debt of fifty pounds or passing by Buckingham Palace I shall drop in to inspect you and claim settlement for your debt to me.

It is so simply done, so simply said. Not a spare word here. Whenever I read this, this ending feels like one of those perfect shots which in a tennis match, make you gasp and you feel it throughout your body. The story is finished.

This, to me, is the ideal example of an ending to a short story that is both surprising and inevitable. It is inevitable from the opening sentence that the insanity of holding a man to a debt of £50 after he was prepared to sacrifice his life would have to be confronted. It could have been straightforward, the father actually doing something about the debt, taking a stand, say, refusing to pay it. Or, conversely, coming to accept it. But this wouldn't really have been surprising. What adds the extra element is the spin Frame puts on the story – it's not about her father and the King; it's about the relationship between father and child. The ending isn't the letter he wrote, but what his daughter, as an adult, imagines he might have written. That's what makes this story shine.

Frame's story makes me cry each time I read it, leaves me reeling. She does this to me without recourse to sentiment or sentimentality, without directly stating anything, without telling me at any point what I must feel. It's an absolute masterclass in short story writing. She trusted her future readers completely and she left space for me to get involved. I was moved by this story not despite the lack of emotion, but because of it. In 770 words this story encompasses life, death, war, children, parents, marriage, love, morality, ethics – and more, I'm sure, something different for each reader. To go on here would be me telling you what to think, and that would seem to undermine my entire argument, so I will leave it there and hope you enjoyed this very close reading of this story.

Publishing short stories

Tania

History of marketing short stories

What about the markets for short stories? In his 2007 article, 'A Brief History of the Short Story in America', Eric Miles Williamson writes of short stories: '[W]hat we now know as a literary form, however, was originally no more high art than is pop music today. Short stories were commercial products written for newspapers and magazines by writers who were trying to make a living at it.' By 1871, says Williamson, 'The literary short story had become an art form, but it was also an art form which paid real money'.

American author Jack London apparently had a contract with *Cosmopolitan* magazine to write a short story a month at a rate of $1,000 per story, which Williamson has calculated is worth 'about $250,000 in today's money'. The situation appears to be the reverse of today's markets: 'When a novelist at the turn of the 20th century needed cash to support the novel-in-progress,' says Williamson, 'he would write a short story and it would sustain him nicely for a long while.'

Today's markets

Today's short story writers – myself included – laugh wryly at the sums in the preceding paragraph. Things have changed if we're looking at the financial side of the picture. But in fact there has never been a better time to be a short story writer. Really. There are so many places to submit your short story to, and the internet makes it easy to both find venues and to send stories off. There are also a plethora of writing workshops and courses, face-to-face and online, and undergraduate and postgraduate courses in creative writing. The short story world is buzzing with activity.

Magazines

When you have a short story you are ready to send out into the world, the first place you can try is the literary magazine. There are now thousands of literary magazines being published worldwide, online, in print and audio. The literary magazine is not – as its name might imply – just for 'literary fiction' (another term that is easier to define by what it's not) but covers all genres. A literary journal may ask for stories that are only in a particular genre or on a particular theme, or be under a certain length, or it may be open to all. There are online databases of writers' markets such as Duotrope.com (which now charges a small annual fee) that allow you to search according to various parameters, such as genre, word length, style.

TOP TIP

Read a publication before submitting and follow their guidelines to the letter.

Literary magazines get hundreds of submissions and one way an editor cuts down on her reading is by instantly discarding those that fail to stick to the guidelines – if the story is double the permitted length, say, or is science fiction and the magazine only publishes realist fiction.

The majority of literary magazines don't charge a fee to submit but most don't pay contributors, other than with a copy of the issue they appear in if it is a print journal. Genre literary magazines, such as those publishing science fiction or horror, seem be in a better position to pay their writers. It is difficult to make a living from publishing in literary magazines, but it's wonderful to see your name in print (or pixels) and to find a good home for your story where it will find readers. It also helps build your reputation as a writer.

There are other magazines that publish short stories, including the periodicals that fall under the 'women's magazines' category, such as (at the time of writing this section) *Women's Weekly* in the UK and *Good Housekeeping* in the US. Science magazines too: *Nature* has a regular weekly paid 'Futures' slot for a very short story.

Radio stories

In the UK, BBC Radio has a small number of short story slots, the 15-minute *Afternoon Reading*, which used to be on every weekday but sadly now is only on twice a week. But the BBC does pay well for a short story; look out for the 'Opening Lines' competition for writers new to radio. In the US, National Public Radio has a 'Three-Minute-Fiction' contest, and Public Radio International has the 'Selected Shorts' programme.

Competitions and awards

Competitions are one way to earn money from your short stories. There is often an entry fee, and I would caution you to check out a competition's reputation before sending off your money and your stories. Look for competition listings in reputable magazines such as *Mslexia*, *Poets & Writers* and others. If something sounds too good to be true, it may well be!

If the competition is being run by a literary magazine, you might get a year's free subscription as part of the entry fee, which is often the same price as a subscription, giving you more for your money. Magazines running competitions on this basis include *Gulf Coast Journal* in the US and *Short Fiction* in the UK.

While prizes can be up to £1,000 for the winning story, sometimes more, there is generally only one winner. But competitions sometimes offer cash prizes – and publication – to finalists as well, and to be published either in the magazine running the contest or in a dedicated competition anthology such as the Bristol Short Story Prize anthology, the Bridport Prize anthology, or the Asham Award anthology – all of which are open to international entries – is a great accomplishment. Competitions often make public not just the winners but the longlisted and shortlisted stories, and to see your short story named in one of those lists can be a great boost to your confidence – no, you didn't win, but your story rose to close to the top out of hundreds, perhaps thousands.

Multi-author anthologies

A third venue for short stories is the anthology – a book containing many short stories by different authors. A publisher (mostly small independent presses) will issue a call for submissions, asking for stories, sometimes on a theme or sometimes an open, unthemed call. If accepted, there may be a small contributor's payment, an honorarium, and you will probably receive one or two copies of the anthology itself. Duotrope is a good place to find these calls for submission in their Theme Calendar.

Live lit events

A very exciting addition to the short story scene over the past few years has been the 'live lit' event, which is where an audience comes to hear short stories being read live. They might either be read by their authors or by actors, and events may feature writers invited in advance, call for submissions – also often on a theme – and include 'open mic' slots, where anyone who has come can read their story.

I believe these events are injecting new life into the short story. People love being read to, and at a short story live lit event they can hear a number of complete stories rather than extracts from longer works. Practising reading your story out loud is a great skill for any writer to hone, and taking part in live lit allows you to connect directly with an audience. If you really don't want to read it yourself, you can find events where an actor will be chosen to read your story if picked by the event organizers.

Dealing with rejection

It is not wise to begin submitting anything until you think you are ready for it. There is never a time in the life of a writer when rejection is a thing of the past. It just gets easier to deal with, to understand that it is not a rejection of you but that there are many reasons why an editor didn't pick your story: it didn't fit with his vision for that particular issue of the magazine; it was a topic she personally doesn't like to read about. Or you haven't quite got the ending right yet (sometimes editors can give marvellous feedback in rejection letters, I have found this very useful!). Not getting anywhere in a competition also doesn't mean the story doesn't work. Competitions, too, are judged by human beings, with their own likes and dislikes. I didn't submit anything for the first seven years of my writing life; I was going to workshops like those run by Arvon in the UK and the Iowa Summer Writers Festival in the US, learning how to write and how to read as a writer. There is no rush. You don't want to risk being put off the entire enterprise by receiving a rejection too soon.

There is also the option these days of avoiding rejection by publishing your short stories yourself – on a blog, say. You can get find readers this way if you put in the work promoting your blog. But you do miss out on the boost to your 'writing CV' to be published in a highly-thought-of publication, and the potential for payment for your work – not to mention the joy and validation of having your short story accepted by an editor, someone else connecting with your work and wanting their readers to read it. This has been a major part of my life as a writer, and editors have also given me excellent feedback. I would recommend this path, since publications have a built-in readership, and your story is likely to be published alongside others, sometimes beautifully illustrated. Also, you should know that the majority of literary magazines and competitions stipulate that short stories must not have been previously published, and appearing on your blog generally counts as previously published.

A few online resources

Duotrope www.duotrope.com – a searchable online database of writers' markets, with an online submissions tracker (charges annual fee).

Poets & Writers www.pw.org – global database of competitions and publications for short stories, poetry and non-fiction, as well as forums for writers.

The Review Review www.thereviewreview.net – news from and reviews of literary magazines worldwide and interviews with editors.

ShortStops www.shortstops.info – listings and news about literary magazines, live lit events, authors and workshops for short stories in the UK and Ireland.

Short story festivals

Cork International Short Story Festival (Ireland, September)
Kikinda Short Story Festival (Serbia, July)
Small Wonder (England, September)

Further reading

Williamson, Eric Miles, 'A Brief History of the Short Story in America', Bookcritics
(http://bookcritics.org/blog/archive/a-brief-history-of-the-short-story-
in-america).

Short story competitions – how to make your story stand out

Tania

I am quite often a first reader, judge or on a panel of judges of short story competitions, and these are enormously instructive experiences. One thing they haven't done is helped me develop a formula for winning said competitions. There isn't one. But reading many unpublished short stories at a time, often hundreds (for one competition where I was the sole judge, I read 849 entries in about six weeks), shows what the common pitfalls are.

I thought I'd illustrate this for you in real time because I have beside me a pile of the first several dozen entries for a short story competition I am judging. Each story has to win me over quickly and go head-to-head with the stories that I read before and after it to make it into the 'Yes' or 'Maybe' pile. It's a tough task. Reading this section may leave you demoralized, but please don't be. It's actually not that hard to stand out – and these are only my impressions. Not rules. Definitely not rules. Just a little peek inside the mind of one particular person reading entries on one day, at one particular hour, for one competition.

Amazingly, the very first story is a definite 'Yes'. The title is unique, never seen anything like it before. Then the first word is a character name and an interesting one, and the first sentence is clear and intriguing, a crisp tone that throws me straight into the story with a 'who' and a 'what' and a scenario. I immediately get the sense of a confident author. There are none of those tentative words and phrases that can signal a less confident writer: 'seems like', 'feels like', 'might'. I start to trust the author to take me wherever this story is going. I am also a sucker for humour, and this story makes me giggle, but its ending is also quite dark and poignant. Lovely.

Story 2 has promise, it also throws me straight in, and the first sentence has some 'who' and 'where'. But then it loses my trust quite quickly by moving to backstory instead of getting to the action, instead of giving me more 'what'. I read on, but then – and this is going to be true of every competition, every editor who reads your work – the subject matter just isn't something that excites me. There is nothing that the writer or I can do about that. This is always, always going to be subjective.

Story 3 turns me off in the first line because it has several clichés in a row. Hard to win me back after that. Lazy language. Story 4 puts me off even before I start reading because I see a whole page in front of me with no paragraph breaks at all. One page of solid text – in fact, the whole story is like this. I read it, but it is a struggle on the eye, and it doesn't do enough to overcome this. Story 5 includes a note to the judge, which I don't really recommend doing. It also is written in an unusual font – this is not a winning tactic with me either, it immediately makes me wonder if the writer felt that the story wasn't going to be great enough and needs some font assistance. Hmm. Then several clichés in the opening para. Also the 'No' pile.

The next story has footnotes, which I rather like if they are ironically done, but here it seems that the writer feels the need to explain some things in a non-ironic way, which serve only to throw me out of the flow of the story. I am happy to read a story I don't quite understand; I'd rather be slightly confused but immersed than have everything clarified but the flow broken. The story after that has a nice title, intriguing, but then it becomes apparent from the first sentence that it refers to a topic that I see so, so often in competition entries: old age and dementia. It is very hard to get excited about this unless it is approached in a new way, and this one doesn't.

So far, all except the first story have gone onto the 'No' pile. A 'Maybe' would be if I enjoyed the story but a few things nagged at me and I wanted to come back to it, read it again. The next story starts like a fable, which is fine, which could be fantastic, but frankly, I get bored. The next story is another 'No' because of lazy language. It started with a bang, a huge and exciting plot point – but in the first paragraph I counted three instances of the same word and it didn't seem that it was repeated for any good reason. Also, after the high-energy first sentence, the author of this story decided to step back and explain a few things – and most of the energy drained away.

The next story has an okay title, and there is 'where' in sentence one, but no 'who', 'what' or 'why'. In fact, there is no main character in the whole first paragraph, no one for me to focus on, to care about. Paragraph two brings in some characters but it's still not clear whose story this is, or what the story is – it's still introduction, setting up. I don't have a lot of patience, I have other stories waiting to be read. Paragraph three gets to the action, but it's now got a harder task to keep my interest, and it doesn't manage it.

The next story has an identical title to its first line, which doesn't really give me much to go on. And then the author loses me because, again, it just wasn't anything I particularly wanted to read about and the writer didn't give me a reason to care. The story after this has a great title, and an intriguing opening paragraph, that begins as if we are already in the middle of something, which I like. But then paragraph two has a complete change of mood, becomes more pedestrian, less magical than it had seemed, and my interest wanes. It also has several names in one paragraph, which is a bit confusing.

Next is a story that seems to be a retelling of a myth, but its language is so flowery and ornate it is hard to read and hard for me to connect with the main character. It seems to push me away. The author also uses bizarre imagery and so much of it that I have a hard time picturing any of it in my mind and get quite lost, quite quickly. The next story does something similar to one of the previous ones in that it implies something quite magical in its opening and then quickly shifts mood to the pedestrian, undermining my expectations and disappointing me. The story afterwards has a spelling mistake in the first sentence which does not endear it to me, and then spends ages getting to any action at all.

Then a story that does something I see quite often: it tells about an event that has already happened but in a way that is so distant as to make me wonder why I should care about this, since it's already done and dusted. Stories in the past tense are fine, can be amazing, but I need to feel involved enough in the story – there needs to be some mystery, some tension, some reason to be talking about something that's been and gone. Using the phrase 'I remember when' can signal to me that we are going down this route — I'd rather know why 'I' is remembering it now. How does it affect the now?

The next story also has a fancy font and also tells me from the outset that it is set in a non-English-speaking country and is being told by a non-English speaker. This is not something I personally am drawn to, but I say to myself, 'Impress me'. Sadly, it doesn't. I am bombarded with names, not sure who the main character is, and then paragraph two over-explains, and momentum has gone.

All the remaining stories also go into my 'No' pile: one falls into the 'I remember' category, another in the 'magical turns to pedestrian' category, several others in the 'lazy language/full of clichés' department, another in the 'old age/dementia' category, and another in the 'not enough action/too much explanation' set. Others have an interesting start but subsequently fail to give me any reason to care about their characters — which doesn't mean I have to like them, but that they be sufficiently compelling, in their nastiness if necessary, to the story! And the penultimate story to go on the 'No' pile wasn't quite a story. It ended just as it was getting exciting.

On the subject of endings, there is one more story I really enjoy reading, a new twist on a familiar plot, but ultimately it doesn't make it into the 'Yes' pile because of its ending, which is a real shame. Short stories turn on their endings, as I've talked about already. Something approaching 'surprising yet inevitable', that gives me a jolt, but then I think, Ah yes, of course. This one let itself down partly because it didn't leave space for me, the reader, to come to a conclusion. The writer decided to tell me what conclusion to come to, what to think about everything that had just happened, right in the last paragraph. A real pity.

I read all these stories in one sitting, which is something judges or sifters probably do quite often, so you can see what your story is up against: sheer quantity competing for my attention, always another one there waiting, one that has the potential to really wow me. So don't give me even one second to put your story down. Grip me — and there are many ways to grip me (none of which includes fancy fonts). I definitely don't just enjoy stories that are in some way similar to the stories I write. I read very widely. I love all kinds and types of story. And, more importantly, once you've gripped me, don't lose me. Don't confuse me, don't stop everything for too long to explain, trust that I will get enough to read on. I don't need for everything to be clear. I just want to be compelled to find out what happens next.

Please send your stories to competitions. We want to read them.

A few final thoughts when you are getting your story ready to send out. Once you've done your spellcheck (and made sure Track Changes has been disabled – yes, I've seen a number of stories with someone else's less-than-complimentary comments still in the margins), think about the sifter, or the judge, with her pile. Think about how to delight him, the smile that will come over her face as she starts reading your story, as your character comes alive in his mind, as your writing moves him or makes him laugh. Listen to the first reader breathe out in relief at a story whose author is in command, is not tentative, is telling the story in the way only that author could tell it, without cliché, without overly fancy language unless necessary, hitting the sweet spot between action and explanation, story and plot.

It can be done. It can be done by you. I see it done so often, by new writers as well as experienced ones, that I know there's no magic trick here. If you write a story that surprises, moves and delights you, there's a good chance it will surprise, move and delight us too.

Harvesting — on writing your collection

Courttia

If, as quoted from Rebecca Solnit earlier in this book, the act of creative writing is an attempt to lose ourselves, then writing a collection is surely a process of accumulating what we have found. An attempt to map the uncharted territory we have chosen for exploration, to acclimatize ourselves to our surroundings. To begin to make sense of it all.

What is a collection?

The collection, unlike the novel, is a series of ruminations on a chosen theme compiled in one of two ways:

- The first is the gathering of all that took place during a chosen period, say two years, or four, or sometimes even as much as ten. They are disparate and random, nothing more coherent linking them together than the stitching of the writer's own experiences, rising and falling like dolphins among waves.

- This method is the instinctive. The writer travels where they may. The terrain is their own emotions; there is the known and the unknown, but it is a recognizable version of *them*, or something they come to accept. This is how I wrote my debut stand-alone collection.

- The second is the intellectual. There is a theme, maybe chosen at random, maybe stumbled over along the way, and once the conceptual model for the collection is set, the stories must conform or be cast aside.

- The writer travels further afield; this is not to say they are not focused on their own emotions, but this could also include territories they might wander to, in the attempt to discover the new. Yet still, this journey is fraught with limitation.

- Whichever method you choose, theme should be prominent in your mind. You must not stray too far from the track; to be led off course is not conducive. Writing a themed collection is to be a meticulous collator of experience. You must possess focus, a steady hand, a sure eye and determination.

- Embrace frustration. The writer, on the whole, is one who is always seduced by the ever-present tug of adventure. The call from elsewhere, the urge to write stories that do not fit the theme of your collection. Stay on the path.

Many writers who work in long and short form agree that the collection is trickier to wrestle with than the novel. Both have their own difficulties, but the collection requires patience, even when going at its best, that novelists only tend to face at their worst. Stephen King speaks of spending weeks going nowhere in his thinking while writing *The Stand*, until he was finally hit with an idea that came from nowhere (citation *On Writing*, 241). If the novel had been shorter, a mere 300 pages instead of 500, he might have let it go completely. Often, when writing a collection, this stopping to take stock and re-evaluate is the norm. Just like the actual short story itself, where gaps and silences can be made to speak as loudly as dialogue and exposition, time spent attaining a picturesque spot on the landscape, pitching a tent and just wallowing in the environment can be as rewarding as doing the work.

EXERCISE

Take a blank, unlined sheet of paper and try to construct an image of your collection. Write your central title in the centre of the sheet of paper. Now, as if in a cloud, write some of the emotional states you think the collection will contain. Detail these states as specifically as possible (i.e. not just 'hate', but 'anger towards a sibling', or 'someone who despises their job'). Find at least a dozen of these ideas.

Make a second cloud that contains the first, and write down a dozen situations that might provoke or contain

---

these emotional states: a fight in the family home, for example, or a bullying boss.

Now create a third cloud that contains the other two, composed of who could actually be telling these stories; think beyond their roles in the story — brother, sister, or boss — to detail who they are as human beings. What do they want or need? What's their favourite food? When did they first fall in love? Cry?

Taking a break

Sometimes there are economic reasons to take a break; you might need to work at something other than writing. At other times, the ideas just won't come. Always, the break becomes a necessary part of the process that actually aids rather than hinders the creation of new work. If you let it. Writing is 95 per cent mental (or, as I joke, you have to be 95 per cent mental to do it), so if you tell yourself you're going to have a block, it's pretty certain you will. Do the exact opposite. Tell yourself everything's going *great*. You'll get to the end of this one for sure, you always do, and any mistakes you make will be ironed out in the end (they always are) and so on and so forth until you get to the end. Then see what you have to show for your efforts.

- Before you begin writing, read collections with a direct link to your own proposed book.
- Work out how they have tackled the subject you wish to explore, and what you can do that perhaps hasn't been done.

TOP TIP

'A novel is never anything but a philosophy expressed in images. And in a good novel the philosophy has disappeared into the images.'

Albert Camus

As Camus wrote a number of stories, and the collection *Exile and the Kingdom* (1957), it's probably fair to believe he felt stories could be composed in much the same way. Philosophy can mean many things for the writer pulling a collection together out of the seemingly unwoven strands of their own experiences and observations, thoughts and feelings; the great, fundamental problems of their own existence, how that rubs up against the greater world. Usually there is one central strand, or conceit. Everything after that becomes a riff, to borrow yet another musical term, a variation on that theme, answerable to the philosophy's central precepts; reality, existence, knowledge, values, reason, mind and language. Each story should become an exploration of one or more of these tenets and its relationship to the wider question posed. This can be done overtly, or otherwise can be submerged so deep into the text that readers are unaware of its presence. What matters is the driving force, that thing that produces the forward movement of exploration.

Why assemble a collection?

A collection offers the opportunity to be in conversation with yourself about what matters to you most, without having to toe your own party line. You can write in the belief of one philosophy in a particular story, and in the next perform a dramatic about-turn, say something new. Collected stories may contradict one another. Diversity of thought is made welcome, explored through intimacy, often using the extreme mind states of multiple protagonists, perhaps whose experiences are vastly different from your own. The multiple narrative – or 'head-hopping', as Julia Bell, senior lecture on the creative writing MA at Birkbeck, calls it – is much prized in the novel. In the collection, multiplicity is inevitable. It works because the stories we're being told are fleeting. We never imagine they will be made whole; indeed, the true lover of the story doesn't want them that way. We expect to begin again, to come to know strangers, to be presented with new ideas, to be surprised, charmed, or even disgusted by what we find on the page, in full awareness that we must move along. We are content with the unknown, attempting to see.

Ways to interlink short stories

Geography

Many writers adopt a geographical setting to underpin philosophical themes. Josh Rolnick, US author of the prize-winning collection *Pulp and Paper*, 'decided' on a New York/New Jersey setting for his stories when his thematic choices — loss, recovery and redemption — met with zero interest from agents. Although he did not initially write the stories with this geographic structure in mind, it was only when he was driving from New Jersey to New York to meet his wife on Broadway that he realized he had subconsciously set four stories in New York, three in New Jersey and one in Pennsylvania. He moved the last to New Jersey so he could have a 4:4 parallel structure and this seemed to work, as far as the marketability of the novel went. The collection has since been compared to *Dubliners*. There are works of wonder such as *Cannery Row* (1945), described in some quarters as a novel but which could be seen as a collection of stories with chapter numbers instead of titles. Some of those chapters are only a page and a half long, featuring a diverse range of characters, some of whom never return.

Single narrative

Alice Munro's *Lives of Girls and Women* (1971) and *Who Do You Think You Are?* (1978), published as *The Beggar Maid* outside Canada, both chronicle the lives of a single character and have also been called novels, or at least a transition between the collection and the novel. Munro describes them as 'a series' that she had tried to write as a novel, but when it failed she pulled it apart and 'put it in story form'. She warns against using force in this shaping of a collection into stories that fit with one another, or using a plan that might overtake the stories (citation *Paris Review*, 'The Art of Fiction', 137).

Junot Diaz, author of the interlinked collections *Drown* (1996) and *This Is How You Lose Her* (2012), which also use Munro's 'series' framing structure, follows the progress of his central character, Yunior, as he discovers an ethical imagination with regard to women. He is a cheater by nature, possibly by hierarchy, his attitudes shaped by the men who surround him. Central to this understanding are his father and brother, both unrepentant misogynists. In the second collection, each of the stories takes place in a different period of Yunior's life, charting his journey through a series of troubled relationships. In a *New York Times* interview Diaz describes the writing process as miserable because the stories wouldn't come; some were a year in the making, 50 pages long, and were in his words 'a miserable botch'. Nevertheless, the collection has been received with almost singular enthusiasm by readers, critics and fellow writers alike. Further in the interview, Diaz lists his favourite 'touchstone collections', which include *Jesus' Son*, *Family Instalments* and *Fort Wayne is Seventh on Hitler's List*.

A social group

Richard Price's debut, *The Wanderers*, follows a gang of friends who live on a housing project in the Bronx, New York. It's composed of 12 interlinked stories, each told from the point of view of a gang member, these main characters reappearing as sub-characters in other stories. They are ugly tales of inner city blight, depravity of mind and environment, the violence of boredom coupled with low prospects. Once again, critics describe the collection as a novel. It seems a trick of the times, a way to market something not quite a collection of stories and not quite a long-form work of fiction, difficult to name or place. This has changed somewhat in contemporary times, although champions of the form might say not enough. At the time of publication some critics described a lack of conventional narrative plot, even while a common thread throughout the collection is each character's individual growth towards maturity. In a 1996 edition of *The Paris Review*, Price describes completing a series of assignments for his creating writing MFA at Columbia. He didn't even know he was working on a book, just that he was working on 'another one of these stories about these guys, The Wanderers' (*The Paris Review*). Even though 'everybody' (meaning his MFA classmates) hated what became the opening story when Price read it, fellow student Dan Halpern asked if he could publish it in his new magazine, *Antaeus*. It took a year, but by that time Price had written ten stories. An editor from Houghton read the magazine and got in contact. He was published aged 24. It's interesting to note that in his interview, Price never claimed to have written a novel. Just stories.

Tradition

The interlinked collection has a rich history. Its tradition stems from texts composed of other texts, such as the Arthurian cycles, and serialized works structured by frame stories like *The Canterbury Tales, The Decameron* and *One Thousand and One Nights.* In the early nineteenth century. genres that became known as village sketch appeared in *Our Village*, a series of over 100 stories about rural life that first appeared in *The Ladies' Magazine* during the 1820s and 1830s. By the 1900s, there was a proliferation of the genre, described by J. Gerald Kennedy as the desire 'to renounce the organizing authority of an omniscient narrator, asserting instead a variety of voices or perspectives reflective of the radical subjectivity of modern experience' (Kennedy pp. x–xi). It is a mode of writing popular among writers who feel they are marginalized in particular, perhaps proven by the US examples given above.

Whatever the approach to your stories as individual works of art, a collection is often the pinnacle of our efforts – an attempt to make cohesion out of what might seem like mere fragments; a collation of altered states housed beneath a permeable construction of intent. Whether you choose to focus on geography, a central protagonist, a collective protagonist, a central theme or pattern, or storytelling, or even a combination of the above is entirely up to you. Tell your story from the heart, and you will tell it well.

EXERCISE

Take a sheet of paper, or if you like index cards, or even post-it notes. Write down the titles of all the stories in your collection, written or yet-to-be. Beneath these titles, write a one-line summary of the theme, or what they are about. Arrange them in the order they will appear on the contents page, or if you've used the index cards or post-it notes, arrange them before you. How does it look? Are there any stories or thematic strands missing? Is there any repetition? How many pages will your collection span? Is that satisfactory or not? Does looking at your collection in this way give you more ideas? Are you finished?

Short story collections – how do they work and how to get one published?

Tania

Short story collections are books full of short stories by one writer. This may seem obvious, but actually it's one of the only clear statements to make about short story collections.

There are various ways that a short story collection comes into being. First, it may simply be comprised of all the stories (or the best stories) a writer has written up to a certain point, each story written with no thought to it being part of a collection. Or you may work towards a collection of short stories which have some kind of link or theme. These collections are often known as 'linked short stories', 'short story cycles' or 'a novel in stories' – there is a growing trend for labelling them as a 'novel', even if their authors think of them as story collections.

Deciding which short stories to include and how to order them within your book is tricky. It is not a given that a reader will read the stories in the order they come in the book. (I tend to look and see which is the shortest story in a collection and read that first!) You, the author, have no control over this, so all you can do, really, is put them in the order you'd like them to be if a reader does choose to read them this way, and then let go. This is one of the questions we ask the short story collection authors we interview for the journal I founded in 2007, *The Short Review*.

AUTHORS TALKING ABOUT HOW THEY ORDERED THE STORIES IN THEIR COLLECTIONS

Niki Aguirre, author of 29 Ways to Drown:

The order was a lot easier to determine. I started with despair and worked my way up to hope. I wanted to be true to my characters' problems, but also include the possibility of an escape route. I believe choices are so important.

Kevin Barry, author of There Are Little Kingdoms:

I had music in mind, actually, favourite albums. I was thinking of how a masterpiece like Marvin Gaye's What's Going On is structured: open with a couple of killer tracks, then let it get all lowdown 'n' weird 'n' smoky.

Josephine Rowe, author of East of Here, Close to Water:

I had many more stories which didn't end up in the collection. Sometimes it's obvious one way or another, which stories belong and which don't. There is one story in particular ... I'm just not sure what it's doing there. Instead of being in conversation with the other stories, it's more or less keeping to itself.

A book full of one author's stories can give you a much fuller picture of that author's work, not just what their stories might have in common, but the diversity of style and voice.

Approaching a publisher

Via established agents

If you have a collection's worth of stories – a minimum of 130 pages or so, roughly 30,000 words – there are several ways to look for a book deal. The traditional route in many countries is through a literary agent. However, agents today commonly respond that it is very hard to sell a short story collection without the promise of a novel. Sending your manuscript straight to one of the large publishing houses will probably elicit a similar response.

Via small publishers

The primary publishers of short story collections today are the small, independent presses, often not-for-profit. You can generally submit to them directly, without an agent, usually a few stories first, and then the full manuscript if they are interested in your writing. Check their submissions guidelines. There is no need to submit only to publishers in your own country; try further afield too.

Enter story collection contests

Enter your unpublished collection for a contest in which the first prize is publication. Examples of this include the Drue Heinz Literature Prize and the Iowa Short Fiction Award. There are also 'chapbook' contests: a chapbook used to refer to slim, often hand-bound, poetry collections, but the term is also now used for collections of short stories or flash fiction. The small presses that publish short story chapbooks often invest a great deal in presentation, hand-stitching the covers and experimenting with different formats. Rose Metal Press and Doire Press both hold short story chapbook competitions.

Tania's experience

My collections are both published by very dynamic small presses, who invest a great deal of love and care into each book they produce.

1 Being published by a small press may not carry the prestige of a 'big name' publishing house.
2 Authors will often have to do a great deal of the book promotion themselves and are unlikely to receive an advance on sales.
3 However, these presses pride themselves on their investment and individual attention to every book and author they publish.
4 Small-press published books do win major literary prizes.

Self-publishing

There is the self-publishing option too, both as a print book and as an ebook, which is becoming more popular, especially among short story writers whose chances of being published by a large publishing house are slim. However, this does cost money and the writer is responsible for every element of the publishing process, including marketing and promotion. If you do head down this path, I would suggest hiring an editor to edit your stories first.

Further reading

Aguirre, Niki, *29 Ways to Drown* (Lubin and Kleyner, 2007).
Barry, Kevin, *There Are Little Kingdoms* (The Stinging Fly Press, 2007).
Rowe, Josephine, *East of Here, Close to Water* (Cherry Fox Press, 2007).

60 favourite short stories

Tania and Courttia

50 favourite collections

Tania and Courttia

Bibliography

The history of the short story

Books – theory

Boddy, Kasia, *The American Short Story Since 1950*, Edinburgh University Press, 2010

Hunter, Adrian, *The Short Story In English*, Cambridge University Press, 2007

May, Charles E. (ed.), *The New Short Story Theories,* Ohio University Press, 1994

— *The Short Story: The Reality of Artifice,* Routledge, 2002

March-Russell, Paul, *The Short Story: An Introduction,* Edinburgh University Press, 2009

McHale, Brian, *Postmodernist Fiction,* Routledge, 1987

Patea, Viorica (ed.), *Short Story Theories: A Twenty-First Century Perspective,* Rodopi, 2007

Patterson Atkinson, William, *The Short-story,* 1916

Poe, Edgar Allen, *The Philosophy of Composition,* 1846

Early short story collections

Aesop, *Aesop's Fables*

Boccaccio, Giovanni, *The Decameron, 1353*

De Cervantes, Miguel, *Novelas ejemplares* (*Exemplary Novels,* 1613)

De La Sale, Antoine, *Les Cent Nouvelles Nouvelles* (*The Hundred New Short Stories*), 1460

Maugham, W. Somerset, *Orientations,* 1899

Melville, Herman, *The Piazza Tales,* 1827

Scott, Walter, *Chronicles of the Canongate,* 1827

The Arabian Nights

The Love Romances of Parthenius of Nicaea

The Seven Sages of Rome

Short stories

Atwood, Margaret, 'Bluebeard's Egg'

Barth, John, 'Lost in the Funhouse'

Brautigan, Richard, 'A Short Story About Contemporary Life in California'

Carter, Angela, 'The Bloody Chamber'

Chekhov, Anton, 'The Lady and the Lapdog'

Davis, Lydia, 'Right and Wrong'

Gass, William, 'In the Heart of the Heart of the Country'

Gordimer, Nadine, 'Six Feet of the Country'

Head, Bessie, 'Looking for a Rain God'

Irving, Washington 'Rip Van Winkle'

Jewett, Sarah Orne, 'The Foreigner'

Joyce, James, 'The Dead'

Kafka, Franz, 'On the Tram'

Mansfield, Katherine, 'Bliss'

Márquez, Gabriel García, 'Very Old Man With Enormous Wings'

Munro, Alice, 'Runaway'

Naipaul, V. S., 'In a Free State'

Poe, Edgar Allen, 'The Tell-Tale Heart'

wa Thiong'o, Ngugi, 'Minutes of Glory'

Articles in print and online

Bowen, Elizabeth, 'Introduction', *Faber Book of Modern Short Stories* (reprinted in May, Charles E. [ed.], *The New Short Story Theories*, Ohio University Press, 1994)

Boyd, William, 'A Short History of the Short Story', *Prospect* magazine, July 2006

Cortázar, Julio, 'Some Aspects of the Short Story' (first published in 1971, included in May, Charles E. [ed.], *The New Short Story Theories*, Ohio University Press, 1994)

Hansen, Arlen J, 'Short Story (Literature)', *Encyclopaedia Britannica*

Crime, tricks and tales: genre and the short story

Books — theory

Amis, Kingsley, *New Maps of Hell: A Survey of Science Fiction*, Arno Press, New York, 1960

Asa Berger, Arthur, *Media, Myth and Society*, Palgrave Macmillan, London, 2012

May, Charles, *The Short Story: The Reality of Artifice*, Routledge, New York, 2002

Early short stories and collections

Aesop, *The Fables of Aesop*, Hodder and Stoughton, London, 1909

Anonymous, 'Epic of Gilgamesh'

—'Tale of the Bamboo Cutter'

—'The Heavenly Bow'

—'The King Who Forgot'

—'Thousand Romances'

—'Urashima Taro'

—'War of the Gods'

Aristides, *The Milesian Tales*

Blicher, Steen Steensen, *The Rector of Veilbye*, Kessinger Publishing, Montana, 2004

Gaselee, S. (trans.), *The Love Romances of Partheius and Other Fragments*, Wildside Press, Maryland, 2008

Gulick, Robert Van, *Celebrated Cases of Judge Dee*, Dover Publications Inc, New York, 1976

Lyons, Malcolm and Lyons, Ursula (trans.), *The Arabian Nights: Tales of 1,001 Nights: (Volumes 1–3)*, Penguin Classics, London, 2010

Maurits, Christopher Hansen, *The Murder of Engine Maker Rolfsen*, 1839

Mohan Ganguli, Kisari, *The Mahabharata of Krishna Dwaipayana Vyasa*, Kessinger Publishing, Montana, 2010

Ovid, *Metamorphoses (Norton Critical Editions)*, W. W. Norton & Company, London, 2010

Poe, Edgar Allen, *The Narrative of Arthur Gordon Pym of Nantucket and Related Tales*, Oxford World's Classics, Oxford, 2008

—*The Murders in the Rue Morgue and Other Tales*, Penguin, London, 2012

Rice Burroughs, Edgar, *Under the Moons of Mars*, Bison, Nebraska, 2003

Sakhawat Hussein, Rokeya, *Sultana's Dream*, Penguin, London, 2005

Shivkumar, K., *Stories from Panchatantra*, Children's Book Trust, New Delhi, 1965

Taylor, Phillip Meadows, *Confessions of a Thug*, Rupa Publications, India, 2010

Short stories and short story collections

Butler, Octavia E., *Bloodchild and Other Stories*, Seven Stories Press, Oakland, 1995

Ellison, Harlan (ed.) *Dangerous Visions*, Orion, London, 2012

Gaiman, Neil, *Angels and Visitations*, Dreamhaven Books, Minneapolis, 1993

—*Smoke and Mirrors*, Headline Review, London, 2005

Hartman, Ivor (ed.), *Afro SF*, Storytime, Johannesburg, 2012

Latimer, Jonathan, *Solomon's Vineyard*, International Polygonics, New York, 1988

Lethem, Jonathan, *The Wall of the Sky, The Wall of the Eye*, Faber & Faber, 2004

Miéville, China, *Looking for Jake and Other Stories*, Pan, London, 2011

Singh, Vadana, *The Woman Who Thought She Was a Planet*, New Delhi, 2014

Thomas, Sheree R. (ed.), *Dark Matter: A Century of Speculative Fiction from the African Diaspora*, New York, 2001

Thomas, Sheree R. and Simmons, Martin (eds), *Dark Matter: A Century of Speculative Fiction from the African Diaspora: Reading the Bones*, New York, 2005

Novels

Bauden, Felix, *Le Roman de L'Avenir*, 1834

Bulwer-Lytton, Edward, *The Coming Race*, Wesleyan University Press, Connecticut, 2005

King, Steven, *Misery*, Hachette UK, London, 2007

Shelley, Mary, *Frankenstein*, Wordsworth Editions Ltd, Hertford, 1992

Tucker, George, *A Voyage to the Moon*, Gregg Press, Boston, 1975

Literary journals

Baird, Edwin (ed.), *Weird Tales*, Rural Publications, Chicago, 1923

Bates, Harry (ed.), *Astounding Stories of Super Science*, Publisher's Fiscal Corporation, New York, 1930

Boucher, Anthony and McComas, Francis. J. (eds), *The Magazine of Fantasy and Science Fiction*, Mystery House, New York, 1949

Carnell, John (ed.), *New Worlds, London*, 1939

Gernsback, Hugo (ed.), *Amazing Stories*, Experimenter Publishing, Lake Geneva, 1926

—*Wonder Stories*, Stellar Publishing Corporation, Lake Geneva, 1929

Gold, H. R. (ed.), *Galaxy Science Fiction*, World Editions, New York, 1950

The Indian Ladies Magazine of Madras, Madras, 1901

Articles in print and online

Hansen, Arlen J., 'Short Story', Encyclopaedia Britannica, http://www.britannica.com/EBchecked/topic/541698/short-story, accessed 8/1/2014

The shorter end of short stories – boundaries with poetry

Books

Armitage, Simon, *Seeing Stars*, Faber & Faber, 2010

Chivers, Tom (ed.), *Adventures in Form*, Penned in the Margins, 2012

Dark, Larry (ed.), *Prize Stories: The O. Henry Awards 2001*, Anchor Books, 2001

Ivory, Helen and Szirtes, George (eds), *In Their Own Words: Contemporary Poets on Their Poetry*, Salt 2012

Maxwell, Glyn, *On Poetry*, Oberon Masters, 2012

McDowell, Gary L. and Rzicznek, Daniel F. (eds), *The Rose Metal Field Guide to Prose Poetry*, Rose Metal Press, 2010

Tate, James, *Return to the City of White Donkeys*, Ecco Press, 2005

Articles in print and online

Bowen, Elizabeth, 'Introduction', *Faber Book of Modern Short Stories* (reprinted in May, Charles E. [ed.], *The New Short Story Theories*, Ohio University Press, 1994)

Collins, Billy, Writers on Writing podcast, http://writersonwriting.blogspot.co.uk/2012/11/poet-billy-collins-on-writers-on.html 2007

Keret, Etgar, *Observer* newspaper http://www.theguardian.com/books/2012/mar/04/etgar-keret-interview-short-stories (4 March 2012).

Stories: those little slices of life

Books — theory

Anonymous, '*Review of Brander Matthews' Philosophy of the Short Story*', Academy, London, 1901

Baxter, Charles, *Burning Down the House*, Graywolf, Minnesota, 2008

Bloom, Harold, *The Anxiety of Influence: A Theory of Poetry*, Oxford University Press, New York, 1973

Chabon, Michael, *Maps and Legends*, Fourth Estate, London, 2010

Forster, E. M., *Aspects of the Novel*, Penguin, London, 1977

King, Stephen, *On Writing*, Hodder and Stoughton, London, 2000

Early short story collections

Aesop, *The Fables of Aesop*, Hodder and Stoughton, London, 1909

Hawthorne, Nathaniel, *Twice Told Tales*, Dent, London, 1967

Short stories and short story collections

Baldwin, James, *Going to Meet the Man*, Penguin, London, 1991

Dahl, Roald, *Kiss Kiss*, Penguin, London, 2011

Dinesen, Isak, *Seven Gothic Tales*, Vintage, London, 1991

Du Maurier, Daphne, *The Birds and Other Stories*, Virago, London, 2011

Joyce, James, *Dubliners*, Penguin Modern Classics, London, 2000

Keenen, Randall, *Let the Dead Bury their Dead*, Abacus, London, 1994

King, Stephen, *Different Seasons*, Hodder and Stoughton, London, 2012

Mowry, Jess, *Rats in the Trees*, Penguin, New York, 1993

Newland Courttia, *Society Within*, Abacus, London, 1999

—*Music for the Off-Key*, Peepal Tree, Leeds, 2006

—*A Book of Blues*, Flambard, Newcastle, 2011

Price, Richard, *The Wanderers*, Bloomsbury, London, 2004

Robinson, Eden, *Traplines*, Abacus, London, 1997

Novels

Carter, Angela, *The Company of Wolves*, Vintage Classics, London, 1995

Chabon, Michael, *Yiddish Policeman's Union*, Harper Perennial, London, 2008

Golding, William, *Lord of the Flies*, Faber, 1997

Joyce, James, *Portrait of the Artist as a Young Man*, Viking Press, New York, 1964

Lee, Harper, *To Kill a Mockingbird*, Arrow, London, 1989

Newland, Courttia, *The Scholar*, Abacus, London, 1997

Steinbeck, John, *Of Mice and Men*, Penguin, London, 2006

Tolkien, J. R. R., *The Hobbit*, HarperCollins, London, 1993

—*Lord of the Rings*, HarperCollins, London, 2007

Reflections on writing and on books on writing

Books

Carlson, Ron, *Ron Carlson Writes a Story*, Greywolf Press, 2007

Gebbie, Vanessa (ed.), *Short Circuit: A Guide to the Art of the Short Story*, Salt, 2013

Goldberg, Natalie, *Wild Mind*, Bantam, 1990

Lamott, Anne, *Bird by Bird: Some Instructions on Writing and Life*, Anchor Books edition, 1995

Stein, Lorin and Stein, Sadie (eds), *Object Lessons: The Paris Review Presents The Art of the Short Story*, William Heinemann, 2012

Tharp, Twyla, *The Creative Habit*, Simon and Schuster, 2007

The Paris Review Interviews Vols 1–4 Picador, 2009

Reflections on the what, when, how, why and where of it for me

Books

Dahl, Roald, *Kiss Kiss,* Penguin, 1962

Daley, Ian (ed.), *Wonderwall,* Route, 2006

Englander, Nathan, *For the Relief of Unbearable Urges,* Faber & Faber, 1999

Goldberg, Natalie, *Wild Mind* (Bantam, 1990)

Lamott, Anne, *Bird by Bird: Some Instructions on Writing and Life* (Anchor Books edition, 1995)

Shapard, Robert and Thomas, James (eds), *Sudden Fiction,* W. W. Norton & Company, 1983

—(eds), *Sudden Fiction International,* W. W. Norton & Company, 1989

—(eds), *Flash Fiction Forward,* W. W. Norton & Company, 2006

—(eds), *New Sudden Fiction,* W. W. Norton & Company, 2007

Smith, Ali, *Other Stories and Other Stories,* Penguin, 1999

Articles

Lehrer, Jonah, 'The Annals of Science: The Eureka Hunt', *The New Yorker* magazine, 28 July 2008

Munro, Alice, 'The Art of Fiction No.137', *The Paris Review,* Summer 1994 http://www.theparisreview.org/interviews/1791/the-art-of-fiction-no-137-alice-munro

Reflections on the evolution of a short story

Books — theory

Budge, Wallis E. A., *The Great Awakening: The Egyptian Book of the Dead,* A&B Publishers Group, New York, 1999

Rinpoche, Sogral, *The Tibetan Book of Living and Dying,* Rider Books, London, 2002

Short stories and short story collections

Chandler, Raymond, *The Simple Art of Murder*, Vintage Books, New York, 1988

Moore, Lorrie (ed.), *The Best American Stories*, Houghton Mifflin Harcourt, Boston, 2004

Newland, Courttia, *A Book of Blues*, Flambard, Newcastle, 2011

Novels

King, Stephen, *The Stand*, Hodder & Stoughton, London, 2011

Saramago, José, *Death with Intervals*, Harvill Secker, London, 2008

The evolution of a short story: 'Under the Tree'

Books

Carlson, Ron, *Ron Carlson Writes a Story*, Greywolf Press, 2007

Gebbie, Vanessa (ed.), *Short Circuit: A Guide to the Art of the Short Story*, Salt, 2013

Kesey, Roy, *All Over*, Dzanc Books, 2007

McKee, Robert, *Story: Substance, Structure, Style and the Principles of Screenwriting*, Regan Books, 2007

O'Reilly, Paddy, *The End of the World*, University of Queensland Press, 2007

Articles in print and online

Wilder, Billy, 'Ten Tips for Writing a Great Screenplay' from *Conversations with Wilder*, Crowe, Cameron, Knopf 2001

Journals

Electric Velocipede http://www.electricvelocipede.com/

kill-author http://killauthor.com/

Reflections: permission and risk

Books

Carlson, Ron, *Ron Carlson Writes a Story*, Greywolf Press, 2007

Gebbie, Vanessa (ed.), *Short Circuit: A Guide to the Art of the Short Story*, Salt, 2013

Kesey, Roy, *All Over*, Dzanc Books, 2007

O'Reilly, Paddy, *The End of the World*, University of Queensland Press, 2007

A note on craft and critique: writing is not a democracy

Books

Carlson, Ron, *Ron Carlson Writes a Story*, Greywolf Press, 2007

Gebbie, Vanessa (ed.), *Short Circuit: A Guide to the Art of the Short Story*, Salt, 2013

From beginning to end

Books — theory

Casterton, Julia, *Creative Writing: A Practical Guide*, Palgrave Macmillian, London, 2005

Sontag, Susan, *As Consciousness Is Harnessed to Flesh: Journals and Notebooks, 1964–1980*, Farrar, Straus and Giroux, 2012

Trilling, Lionel, *Authenticity and the Modern Consciousness*, Commentary, New York, 1971

Short stories and short story collections

Carver, Raymond, *What We Talk About When We Talk About Love*, Vintage, London, 2009

Joyce, James, *Dubliners*, Penguin Modern Classics, London, 2000

Newland, Courttia, *A Book of Blues*, Flambard, Newcastle, 2011

Novels

Mosely, Walter, *Gone Fishin'*, Serpent's Tail, London, 1998

Tolkein, J. R. R., *Lord of the Rings*, HarperCollins, London, 2007

Where to start – ideas and inspiration
Books
Carlson, Ron, *Ron Carlson Writes a Story*, Greywolf Press, 2007
Gebbie, Vanessa (ed.), *Short Circuit: A Guide to the Art of the Short Story*, Salt, 2013

Where to start: titles, beginnings and endings
Books
Doerr, Anthony, 'Memory Wall', *Memory Wall* (Scribner, 2010)
Hall, Sarah, 'Butcher's Perfume', *The Beautiful Indifference* (Faber and Faber 2012)

Short stories
Emshwiller, Carol, 'Grandma', Fantasy and Science Fiction magazine, 2002
Davies, Carys, 'The Redemption of Galen Pike', Prospect magazine http://www.prospectmagazine.co.uk/magazine/fiction/the-redemption-of-galen-pike/#.Uup8LqHh-mg, and in *The Redemption of Galen Pike* (Salt, 2014)
Wolff, Tobias, 'Bullet in the Brain', *The New Yorker*, September 1995

Movement and syncopation in fiction: writing the long short story
Books – theory
Aristotle, *Poetics*, Penguin, London, 1996
Solnit, Rebecca, *A Field Guide to Getting Lost*, Canongate Books Ltd, Edinburgh, 2006

Short stories and short story collections
Carver, Raymond, *Elephant*, Vintage, London, 2009
Milhauser, Stephen, *The Knife Thrower*, Phoenix, London, 1999
O'Brien, Edna, *Saints and Sinners*, Faber and Faber, London, 2012

Plot versus story – where's the tension?

Books

Carlson, Ron, *Ron Carlson Writes a Story*, Greywolf Press, 2007

Gebbie, Vanessa (ed.), *Short Circuit: A Guide to the Art of the Short Story*, Salt, 2013

Editing and revising

Books – theory

Orwell, George, *Politics and the English Language*, Horizon, London, 1946

Tenses

Short stories

Smith, Ali, 'The Child', online in Blithe House Quarterly (http://www.blithe.com/nhq9.1/9.1.01.html) or in her collection, *The First Person & Other Stories* (Hamish Hamilton, 2008)

Step into a world – thoughts on structure

Books – theory

Dunne, Will, *The Dramatic Writer's Companion*, The University of Chicago Press, Chicago, 2009

Lodge, David, *Consciousness and the Novel*, Harvard University Press, Massachusetts, 2004

Poetry, short stories and short story collections

Bloom, Valerie, *Refuelling*, Hamish Hamilton, London, 2000

Structure and how to use it

Short stories

Chasin, Alexandra, 'They Came From Mars,' from *Kissed By*, FC2, 2007

What gets left out and minimalism

Articles

Peterson, Adam, interview, Smokelong Quarterly, http://smokelong.com/interview/adampeterson42.asp

Speaking their minds – character and voice

Books – theory

Alvarez, Al, *The Writer's Voice*, Bloomsbury, London, 2005
Wood, James, *How Fiction Works*, Jonathan Cape, London, 2008

Writing flash fiction, liberation through constraint

Articles

Gaffney, David, 'How to Write Flash Fiction', *Guardian*, May 2012, http://www.theguardian.com/books/2012/may/14/how-to-write-flash-fiction
Shapard, Robert, 'What is Flash Fiction?', Flashfiction.net, Feb 2013 http://flashfiction.net/2013/02/what-is-flash-fiction-robert-shapard-james-thomas.php

Collections of flash fiction

Brautigan, Richard, *Revenge of the Lawn*, Jonathan Cape, 1972
Freele, Stefanie, *Feeding Strays*, Lost Horse Press, 2009
Gaffney, David, *Sawn-Off Tales*, Salt, 2006
Meyer, Angela, *Captives*, Inkerman and Blunt, 2014
Ní Chonchúir, Nuala, *Of Dublin and Other Fictions*, Tower Press, 2013
Shapard, Robert and Thomas, James (eds), *Sudden Fiction*, W. W. Norton & Company, 1983

—(eds), *Sudden Fiction International*, W. W. Norton & Company, 1989

—(eds), *Flash Fiction Forward*, W. W. Norton & Company, 2006

—(eds), *New Sudden Fiction*, W. W. Norton & Company, 2007

Wild, Peter (ed.), *The Flash: A Flash Fiction Anthology*, Social Disease, 2007

Books on flash fiction

Gebbie, Vanessa (ed.), *Short Circuit: A Guide to the Art of the Short Story*, Salt, 2013

Masih, Tara (ed.), *The Field Guide to Writing Flash Fiction*, Rose Metal Press, 2009

Journals

FlashFiction.net http://flashfiction.net/

Flash: The International Short Short Story magazine, www.chester.ac.uk/flash.magazine

Smokelong quarterly www.smokelong.com

A brief history of time in the short story

Short stories

Hall, Sarah, 'Butcher's Perfume', from *The Beautiful Indifference*, Faber and Faber, 2012

Orner, Peter, 'Initials Etched on a Dining Room Table, Lockeport, Nova Scotia', from *Esther Stories*, Mariner Books, 2001

Wolff, Tobias, 'Bullet in the Brain', *The New Yorker*, September 1995

Another perspective — point of view in the story

Books — theory

Le Guin, Ursula, *Steering the Craft*, Eighth Mountain Press, Oregon, 1999

Short stories and short story collections

Everett, Percival, *Damned if I Do*, Graywolf, Minneapolis, 2004

Gray, Stephen, *The Picador Book of African Short Stories*, Picador, London, 2000

Jackson, Shirley, *The Lottery and Other Stories*, Penguin, London, 2009

Milhauser, Stephen, *The Knife Thrower*, Phoenix, London, 1999

O'Brien, Edna, *Saints and Sinners*, Faber and Faber, London, 2012

Novels

Chikwava, Brian, *Harare North*, Jonathan Cape, London, 2010

Experimenting and experimental short stories

Journals and publishers

Breadless Crust http://breadlesscrust.co.uk/

Cafe Irreal http://cafeirreal.alicewhittenburg.com/

The Capilano Review http://www.thecapilanoreview.ca/

Cease, Cows http://ceasecows.com/

Conjunctions http://conjunctions.com/

Contrary magazine http://contrarymagazine.com/

Diagram http://www.thediagram.com/

FC2 http://www.fc2.org/

HARK magazine http://www.harkmagazine.org/

HOAX http://www.hoaxpublication.co.uk/

Itch http://itch.co.za/

Redivider http://www.redividerjournal.org/

Sein Und Werden http://www.kissthewitch.co.uk/seinundwerden/sein.html

Streetcake http://www.streetcakemagazine.com/

Unsaid magazine http://unsaidmagazine.wordpress.com/

Valve http://www.valvejournal.co.uk/

Word Bohemia http://wordbohemia.co.uk/

Publishing short stories

Websites

Duotrope www.duotrope.com
Poets & Writers www.pw.org
The Review Review www.thereviewreview.net
ShortStops www.shortstops.info
Writers & Artists https://www.writersandartists.co.uk/

Articles

Williamson, Eric Miles, 'A Brief History of the Short Story in America', Bookcritics (http://bookcritics.org/blog/archive/a-brief-history-of-the-short-story-in-america)

Harvesting — on writing your collection

Books — theory

Kennedy, J. Gerald (ed.), *Modern American Short Story Sequences: Composite Fictions and Fictive Communities*, Cambridge University Press, 1995
King, Stephen, *On Writing*, Hodder and Stoughton, London, 2000
Solnit, Rebecca, *A Field Guide to Getting Lost*, Canongate Books Ltd, Edinburgh, 2006

Early short story collections

Boccaccio, Giovanni, *The Decameron*, Penguin, London, 2003
Chaucer, Geoffrey, *The Canterbury Tales*, Penguin, London, 2003
Lyons, Malcolm and Lyons, Ursula (trans.), *The Arabian Nights: Tales of 1,001 Nights (Volumes 1–3)*, Penguin Classics, London, 2010
Russell Mitford, Mary, *Our Village*, Serenity Publishers, Maryland, 2009

Short stories and short story collections

Camus, Albert, *Exile and the Kingdom*, Penguin, London, 2006
Diaz, Junot, *Drown*, Faber, London, 2008
—*This Is How You Lose Her*, Faber, London, 2013

Johnson, Denis, *Jesus Son*, Granta, London, 2012

Martone, Michael, *Fort Wayne is Seventh on Hitler's List: Indiana Stories*, Indiana University Press, Indiana, 1990

Munro, Alice, *Lives of Girls and Women*, Penguin, London, 1989

—*Who Do You Think You Are?*, Penguin, London, 1996

Price, Richard, *The Wanderers*, Bloomsbury, London, 2004

Riviera, Edward, *Family Installments: Memories of Growing Up Hispanic*, Penguin, London, 1983

Rolnick, Josh, *Pulp and Paper*, University of Iowa Press, Iowa, 2011

Steinbeck, John, *Cannery Row*, Penguin, London, 2000

Novels

King, Stephen, *The Stand*, Hodder & Stoughton, London, 2011

Articles in print and online

Anderson, Sam, 'Junot Diaz Hates Writing Short Stories', *New York Times*, New York, 2012

Camus, Albert, 'Review of Sartre's *Nausea*', *Alger Républicain*, Algiers, 1938

Munro, Alice, 'The Art of Fiction No. 137', *The Paris Review 131*, New York, 1994

Price, Richard, 'The Art of Fiction No. 144', *The Paris Review 138*, New York, 1996

Short story collections — how do they work and how to get one published?

The Short Review Author Interviews http://thenewshortreview.wordpress.com/interviews/

Index